Apartheid's Last Stand

The Rise and Fall of the South African Security State

Chris Alden
Lecturer in International Relations
University of Witwatersrand
Johannesburg

First published in Great Britain 1996 by
MACMILLAN PRESS LTD
Houndmills, Basingstoke, Hampshire RG21 6XS
and London
Companies and representatives
throughout the world

A catalogue record for this book is available
from the British Library.

ISBN 0–333–63795–X

First published in the United States of America 1996 by
ST. MARTIN'S PRESS, INC.,
Scholarly and Reference Division,
175 Fifth Avenue,
New York, N.Y. 10010

ISBN 0–312–12666–2

Library of Congress Cataloging-in-Publication Data
Alden, Chris.
Apartheid's last stand : the rise and fall of the South African security state / Chris Alden.
p. cm.
Includes bibliographical references and index.
ISBN 0–312–12666–2 (cloth)
1. Apartheid—South Africa—History. 2. South Africa—Politics and government—1978–89. I. Title.
DT1963.A43 1996
30-5.8 '00968—dc20

95–14916
CIP

---

10 9 8 7 6 5 4 3 2 1
05 04 03 02 01 00 99 98 97 96

Printed and bound in Great Britain by
Antony Rowe Ltd, Chippenham, Wiltshire

APARTHEID'S LAST STAND

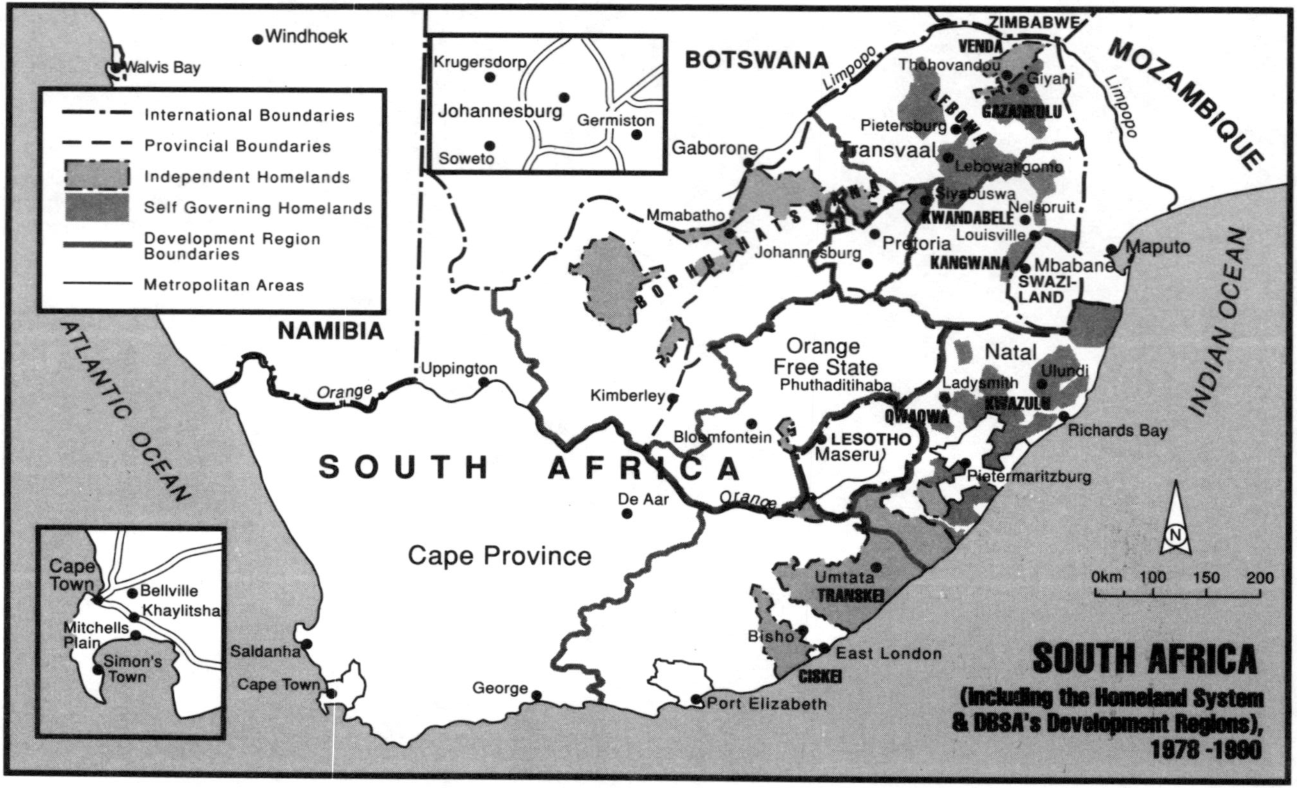

SOUTH AFRICA
(Including the Homeland System & DBSA's Development Regions), 1978 -1990

To my parents

Contents

Acknowledgements

As is the case in all such ventures, this book would not have been possible without the support and assistance of a whole host of people. In the United States, I was lucky to have a first-rate adviser in Professor Richard Shultz. His support for my long-distance research project in South Africa was absolutely invaluable and his judgement always sound. Professor Arpad von Lazar and Professor Robert Pfalztgraff provided support and commentary at crucial stages in the process.

In the United Kingdom, Professor Jack Spence kindly offered commentary and advice as I moved towards completion of this project. Kato Lambrechts spent valuable hours giving the sometimes unreadable manuscript a needed critical reading. Macmillan's Annabelle Buckley and Tim Farmiloe, as well as Anne Rafique, and Cory Voigt (in South Africa) deserve my thanks for their support in turning the manuscript into a book.

In South Africa, my colleagues at the Department of International Relations at the University of the Witwatersrand helped me at different stages and in innumerable ways but in particular by looking over aspects of the text as it was in progress. A special note of gratitude goes to Dr Daan Prinsloo, whose knowledge of the Botha years was critical to my understanding of this complex period. There are many others, some of whom are listed at the end of this book in the interview section and others who wish to remain anonymous, who gave generously of their time to a foreigner and deserve my thanks.

I would like to thank the William H. Donner Foundation, without whose generous financial support I would not have been able to conduct my research. The Anglo-American/De Beers Chairman's Fund also provided financial support for travel.

Finally, my whole family has provided unstinting support throughout this lengthy endeavour. Barbara, Deborah and Allison have always listened and assisted me whenever possible as have Jay Jones and Steve Bowen. But I must save a special thanks for my parents, Alice and John, whose guidance, support – which included answering numerous requests and reading documents in progress – and patience have seen me through literally decades of schooling. I dedicate this book to them.

Abbreviations

ANC	African National Congress
APMC	Area Political Military Councils
AWB	Afrikaner Weestandsbeweging
AZAPO	Azania People's Organization
BLS	Botswana, Lesotho, Swaziland
BOSS	Bureau for State Security
CAAA	Comprehensive Anti-Apartheid Act
CODESA	Convention for a Democratic South Africa
CONSAS	Constellation of Southern African States
COSAS	Congress of South African Students
COSATU	Congress of South African Trade Unions
CRC	Coloured People's Representative Council
DCD	Department of Cooperation and Development
DCDP	Department of Constitutional Development and Planning
DFA	Department of Foreign Affairs
EPG	Eminent Persons Group
FAPLA	Forças Armadas Populares de Libertação de Angola
FNLA	Frente Naçional de Libertação de Angola
FOSATU	Federation of South African Trade Unions
FRELIMO	Frente de Libertação de Moçambique
HNP	Herstigte Nasionale Party
IDASA	Institute for a Democrative Alternative in South Africa
JIC	Joint Intelligence Centre
JMC	Joint Management Centre
JOC	Joint Operation Centre
MK	Umkhonto we Sizwe
MPLA	Movimento Popular de Libertação Angola
NECC	National Education Crisis Committee
NF	National Forum
NI	National Intelligence
NJMC	National Joint Management System
NP	National Party
NSMS	National Security Management System

NWMS	National Welfare Management System
OAU	Organization of African Unity
PAC	Pan Africanist Congress
PEBCO	Port Elizabeth Black Civic Organization
PFP	Progressive Federalist Party
PWV	Pretoria-Witwatersrand-Vereeniging
RENAMO	Resistênçia Naçional Moçambicana
RPMC	Regional Political Military Councils
RSA	Republic of South Africa
RSC	Regional Services Council
SACP	South African Communist Party
SACTU	South African Congress of Trade Unions
SADF	South African Defence Force
SAIC	South African Indian Council
SAP	South African Police
SCA	Soweto Civic Association
SWAPO	South West African People's Organization
SWATF	South West African Territorial Force
TGNU	Transitional Government of National Unity
UDF	United Democratic Front
UNITA	União Naçional para a Independência Total de Angola
ZANU	Zimbabwe African National Union
ZAPU	Zimbabwe African People's Union

'n Boer maak 'n plan.

– Afrikaans saying

Introduction

> *The use of force alone is but temporary. It may subdue for a moment but it does not remove the necessity of subduing again; and a nation is not governed which is perpetually to be conquered.*
>
> Edmund Burke

> *It should be borne in mind that there is nothing more difficult to handle, more doubtful of success, and more dangerous to carry through than initiating changes in a state's constitution. The innovator makes enemies of all those who prospered under the old order, and only lukewarm support is forthcoming from those who would prosper under the new. Their support is lukewarm partly from fear of their adversaries, who have the existing laws on their side, and partly because men are generally incredulous, never really trusting new things unless they have tested them by experience.*
>
> Niccolo Machiavelli

This book is an investigation into the formulation and implementation of the South African government's security-based reform programme under P.W. Botha. Specifically, it will examine the role of the National Security State, that is to say a state recast in terms of counter-revolutionary strategy, as a transformative agent in the volatile topography of modernization and revolution. The case of the South African security state from 1978 to 1990, the period in which the former Defence Minister took up the reins of power under the anthem of reform and finally fell disgraced as a perpetuator of the status quo, will serve as the focus of this book.

The process of integration of the Third World into the Western international system, characterized by the rapid and forcible imposition of the Western market economy and political suzerainty over existing systems, ushered in a period of extreme crisis for these regions of the world. Having begun in earnest with the advent of European colonialism, this integrative process profoundly transformed the traditional economic and political systems as well as existing structures of authority in Africa, Asia and Latin America. The subsequent retreat of the colonial powers from their imperial strongholds in the aftermath of World War II, actively encouraged by the United States and the Soviet Union, did not signal a concomitant withdrawal from either the global economy or politics rooted in the European state system. The anti-colonial rhetoric of autarky and non-alignment notwithstanding, the enduring circumstances of a captive economy and weak political structures continued to impact negatively upon societies still very much in the throes of socio-economic and political transformation.

It was this volatile process which came to assume a central position within the strategic calculus of competition and conflict between the two superpowers in the Third World. Utilizing an array of means at their disposal, the Soviet Union and its allies gave support to anti-colonial and anti-Western movements and regimes; for its own part, the United States and its allies responded by throwing their considerable resources behind regimes or movements with an explicitly anti-communist bias. The result of this intervention was that the complexities of the transformation from traditional to Western economic and political systems in the Third World were often held hostage to exigencies of policies developed in the service of bipolar politics.

The scholarly literature on this transformative process, originating in the context of this growing ideological competition between the United States and the Soviet Union in the Third World, also reflected the beliefs and strategic preoccupations of the superpowers. Modernization theory, rooted in classical liberalism, and Marxist-Leninist theory, rooted in a critique of classical liberalism, became the ideological pillars around which the debate on the Third World took place. Broadly speaking, the scholars associated with the modernization school identified socio-economic forces emerging out of the movement from traditional society to modernity as posing a challenge to the established political order in developing countries.[1] This interpretation contrasted with Marxism-Leninism, which placed the process of modernization within the context of its cosmopolitan socio-economic theory, one which saw communist revolution as the ultimate (and inevitable) political expression of changing socio-economic conditions.[2] In each of these approaches traditional society and its political manifestations was set against the revolutionary forces of modernization; where they principally differed lay in the competing prescriptive formulas which grew out of this analysis and corresponded with their opposing ideological agendas. Despite these differences, the two schools shared a belief in the fundamentally beneficial and positive nature of integration into the Western international system (capitalism for modernization theorists and socialism for Marxists).

For proponents of the modernization school, whose work reflected an imperative towards activism, personal involvement in American politics allowed for the translation of their interests from political science and into the realm of public policy.[3] Walter Rostow, author of *The Stages of Economic Growth: A Non-Communist Manifesto,* became the Kennedy administration's chief theorist on modernization. He perhaps best exemplified this shift from scholastic concerns of the political scientist to those of the policy-maker. Accepting that the socio-economic changes engendered by modernization were inevitable and, in fact, represented a positive step towards the political development of the polity,[4] modernization theorists suggested (implicitly and explicitly) that the state could function as a stabilizing and transformative agent in that process. Thus, for these scholars the dominant issue emerging out of the challenge of modernization, and in particular that of revolutionary movements, came to be how the state could retain control and stability under these adverse circumstances while simultaneously addressing the underlying causes which motivated revolution.

By way of contrast, Marxism-Leninism promised both development and stability through the institutionalization of a centralized state structure along socialist lines. Citing the Soviet Union as an exemplary model of rapid modernization of a traditional society, this school of thought upheld the socialist path of development as a superior and equitable means of guiding the Third World into modernity. In 1960 the Soviet Union unveiled a programme that laid out in specific terms the means and goals for the creation of socialist-oriented states amongst developing countries, the transitional 'national democratic state'.[5] Concurrently, with the consolidation of the People's Republic of China in the late 1950s, an alternative path to revolutionary socialism increasingly challenged the Soviet Union's own experience. As with the proponents of modernization, the call to activism – in particular the idealization of revolution itself as a transformative agent for society – was an crucial and distinguishing component of Marxism-Leninism.[6] As such, this approach was inherently attractive to Third World leaders concerned with issues ranging from national development to political consolidation.

As noted above, this debate took shape and was sharpened in the context of the Cold War, which saw the United States and the Soviet Union increasingly challenging one another in the decolonized terrain of the Third World. The forces unleashed in the process of modernization, linked with those of nascent nationalism, threatened the political and economic position of the West in the emerging Third World. Turning to the strategy of revolutionary warfare espoused by the leading communist states to assist their cause, Third World revolutionaries and nationalists alike found an established path to power based on the leadership of an elite cadre, the utilization of a populist ideology, the construction of a disciplined mass base, the creation and use of military forces, and the establishment of an external support network.[7] This they put into service of their specific political agendas, ousting colonial governments or those explicitly aligned with Western interests through the application of the strategy and techniques of revolutionary war. Upon taking power, as was the case in the People's Republic of China and Algeria, these revolutionaries usually proclaimed a foreign policy predicated on hostility to traditional Western political and economic concerns – if not outright alignment with the Soviet Union – and domestic policies which took centralized state control of the economy and other aspects of life in the polity as their starting point.

With Third World revolutionaries drawn to the proven strategies derived from the experience of the Soviet Union, the People's Republic of China and its allies – not to mention material and other forms of support from the East – the logic of the Cold War required that the West respond in kind towards those states threatened by revolution. The development of a counter-revolutionary strategy by the United States and its allies, one which drew upon both the insights and experiences of contact with revolutionary warfare as well as the propositions of modernization theory, provided the state with a formula for combating such threats. Sir Robert Thompson, General André Beaufre and Colonel J.J. McCuen were among the many strategists who attempted to develop a strategic response to the appeal of revolutionary warfare.[8] While their individual approaches to opposing revolutionary war varied from the theoretically abstract to the detailed explication of military science, nonetheless all of these strategists felt compelled to fix counter-revolutionary strategy within the framework of the pursuit of security and reform by the state.

With the security threat posed by revolutionary warfare as a spur to action, states as diverse as colonial Malaya, the Philippines, South Vietnam, South Africa, Chile and El Salvador turned to counter-revolutionary strategy as a panacea for the ills induced by modernization. Taking the central principles of counter-revolutionary strategy as their starting point, these states – which were overwhelmingly authoritarian in terms of their political systems – introduced policies in the spheres of security and reform which were designed to both combat and undercut the appeal of revolutionary-inspired change. In the case of the majority of these states, the governing authorities chose to adopt those aspects of counter-revolutionary strategy which met their security requirements while fundamentally ignoring the reformist imperatives of the strategy. However, in the case of some of the colonial territories and a select number of independent states, the governing authorities actually remade their polity and themselves in the image of the exigencies of counter-revolutionary strategy. This process consisted not only of implementing the security directives of counter-revolutionary strategy but of introducing significant reforms to the state itself. French Algeria and British Malaya are prime examples of colonial territories remade along these strategic lines while the Philippines (at various times), Chile and South Africa are salient examples of independent states refashioning themselves according to the dictates of counter-revolutionary strategy. It is this latter phenomenon which can be characterized by the theoretical construct known as the National Security State.

THE NATIONAL SECURITY STATE: A THEORETICAL CONSTRUCT

The establishment of the National Security State represented a distinctive variant of the emerging state in the Third World.[9] As a product of the Cold War's intrusion into Asia, Africa and Latin America, this new type of state reflected the West's preoccupations as transposed into the context of a traditional society in the throes of modernization. With these elements featuring as background to the development of the National Security State, a preliminary exposition of the concept highlights three characteristics which serve as defining attributes of this theoretical construct. They are: the governing authorities' acceptance of counter-revolutionary strategy, with its twin pillars of security and reform, as the foundation or basis of national policy; the implementation of the security and reformist measures contained within counter-revolutionary strategy by the state; and, at the policy-making level, the constant and evolving tension between security concerns and reform imperatives in response to the environment into which they were thrust.

The first defining characteristic of the National Security State was that the governing authorities must have accepted counter-revolutionary strategy as the foundation or basis of national policy. The overt development of a threat-perception which cast the state as the object of revolutionary aggression, thereby serving as the justification for the reversion to extraordinary means inherent in counter-revolutionary strategy, was a public manifestation of this acceptance. This generally took the form of ideological affiliation with the West and against that of the Soviet Union. The military, as guardian of state security interests and the most self-consciously national institution in the developing state, played a crucial role in both the definition of the crisis facing the state and the formulation of a response. Though not necessarily wielding ultimate power in the National Security State, by virtue of its pre-eminence in matters of security the military was capable of exercising a decisive influence on state policy. The implications of the adoption of counter-revolutionary strategy as the guiding principle of state policy ranged from the formulation of policies consciously informed by counter-revolutionary strategy to the restructuring of the state to reflect counter-revolutionary considerations.

With counter-revolutionary strategists calling for the institutionalization of a unified politico-military structure to provide a basis for the development of state policy in accordance with strategic dictates, as well as to coordinate the implementation of state policy, the governing authorities usually accompanied the adoption of counter-revolutionary strategy with the establishment of a centralizing policy-making body. It was here that the two poles of counter-revolutionary strategy – security and reform – were translated into national strategy and subsequently into specific policy proposals by a bureaucratic elite consciously remoulded as 'counter-revolutionaries'. The formulation of a national strategy was characterized by an effort on the part of the state to strike a balance between transforming the polity without relinquishing the mechanisms of control of the process. Developing an approach to state-led reform which best enabled the state to maintain this control, whether it be through the application of an incrementalist approach or through the introduction of 'fabian strategy and blitzkrieg tactics',[10] was at the heart of the formulation of this national strategy. The degree to which the envisaged reforms represented a definitive shift away from the established situation, a measure of the limits of the transformative nature of state-led reform itself, were to play a significant part in the success of the venture. Coupled with this, the chosen approach to reform lent or detracted from the legitimacy of the reforms introduced by the state. These factors became most clearly visible in the implementation phase of counter-revolutionary strategy.

The second determining characteristic of the National Security State was the implementation of the security and reform measures contained within counter-revolutionary strategy by the state.

With respect to security measures, these ranged from the

introduction of emergency regulations or extraordinary legislative powers for the security forces to the activation of civic action programmes predicated on 'winning the hearts and minds' of the population. The security component of counter-revolutionary strategy drew its primary inspiration from the strategies and tactics employed by the practitioners of revolutionary warfare. Lenin, Giap, Guevara and most particularly Mao Tse-tung, all influential to the development of the theory of counter-revolutionary warfare, advocated the selective use of coercion against both the population and the state as a means of attaining political ends; this approach founds its way into the security approach of the counter-revolutionary strategists. Extended legislative authority for the security forces was coupled with their numerical expansion. Typically, this involved an increase in police and local militia, as well as the establishment of elite counter-insurgency units. Finally, these changes in the composition of the security forces were also reflected in a transformation of their mission. No longer devoted exclusively to conventional police and military operations, the security forces (or at least select elements amongst them) were enlisted into civic action programmes aimed at gaining the support of the population.

The implementation by the state of the reformist concerns contained within counter-revolutionary strategy ranged from essentially 'cosmetic' policy changes in the socio-economic and political spheres to fundamental restructuring of the existing political order. The reform component of counter-revolutionary strategy was rooted in the insights of modernization theory. An emphasis was usually placed on development projects designed to ameliorate the detrimental socio-economic conditions which were believed to foster political upheavals. Coupled with this were political reforms of varying degrees of substance which were directed at meeting some of the political grievances of the population. Generally speaking, land reform featured prominently amongst the National Security State's reformist policies as the economies of these states were predominantly rurally based, a fact which was reflected in their traditionalist political relationships and structures. However, unlike the translation of security concerns into state policy, the introduction of reformist measures represented the initiation of a process of restructuring of the polity which ultimately had implications for both the maintenance of control of the process of reform and the retention of the state as constituted.

And finally, the last defining characteristic of the National Security State was in the realm of the policy-making process itself. As counter-revolutionary strategy was built around the two poles of security and reform, there developed a dynamic tension between the security-reform matrix which necessarily guided and impacted upon the specific content of that strategy. The shifting balance between these two variables, which marked everything from changes in policy emphasis to adoption of new strategies, was a response to the environment into which the strategy of reform was introduced. Depending on a number of factors – the vitality of the state, the strength of the opposition to state-led reform, the ability of these actors to exert influence over the relevant secondary actors such as those in the international context – the environment imposed restrains on the implementation of reform or even caused the state to reformulate its national strategy. This dynamic process of formulation and implementation ('praxis', to use the Marxist parlance), effecting both the strategies of the state and of the revolution itself, introduced new or modified variables into the policy-making equation and ultimately resulted in both a redefinition of the meaning of reform and a transmutation of the terrain in which it took place. A failure on the part of state strategists (or, to a lesser degree, strategists of the revolution) to respond to the changing terrain of reform could potentially freeze the dynamic process initiated by the state. The development of this situation would allow the *sine qua non* of state-led reform, that is the maintenance of control over the process, to slip from the hands of the state and, if the opposition proved capable of taking advantage of this opportunity, shift the initiative to the revolutionaries. Thus, inherent within the policy-making process of the National Security State was a constant and evolving contradiction between security concerns and reform imperatives which, under certain circumstances, paralysed the process of state-led reform and ultimately threatened the viability of that state.

THE SOUTH AFRICAN CASE

South Africa in the eighties represented a singularly vivid institutional expression of the National Security State. With much of the theoretical literature on counter-revolutionary warfare having been written in the period between the late fifties to the early seventies, South African policy-makers were uniquely placed to draw upon an existing body of literature in formulating their analysis and response to the threat of revolutionary warfare. Coupled with this were the practical experiences garnered from observing neighbouring states in similar circumstances, among them Rhodesia and the Portuguese territories of Angola and Mozambique. This was particularly true in the case of the South African administered territory of South West Africa (or Namibia) which deliberately operated as a testing-ground for both the South African Defence Force's preliminary efforts at counter-revolutionary warfare and the South African government's broader programme of economic, social and political reforms. With Defence Minister P.W. Botha's analysis that the state faced a 'total onslaught' against it serving as a foundation, the state itself was restructured along lines which supported coordination between security and reform bureaucracies while concurrently highlighting the tension between security and reform policies. In short, the South African state as restructured under Botha exhibited all of the basic conceptual criteria of the National Security State outlined above.

This book is an explicit effort to investigate the evolution of the National Security State in South Africa, focusing specifically on its role as a transformative agent in the explosive topography of modernization and incipient revolution. By examining the South Africa case from the early 1970s to the dawn of the nineties – the period in which Botha recast the state in terms of counter-revolutionary strategy – through this theoretical construct, it is believed that a number of facets of the South African state policy under Botha will be brought into focus. Among the most important of these is the fact that the utilization of this theoretical construct will serve as a useful interpretive device enhancing an understanding of the Botha era which has heretofore been lacking in the literature on that period. This is especially true of the volatile process of policy-making within the National Security State, hidebound by the parameters of security and reform. The impact of this approach, translated in policy terms as the setting of distinct limitations on the scope of reform, was one of the major factors inhibiting the complete transformation of the apartheid state. Another notable facet which will be illuminated by this study is the nature of the long-term strategic vision which informed the policies promulgated by the Botha administration. Contrary to popular belief at the time, there was a strategic plan for the reform of apartheid, one which was grounded in the particular variant of counter revolutionary strategy espoused by Botha – total onslaught and total strategy – which was given voice through the South African government's Twelve Point Plan in 1979. It is a measure of both the inherent flexibility built into the strategic plan and the tenacity of its main proponent that the Twelve Point Plan could credibly serve as a guideline for the trajectory of the reform process well into the mid-eighties. Predicated on the maintenance of a narrowing band of white interests, including a host of 'non-negotiables' such as separate education and political veto power, this blueprint for reform apartheid was itself to be reformulated after 1986 and ultimately abandoned in the face of mounting opposition across South African society. And yet, elements of it were to reappear in F.W. de Klerk's own strategy for negotiating with the African National Congress as the two former enemies strove to rework the apartheid polity into the substance of today's new South Africa. Another notable facet which will be illuminated in this study is the nature of the long-term strategic vision which informed the policies promulgated by the Botha administration.

1 The Rise and Crisis of Apartheid

What we demand for ourselves, we do not begrudge the Bantu.
Prime Minister H. Verwoerd debating separate development before Parliament in 1959.[1]

A mere thirty years separates the unexpected triumph of the National party in the general elections of 1948 and the emergence of dark horse candidate P.W. Botha as victor in the bitter party caucus struggle to succeed fallen Prime Minister John Vorster. The intervening period saw the rapid introduction of National party leader D.F. Malan's doctrine of apartheid (and its extension under Prime Minister Hendrik Verwoerd) further entrenching white power and privilege – particularly Afrikaner power and privilege – in a society heir to a colonial legacy of racial segregation and white domination. The rise and implementation of 'apartheid' as state doctrine under the tutelage of the National party and the subsequent crisis engendered by events in the 1970s formed the background to the reform impetus that was to emerge under Botha's administration.

This chapter will briefly examine the development of the National party and its ideological programme of 'apartheid', the adoption and implementation of 'apartheid' as state doctrine by the National party upon taking power, and the crisis enveloping the South African state in the mid-seventies.

THE NATIONAL PARTY AND THE DEVELOPMENT OF THE IDEOLOGY OF APARTHEID

The rise of the National party (NP) and the development of the ideology of apartheid are intertwined with the history of the Afrikaner people in South Africa itself. Principally of Dutch origin, the Afrikaners had struggled in one form or another to retain their cultural and political identity in the alien environment of Southern Africa since landfall in 1652.[2] With the coming of British suzerainty in the early nineteenth century, a conflict developed within the Afrikaner community between assimilation into the politically dominant but numerically inferior Anglo-Saxon world and the maintenance of the society which had developed over the last one hundred and fifty years. A large contingent of Afrikaners, angered at the failure of the British administration in Cape Town to provide support against the Xhosa people on the eastern frontier and its unilateral imposition of manumission, trekked into the wilderness to the north-east and established fledgling pastoral republics. With the discovery of diamonds and gold in these Boer Republics in the 1870s, British imperialists cast their ambitions towards the Transvaal and Orange Free State and, after instigating two wars, succeeded in absorbing these territories into the British Empire. The second war, lasting from 1899 to 1902, was a particularly bitter affair which was only brought to a close through the employment of Lord Kitchener's 'scorched earth' policy and the introduction of concentration camps for Afrikaner women and children. The resultant deaths, upwards of 26,000, emblazoned a lasting animosity towards the British for many Afrikaners and was to shape the development of modern Afrikaner nationalism in the newly formed Union of South Africa.

Under the tutelage of General Jan Smuts, an Afrikaner and former opponent who had won the trust and admiration of the British, the South African state struggled to revive the devastated economy and heal the wounds of war. The growing trend towards urbanization of the rural South African population, brought on in part by the ruination of farming during the recent conflict, engendered a crisis in Afrikanerdom. Lacking the skills demanded by the urban environment, Afrikaners found themselves in the situation of living with and competing against newly urbanized black South Africans for jobs and housing.[3] Coupled with this was a growing trend towards the abandonment of Afrikaans in the home in favour of English. Afrikaner leaders such as D.F. Malan viewed these developments with alarm, seeing in them an erosion of hundreds of years of Afrikaner culture and society.

Spurred on by these circumstances, organizations like the

Broederbond (Brotherhood) – a secret society of elite Afrikaner men – were established to promote distinctly Afrikaner values through the creation of separate bilingual educational facilities and the founding of Afrikaner cultural organizations. A new ideology was consciously developed by Afrikaner nationalists around the notion that the Afrikaner people constituted a special *volk* with a divinely inspired civilizing mission amongst the heathen tribes of the African continent. Tested by God through such tribulations as warfare with the Zulus and oppression by British imperialism, according to the proponents of Christian National education, the fulfilment of Afrikanerdom's destiny lay in the re-establishment of the Boer Republics in South Africa.[4] The recognition that obtaining political power was the key to asserting their vision of society over that of English liberalism led the men who engineered the Afrikaner nationalist revival to give active support to Albert Hertzog's NP. When Hertzog committed the unpardonable sins of colluding with Smuts government at the height of the depression and compromising on Afrikaner nationalist issues with the British government, the more extreme Afrikaners withdrew their support and, in 1933, formed the Purified National party.

It was this 'purified' version of the NP, spearheaded by Malan, which became the primary vehicle for Afrikaner nationalist aspirations for the next fifty years. South Africa's entry into the Second World War, a move adamantly opposed by Malan's Nationalists, saw further changes in the industrial and social landscape of the country. Under conditions of a wartime boom, black South Africans joined the labour force in greater numbers, winning modest concessions in the economic sphere from the South African government. The spectacle of growing black domination of the white community thrust itself into the political debate as never before and, armed with a clear ideological perspective founded on racial exclusivity, the NP stood ready to exploit this new development. While Smuts' government professed to be unable to contain African urbanization, the NP's own programme called for specific legislative action to curb urbanization along with a broader programme of consigning black South Africans to the rural areas.[5] 'Apartheid', or 'separateness', became the NP's watchword for its proposed enforcement of racial segregation in all facets of South African society in the name of the preservation of cultural diversity.[6] With a national election looming in May 1948, the lines were drawn for a contest which would ultimately shape the history of the country for years to come.

Smuts and the Union party, seemingly unaware of the mounting concerns in the white community, conducted an enervated campaign for re-election. Against all expectations, Malan and the NP won a slender five-seat majority in Parliament, ousting the Unionists and ushering in an unbroken sequence of electoral victories up to the nineties.

APARTHEID IMPLEMENTED AS STATE DOCTRINE

Malan, a former minister in the Dutch Reformed Church, wasted little time in turning the hard-fought victory into legislative action. Building in many instances upon existing legislation promulgated under previous governments, the NP pushed through what were to become the pillars of apartheid legislation. In the area of social relations, the government decreed through the Prohibition of Mixed Marriages Act of 1949 and the Immorality Act of 1950 that sex and marriage between whites and blacks would no longer be officially tolerated.[7] As a necessary prerequisite to its overarching programme of instituting racial separation, the government passed the Population Registration Act of 1950 calling for the categorization of all South Africans in accordance with the government's established racial criteria.[8] This was followed by the passage of the Group Areas Act of 1950 which sanctioned the establishment and enforcement of separate residential areas for the racially categorized population groups.[9] The Reservation of Separate Amenities Act of 1953 set out the legal framework for the promotion and maintenance of a range of segregated and unequal facilities.[10] And, finally, the Bantu Education Act of 1953 put African education in the hands of the central government, allowing it to deliberately promote inferior training amongst Africans in line with the government's perception of their future occupational status.[11]

While many of the NP ideologues at that time wanted to

introduce a policy of full territorial separation of the different ethnic communities in South Africa, Malan himself was opposed to this on pragmatic grounds.

> If one could attain total territorial apartheid, if it were practicable, everybody would admit that it would be an ideal state of affairs . . . but that is not the policy of our party. [Total territorial separation is] impracticable under present conditions in South Africa, where our whole economic structure is to a large extent based on Native labour.[12]

It was therefore left to the former Minister of Native Affairs, Hendrik Verwoerd, to develop the doctrine of apartheid to its fullest extent. Verwoerd, a former theologian and Minister of Native Affairs under Malan, was possessed by a singular vision of the direction that the South African state should follow. Assuming office in 1958, Verwoerd took the inherited concept and preliminary structure of apartheid and proceeded to put his own stamp on it. Under Verwoerd, apartheid (which he had come to view as essentially negative in the sense that its focal point lay in establishing restrictions on the African population) was eschewed in favour of 'separate development', a grandiose term which called for the devolution of political control over specified territories within the Republic established on an ethnic basis (called Bantustans or homelands) to the respective African authorities.[13] These would constitute the forum for the exercising of African political aspirations and, ultimately, would be granted full independence by the government. The establishment of 'border industries' alongside the homelands would both act as a magnet for African employment otherwise destined for the white urban areas and provide the territories with economic wherewithal. As those Africans unable to meet the criteria for employment and housing in white South Africa were to be removed to their respective ethnic homelands, the phenomenon of African urbanization would be reversed by the 1970s. The passage of the Promotion of Bantu Self-Government Act of 1959 and establishment of the Bantu Investment Corporation in 1960 were the key events which set separate development in motion. Thus South Africans of African origin, while residing and working in the 87 per cent of South Africa reserved for the white population, were accorded restricted economic, social or political rights in South Africa on this basis. The whole process would be monitored through the application of a system of restrictions and passes (influx control) enforced by the security police. The problematic of the so-called Coloured community was dealt with by officially putting them on a path of 'parallel development', that is to say, according to the prescriptions of separate development the Coloured community was sufficiently advanced as to have in the future its own political institutions within white South Africa. No territorial base comparable to that accorded the African population was envisioned by the government, though recognition of the pre-eminent position of the Coloured community in the Cape province resulted in legislation promoting Coloured employment in that region.[14] No provisions were to be made for the 800 000 Indians residing in South Africa and they were encouraged by the government to emigrate back to India. Underpinning this entire process was the emergence of a weighty bureaucracy of Bantu Affairs and security officials whose primary function was to oversee the increasingly byzantine regulatory environment which accompanied the efforts to implement separate development.

The imposition of the NP's vision of categorization and separation of South Africa's many ethnic groups did not pass without incident. Both domestically and internationally, the South African government came under increasing criticism for what was – particularly in the context of the post-war era of decolonization – perceived to be morally reprehensible policies based on an anachronistic doctrine of paternalistic racism.

Within South Africa itself groups like the African National Congress (ANC), the Pan-Africanist Congress (PAC), the South African Indian Congress (SAIC), the South African Communist party (SACP), Black Sash, and others mobilized to fight the NP's programme.[15] The late 1950s saw the emergence of a united front strategy acting under the banner of the Congress of Democrats and involving many of the aforementioned groups which sought – emulating the philosophy and experience of the Indian nationalists, African nationalists to the north, and the American civil rights movement – to utilize the tactics of non-violent protest in pursuit of the acquisition of civil rights. The launching of the Defiance Campaign in 1952 was the high water mark of this approach. Massive demonstrations, the burning of the hated passes critical to the maintenance of influx control, boycotts and other acts of civil disobedience were conducted under the leadership of the Congress of Democrats. For a brief moment in history, it seemed that South Africa would go the way of the some of the other white-dominated states to the north.

The euphoria generated by the Defiance Campaign was misplaced. After an initial period of uncertainty, the South African government clamped down hard on the protesters, banning many of their organizations and jailing their supporters. The killing of 69 protesters in Sharpeville township in March 1960, followed by the imposition of a partial state of emergency and the banning of the ANC and PAC[16] underlined the government's intransigence on any contemplated reform of its policies. Verwoerd's determination to withstand the challenge was captured in his admonition to white South Africans to 'stand like walls of granite because the survival of a nation is at stake'.[17] As a result, in June that same year the decision was taken by members of the ANC to eschew non-violence and activate an underground network to continue with the anti-government campaign. With the SACP providing training and support, the military wing of the ANC ('Umkhonto we Sizwe') attempted to pressure the government over the next eighteen months through a series of acts of sabotage. Riddled with government informants as well as plagued by inexperience, the military campaign was cut short after a spate of over two hundred incidents.[18] On 11 July 1963, the remaining ANC leadership (Nelson Mandela had been picked up the previous year) was captured while meeting at a farmhouse on the outskirts of Johannesburg. The subsequent trial and imprisonment of Nelson Mandela, Walter Sisulu, Govan Mbeki, and others effectively spelled an end to significant domestic resistance to the South African government for nearly a two decades.

At the same time that the internal environment was erupting, internationally South Africa found itself increasingly on the defensive. At the United Nations, the newly independent state of India had pressed the Western powers into taking a stance against South Africa's racial policies. Resolutions condemning apartheid were drafted on a regular basis by the world body, including a voluntary ban on arms sales passed by the Security Council in 1963, and were seconded by the work of anti-apartheid activists in Europe.[19] The visit by British Prime Minister Harold Macmillan in early 1960, marked by his 'winds of change' speech to a stunned South African Parliament, signalled Britain's determination to carry forward the decolonization process irrespective of white settler sentiments. The animosity generated by this policy ultimately culminated in South Africa's departure from the Commonwealth a year later.[20] With the revelations surrounding the Sharpeville Massacre in 1960, international pressure levelled against the country increased further.

Verwoerd's assassination in 1966 paved the way for John Vorster to take up the premiership. Vorster's ascendancy to power coincided with the halcyon days of the apartheid state. With the economy booming at an annual rate only surpassed by Japan, political dissent amongst the blacks muted since the Rivonia Trial, and the NP garnering ever higher percentages of the white vote, the position of the South African government appeared to be well-nigh invincible. The only troublesome note heard came from the outside world where African colonial independence had resulted in South African being ostracized from continental bodies such as the Organization for African Unity and a growing number of other international organizations. South Africans, however, could take comfort from the fact that a belt of countries to the immediate north consisting of the Portuguese colonies of Angola and Mozambique, as well as the rebel white settler state of Rhodesia, served as a *cordon sanitaire* against the infection of independence fever.

With respect to domestic policy, Vorster initially continued to pursue the policies of separate development as outlined under his predecessor.[21] These included tightening outstanding legal loopholes which hampered the racial classification of persons, removing 'black spots' (areas of black South African settlement in designated white areas), the enforcement of influx control measures, the regulation of labour and a host of other measures. In keeping with the dictates of separate development, Vorster granted self-government to the homelands, and, on the eve of the upheaval in Soweto in 1976, was preparing to grant full independence to the Transkei. In the area of foreign policy, the Vorster administration embarked on an assertive programme that sought to gain diplomatic support within Africa as a precursor to re-establishing normal ties with the West. This 'outward policy' soon came in conflict with strict Verwoerdian apartheid as the government attempted to conduct diplomatic relations within the restrictive framework of separate development.

The first crack in the heretofore impenetrable front presented by Afrikanerdom to the world since coming to power occurred in 1969. It centred around the seemingly innocuous issues of sports and the hosting of African diplomats. With South African sports teams increasingly excluded from international competition as part of the anti-apartheid campaign, a frustrated government announced changes in apartheid policy allowing blacks from other countries to compete on South African soil. This action was coupled with the government's decision to grant those African diplomats who had responded to Vorster's 'outward policy' initiative facilities and accommodation within the country. The storm of protest that erupted within the NP from this step ultimately generated a split as Albert Hertzog led a walkout of MPs to form a new party.

Emerging out of this tempest came the first outlines of the reform debate within the NP, pitting the *verkrampte* (conservative) perspective against the *verligte* (enlightened) perspective. This debate, mirrored in Vorster's cabinet, came to be the first official acknowledgement that some manner of reform of the Verwoerdian system was necessary if it was to survive and prosper. Specifically, NP pundits had come to question the efficacy of government policy in economic, social and political terms.

In the economic sphere, the continued adherence to apartheid policies posed a direct threat to the maintenance of economic prosperity in South Africa. Agriculture and mining had been the traditional sources of economic well-being since the early part of the century, and, given their seasonal or unskilled labour requirements, had supported the imposition of apartheid laws on everything from migratory labour to racially-based job reservation. By the late 1960s, growth in the manufacturing sector had begun to outstrip all other sectors of the South African economy, and given its requirements of an educated and skilled labour force, pressures began to build for changes in the traditional apartheid system. With white immigration unable to provide the requisite numbers of skilled labourers for manufacturing to grow, industrialists and economists called for the loosening of the 'colour bar' on skilled employment and a reorientation in the inferior educational system provided to black South Africans. At the same time, agriculture and mining themselves had become more capital intensive, lessening their need for migratory or unskilled labour. Coupled with this was the fact that overall economic growth was stymied by the artificially small domestic market – a product of low wages and migratory status of black South Africans deliberately fostered under apartheid. The forswearing of a massive domestic market for manufactured goods, which was not overcome by a conscious export-oriented approach to the region, made little economic sense. As the South African economy began to cool off in the early seventies, it became increasingly imperative to the maintenance of its high growth rates to open and expand that market.

In the social sphere, the purported objectives of separate development, that of stemming the tide of African migration to the cities, had been largely unsuccessful. Despite the most vigilante of efforts by the government, Africans resided – either legally or illegally – in all of South Africa's urban areas in numbers which exceeded that of the white population. The economic costs which accompanied the establishment and maintenance of segregated facilities, as well as the costs associated with the forced removal of racial groups, were evident as the South African economy began to stall. Finally, the patent absurdity of social engineering on racial lines, laced with the manifest tragedy of apartheid experienced by many South Africans black and white, pricked the moral conscience of a growing number of members of the white community.

Lastly, in the political sphere, Verwoerdian separate development was not seen to be a resounding success by even those supporting it. Lacking international legitimacy, territorial unity and the economic wherewithal to function as autonomous units, the homelands remained little more than dumping grounds for black South Africans without legal standing in white South Africa. In the wake of the Soweto uprisings of 1976, a major step was taken with the granting of independence to the most viable of the homelands, Transkei; this effort was, however, met with hostility and indifference on the part of the international community. Another political challenge to state doctrine was the problematic of the Coloured community – Afrikaans-speaking and historically linked to the Afrikaner *nasie* (nation).[22] Ostensibly on a separate path of political development ('parallelism'), by the end of the sixties the Coloured and Indian communities had been stripped of all significant political rights without fulfilling the stated requirements of separate development of providing alternative forms of political expression. Concomitant with this issue was the seemingly insurmountable question of the urbanized African population, which continued to defy the government's attempts to curb its growth. Finally, the changing socio-economic composition of the NP's primarily Afrikaans-speaking electorate, which had moved from its working-class and agricultural origins to white-collar professions in the city, coincided with a change in its political orientation. Less inclined to insist on the immutability of aspects of apartheid, the white electorate was ready – up to a point – to contemplate modifications to the existing structure of society.

The result of all of these factors was the launching of a tentative reassessment of selected aspects of state doctrine. This preliminary reappraisal of separate development by the Vorster administration was given content through two events: the outbreak of black labour unrest in 1973 and the convening of a government committee to re-evaluate government policy towards the Coloured population (see Chapter 3). In the wake of the country's first significant labour unrest in decades, protests which underlined the grievous conditions under which black labour was forced to work, the legislation governing labour – in particular the job reservation legislation – was put under review. Concurrently a committee of inquiry into the possibility of changes in constitutional status of the Coloured community, which had recently been stripped of its political rights, was established. These steps, marking a break from the single-minded pursuit of the Verwoerdian vision, were soon to be swept up in a general revaluation of government policy which accompanied the emergence of the crisis facing the state in the mid-seventies.

APARTHEID STATE DOCTRINE IN CRISIS

The mid-seventies proved to be watershed years in South African history. The sudden collapse of Portuguese suzerainty in Africa in April 1974 signalled the disappearance of South Africa's *cordon sanitaire* and the concomitant exposure of the state to hostile and revolutionary forces. By the end of the following year, the South African Defence Force was embroiled in a dangerous regional conflict in Angola, pitting it against the Soviet Union and its proxies, while in neighbouring Mozambique the advent of the Frelimo government gave the African National Congress direct access to South African borders. At home, the long hiatus of black unrest was abruptly shattered by the schoolchildren's revolt in Soweto and its bloody aftermath. Finally, the Vorster government's attempts to grapple with the crisis facing the state were themselves jeopardized by the unfolding of a scandal that shook the very foundations of the NP.

The officers' coup in Portugal, engineered on 25 April 1974 by radicalized elements within the Portuguese armed forces, spelled an end to almost 500 years of Lusitanian involvement in Africa. Following in swift succession was the demise of half-hearted attempts at retaining a measure of Portuguese influence in the colonies, resulting in the installation of a Marxist-Leninist regime in Mozambique and a scramble for power between competing guerrilla movements in Angola. For the South Africans, the impact of the collapse of Portuguese rule was as much psychological as strategic. It meant that Black Africa would now be at the doorstep of the Republic. In the ensuing months, where there had once been a series of white buffer states to the North, now Soviet-backed guerrillas were negotiating the transfer of sovereignty in Mozambique and Angola with sympathetic members of the Portuguese Armed Forces Movement.

In the case of Mozambique, the initial response of Vorster's government was to redouble its efforts to pursue a policy of détente with the vain hope that peaceful coexistence could be established between the neighbouring state and the Republic. Assurances were given to the incoming Frente para Liberação de Moçambique (Frelimo) government that South Africa would not interfere in that country's internal affairs as long as it followed a similar policy with regard to South Africa.

> All that we are really interested in is good rule. It is not in our interest that there should be chaos in any neighbouring country. We want stability. It is not for us to prescribe what sort of rule.[23]

This 'hands off' policy of the government was underlined when five months after the officers' revolt in Lisbon, Portuguese settlers attempted to instigate their own 'unilateral declaration of independence'. Vorster's response was to eschew South African involvement and the counter-coup withered and died. Thus it appeared, at least in those first years, that South African–Mozambican relations would be cordial, if not friendly.

The same could not be said for the other Portuguese colonial possession, Angola. Frelimo's near-total dominance of the revolutionary environ in colonial Mozambique was not replicated in Angola. Three revolutionary movements, roughly corresponding to ethnic divisions within Angola, vied for control of Portugal's wealthiest colony. Competition between the Movimento Popular de Libertação de Angola (MPLA), the Frente Naçional de Angola (FNLA), and the Uniao Naçional para a Independênçia Total de Angola (Unita) over the years had resulted in internecine struggle as each group sought to displace the other in the battle against the Portuguese government. The sudden collapse of the Caetano government in 1974 served to sharpen existing tensions between these groups.

With the encouragement of the American government, Vorster manoeuvred the South African Defence Force (SADF) into a position to render support to the anti-MPLA coalition of FLNA and Unita. The MPLA's avowedly Marxist-Leninist orientation, coupled with overt and covert support from the Soviet Union and its allies, set the stage for the first major superpower confrontation in Sub-Saharan Africa. Conscious of the narrow margin between cooperation and civil war, Portuguese negotiators desperately attempted to put together a compromise settlement that would avert the impending conflict. The Alvor Agreement, hammered together in January 1975, was to have provided the basis for free elections in Angola. However, fighting broke out between MPLA and FNLA forces in April, jeopardizing the already shaky truce that had existed. Full-fledged civil war reigned in the country by May and the three liberation movements scrambled to win support that would match or surpass that of their rivals. As the target date of independence, 11 November, drew nearer it appeared that the FNLA was jockeying itself into a position to take the MPLA stronghold of Luanda. With the MPLA garnering further assistance from its Eastern Bloc sponsors, including a growing contingent of Cuban troops, South Africa and the American Central Intelligence Agency increased their logistical support to the newly allied FNLA-Unita forces to counter such steps. By August, two armed divisions of the South African Defence Force were moving north towards Luanda, sweeping the MPLA troops before them.

However, both Kissinger and the South African government misjudged the mood of the United States Congress for American involvement in Angola. Coming on the heels of the ignoble experience in Vietnam, Congressional doves sought to curtail American 'adventurism' in Africa. The result was the Clark Amendment, passed in December of 1975, which effectively cut American assistance to the joint American–South African campaign to thwart the MPLA's ambitions. For a time, the SADF maintained its forces within striking distance of Luanda; however, with the recognition of the MPLA government by the OAU in early 1976, Pretoria elected to pull out its forces.

The Angolan intervention was to have a profound effect on all aspects of international relations conducted by the South African government. The perception of American duplicity, or at least prevarication in the face of congressional pressure, cast a shadow on South Africa's belief in the reliability of its Western allies. This attitude would increase as the sanctions movement gathered momentum. At the same time, the Angolan intervention highlighted the shortcomings of Vorster's style of government by ad hoc measures and cronyism. Better information and coordination between interested government departments – the Department of Foreign Affairs was particularly incensed that it had not received any notification of action – would, it was felt in the SADF, result in better policy decisions, avoiding further Angolan debacles.

On the heels of the momentous changes in the foreign environment came the first significant eruption of violence within South Africa itself in a decade and a half. Galvanized by the coup in Portugal, black South Africans began to emerge out of their political torpor and engage in protest against the state. Political activity in the townships increased markedly as activists sought to capitalize on the momentous changes in the region. Concomitantly, an economic downturn served to highlight the deprivation that was characteristic of the majority of black South African lives. Pressed by poor wages, deteriorating conditions in the townships themselves, and laws that impeded everything from freedom of movement to the ability to own housing, by the mid-seventies black grievances had reached the boiling point.

Violence finally erupted in the sprawling black township of Soweto situated on the outskirts of Johannesburg. The governing apparatus for the townships, the Bantu Administration Development Boards, acting in a characteristically capricious manner, declared that henceforth black education at the secondary level would be conducted in Afrikaans. On 16 June 1976, a group of students marching to protest the decision were met by a contingent of the South African police force. In the ensuing mêlée, sixty of the youngsters were killed. The news shocked the complacent white community, which had grown accustomed to a quiescent black population, and inspired outrage and further protest within the townships. Across the country black protest and violence was countered by the police, whose heavy-handed response often evoked further violence. The situation was not brought under effective government control until the following year but, from the perspective of both the South African government and the black activists, a rubicon of sorts had been crossed.

For black activists, the death of over six hundred persons in the six-month uprising represented a turning point in a number of respects. First, it was the first major protest action directed towards the government since the crushing of the Defiance Campaign and the subsequent launching of the ANC's guerrilla insurgency. Out of that emerged a new, more militant generation of activists, many of whom fled north to join the exiled and indeed near legendary ANC. Secondly, while the ANC was caught napping on the specifics of the education issue which triggered the unrest in Soweto,[24] it quickly moved to reassert its position as spokesperson for the anti-apartheid movement. A revitalized and reactivated guerrilla insurgency was soon to follow. Finally, the mobilization of international support for the anti-apartheid movement – both directly in the form of condemnation and sanctions in the United Nations, and indirectly in the form of slackening of business investment and support in the country – demonstrated to activists that domestic protests could impact negatively upon the South African government's ability to exercise its will as it saw fit. International pressure, essentially a moribund tool since the Sharpeville incident, increasingly became of focus of anti-apartheid activism and was to achieve crucial results by the mid-eighties.

In the case of the South African government, the events of 1976 rendered it unable to deny the extent of significant black grievances with the existing system and as a result it was forced to reassess the viability of maintaining aspects of existing policy in the face of massive rejection by the bulk of the black population. At the same time, it was clear that the half-hearted reforms of the recent past, focused primarily in such areas as sports policy, were insufficient to placate the scope of black unhappiness with apartheid policy. Building on the recent initiatives in labour policy and the status of the Coloured community, Vorster launched an investigation into government policy by commissioning inquiries into the volatile areas of industrial relations and urban policy. Coupled with the official investigation into the status of the Coloured population – which was to have significant constitutional ramifications – these initiatives together represented a major reassessment of Verwoerdian apartheid. The publication of the recommendations of these committees a few years later, coming at a time of crisis for the South African state, were to have a profound influence on the reformist regime enacted by P.W. Botha in years to come.

With Vorster's departure from the premiership in September 1978, coming on the heels of the 'Information Scandal' which shook his government, a path was cleared for the introduction of a major shift in government policy. Defence Minister P.W. Botha, a 'hawk' on defence issues whose role in drawing up the constitutional proposals of 1977 was largely unheralded by the South African public, lobbied hard within the NP caucus to succeed Vorster. Competing against conservative Connie Mulder and liberal R.F. 'Pik' Botha, the caucus narrowly voted in Botha.[25]

CONCLUSION

With the failure of apartheid to realize its purported goal of total separation evidenced by the constant 'illegal' migration of Africans to the urban areas – in spite of the most vigilant and repressive efforts by the government – and the development of a growing conflict between the increasing labour needs of industry (restricted by the 'colour bar' on types of labour) and the prescriptions of separate development, as well as the emergence of moral qualms about apartheid in certain sectors of the Afrikaner community, a tentative reassessment of key aspects of NP policy officially commenced.[26] Vorster's revisionist approach to separate development, while implicitly challenging some of the precepts of Verwoerdian apartheid, nevertheless remained very much within the narrow confines of the policy of separate development. Vorster's own characterization of the parameters of his government's reassessment highlighted this fact.

> The identity of each of the (statutory) groups must be preserved, friction points must be eliminated and each group must get the opportunity for development.[27]

Under Vorster, the principal policy expression of this reassessment of apartheid was seen in the development of a multiracial sports policy, the establishment of the principle of equal treatment with African diplomats and the relaxing of aspects of the colour bar in the labour field. However, the clearest indication that Vorster was readying to move the country beyond these elementary reforms can be found in the convening of several committees of inquiry into social, economic and constitutional issues in the mid and late seventies. Further evidence of Vorster's reformist intentions can be seen in the fulfilment of aspects of the Theron commission report on the status of the Coloured community, contained within the stillborn constitutional proposals of 1977 (see Chapter 3). It was left to P.W. Botha to put content to and further extend the preliminary revisionism of separate development articulated by Vorster.

2 Total Onslaught and Total National Strategy: The Military Response to Crisis

The Western World – or the Free World, to put it more broadly – is being threatened by the global and total strategy under the leadership of aggressive communism . . .

P.W. Botha to the House of Assembly in July 1970.[1]

The military struggle is merely a part of the total struggle in which South Africa is involved. We shall have to fight in all other fields if we want to protect the hearts and minds of our people against communism . . .

P.W. Botha at the National Party Congress in September 1976.[2]

From the late 1960s onwards, certain observers within the South African defence establishment had watched with growing trepidation as the external threats to South Africa's cordon sanitaire multiplied. Insurgency movements, with the support of Eastern Bloc countries, gained ground in neighboring Rhodesia, Mozambique, Angola, and South West Africa (Namibia), putting increasing pressure on white minority governments there and giving rise to a perception of a Soviet inspired assault on white South Africa itself. With the collapse of Portuguese Africa in 1974, this notion of a Soviet-orchestrated threat gained wider currency within the defence establishment, articulated as the concept of 'total onslaught'. Seeking to devise a response to this phenomenon, South African strategists turned to General André Beaufre, a Frenchman whose work on counter-revolutionary strategy in the third-world context seemed to provide a model for South Africa. Using Beaufre's work as a starting point, the SADF developed a comprehensive strategic doctrine – embodied in the 1977 White Paper on Defence – that called for the marshalling of all state resources to combat revolutionary warfare while simultaneously engaging in substantive domestic reforms. It was this military doctrine that was to serve as

asis of the South African military's response to revol-
iary turmoil in the region and, later, exert a profound influence on Botha's policies as Prime Minister.

This chapter will first examine the rise and development of the concept of total onslaught. This will be followed by a brief investigation into the strategic works of Beaufre. The chapter will conclude by looking at the development and adoption of Total National Strategy, focusing on the Defence White Paper of 1977 which heralded the introduction of the SADF's radical new strategic doctrine.

THE DEVELOPMENT OF THE CONCEPT OF TOTAL ONSLAUGHT

The perception of a Soviet-orchestrated assault on South Africa, later fully articulated as the concept of total onslaught, evolved gradually within the South African defence community. The initial source of total onslaught, providing the construct with much of its conceptual framework, was the ideological conflict that dominated the post-war environment and South Africa's attempts to fit itself within the Cold War framework.

The origins of the total onslaught theory are first and foremost rooted in the West's perception of the Soviet Union's oft-stated global ambitions. As related in numerous scholarly works, since its inception the Soviet Union had declared its belief in the inevitability of the victory of socialism and, through its support of revolutionary movements worldwide, demonstrated a willingness to act on such statements. The speedy triumph of Mao's forces in China in 1949, coupled with the outbreak of communist-inspired revolutions in Greece, Malaya, Korea and Indochina caught a war-weary West by surprise. This gave rise to the American doctrine of 'containment', which took the form of a network of regional defence pacts under the aegis of American support, designed to thwart further expansion by the Soviet Union and its allies. Undaunted, Nikita Khruschev reiterated Soviet support for 'wars of national liberation' in the 'colonial and semi-colonial world' at the Twentieth Party Congress in 1956, and, with the establishment of friendly regimes in those areas in subsequent years, this gave additional credence to the threat posed by the Soviet Union to Western interests.[3] Among the remaining bastions of colonial rule, the twining of communism and indigenous nationalism proved to be an increasingly potent force for challenging the status quo.

South Africans too were drawn into the polarizing web of Cold War politics. In white South Africa's bifurcated society, the English-speaking community – which placed a premium on maintaining political, economic and cultural links with the West – overwhelmingly supported Smuts' efforts to couple South Africa's security concerns with those of the West and Britain in particular. Amongst Afrikaners – to whom anti-communism was a cardinal principal but who nonetheless retained an enduring animosity towards Britain – a studied neutrality in the Cold War was the preferred course.[4] However, on the eve of the election in 1948, the NP engineered a major shift in their prospective foreign policy goals, coming out in strongly in favour of cooperation with the West in the event of an East–West conflict. Critical to this change in policy was the recognition that communism posed a grave and immediate threat to South Africa's internal security and that South Africa lacked the resources to combat a sustained assault alone.[5] As NP leader D.F. Malan noted:

> Communism can be more destructive in South Africa than elsewhere not merely because of its ideology, but because of the fact that it makes a special appeal to the country's non-European population, and if the communists achieve in South Africa what they want to achieve as far as the non-European population of the country is concerned, the death knell will have been sounded for white civilization in South Africa.[6]

With their electoral victory in 1948, the NP found themselves in a position to both formulate and implement national security policy. The principal security objective that guided the NP from Prime Minister Malan through his successors Strydom, Verwoerd and Vorster was the achievement of integration of South African security concerns into the larger framework of the Western alliance structure.[7] Conscious of South Africa's dependence on Western sources – principally British due to the enduring legacy of imperial involvement and through Commonwealth commitments – for armaments, training and security, South African governments of the post-war period sought to convince Western governments both of its strategic importance and willingness to participate in Western actions against the communist threat. The Cape route, as many British strategists of the day readily agreed, was touted as strategically vital to a Western Europe dependent upon oil from the Middle East.[8] Nasser's nationalization of the Suez Canal in 1956 – and still later its closure with the advent of the Six Day War in 1967 – seemed to provide further proof that Western control of the Cape route was critical to its long-term survival. In subsequent years, the argument was extended to include minerals utilized in the production of a variety of militarily and industrially strategic processes. Finally, Western military action against the Soviet threat in Berlin and Korea prompted the sending of token South African forces to assist and served to demonstrate South Africa's commitment to Western security interests.[9]

The results of the government's efforts to link South African security concerns with those of the West were disappointing. The growing international opprobrium for the NP's apartheid policies, heightened by the shootings at Sharpeville in 1960, initially found expression in numerous United Nations resolutions condemning the South African government. 1962 saw a further strengthening of international resolve against South Africa with the founding of a Special Committee on Apartheid within the UN. The following year, the UN Security Council passed a voluntary arms embargo against the country.[10] South African attempts to gain international approval for the absorption of South West Africa, a League of Nations mandate, were persistently thwarted. The leader of the West, the United States, professed a policy of relative neglect of the region and coolness towards South Africa itself – partly a function of its hostility towards colonialism and a reflection of America's own domestic civil rights policy – which obviated the need for overt security arrangements of the kind established elsewhere in the world.[11] South Africa's ties with the Commonwealth – cherished by General Smuts as an alternative source of world stability – became increasingly problematic for the government as newly independent colonies, particularly India, used the Commonwealth forum to criticize South African domestic policies. Commonwealth censure and the institutional crisis it produced eventually prompted Verwoerd to withdraw from the organization in 1961. This action was further bolstered by Harold Macmillan's shocking 'winds of change' address to the South African parliament that same year, culminating in the NP's successful campaign to sever the 'imperial connection' and establish a Republic.

Much to the chagrin of die-hard Afrikaner Nationalists, it was the 'imperial connection' with Britain that held out the best hope for establishing a formal association within Western security arrangements.[12] As the dominant Western power in Sub-Saharan Africa, Britain retained a myriad of economic and political interests in the region that needed to be safeguarded against both internal and external threat. Recognizing this, successive British and South African governments attempted to find institutional expression for their common concerns. Periodic discussions over a British-sponsored Middle East Defence Organization came to naught, as did a series of conferences sponsored by the colonial powers held in Nairobi in 1951 and Dakar in 1954.[13] It was uncertainty within British circles over the future of the Empire, the ill-prepared nature of the South African military itself, and South Africa's reluctance to allow its troops to be incorporated within the racially integrated force structures proposed at Nairobi that scuttled these endeavours.[14] An Anglo-South African agreement over the use of the naval base at Simonstown signed in 1955 included a memorandum promising British support in defence of the Union and South African assistance against aggression in the Middle East. Nevertheless, despite South African efforts to inflate the importance of the Simonstown Agreement, it did not represent the formal security commitment that South Africa had been seeking.

The frustration experienced by the South African government in broadening their security links with members of the Western Alliance, as well as the rising tide of international criticism of the state, continued unabated into the sixties. Nevertheless, the economic prosperity and internal stability experienced by South Africa during this period found expression in a renewed effort to secure Western support by establishing the Republic as a regional power. Under Prime

Minister John Vorster, South Africa embarked on an aggressive policy course that centred on the formation of working relationships with African states, emphasizing the economic and technical benefits that South Africa could offer to these countries. Labelled South Africa's 'outward movement' policy, the government's hope was that Western support could be won by demonstrating South Africa's acceptability amongst moderate African states.[15] This policy was seconded by the maintenance of a modest military build up and drive towards a degree of self-sufficiency in armament production. Towards the first end, the newly appointed Defence Minister P.W. Botha retained defence spending at a steady 3 per cent of the state's GNP throughout the sixties (in contrast with pre-1960 defence expenditures of less than 1 per cent of South Africa's GNP).[16] The effort to establish a domestic source of military hardware culminated in the founding of the state armament production corporation, Armscor, in 1966.[17] Finally, the Vorster administration sought to construct a South Atlantic Treaty Organization from amongst willing Western states and lesser powers in Latin America.

For all the promise that these endeavours seemed to hold for South Africa, in most respects the 'outward movement' policy was a grave disappointment. Only the smaller nations in the immediate region risked formal recognition of South Africa, and while leading states in francophone Africa proclaimed their interest in the process of dialogue, their effort failed to sway the OAU's enmity towards South Africa. Broadening contacts with Latin America did not result in an alliance; neither did South African attempts to woo France by touting the virtues of the expanded naval facilities available at Simonstown. Only the military build-up and Armscor produced tangible results, increasing the capacity of the state to supply its own military hardware needs. Utilizing the example of France's development of self-sufficiency and a domestic arms industry under General de Gaulle and his successors,[18] the Ministry of Defence was able to boast that South Africa was able to manufacture everything from tanks to fighter planes by the late seventies.[19] In fact, on the eve of the UN's mandatory arms embargo in 1977 it was estimated that approximately 45 per cent of South Africa's military procurement was domestically produced.[20]

Considered against the background of adherence to the voluntary arms embargo by its traditional ally, Britain, the commencement of guerrilla insurgencies in neighbouring states, the introduction of the Soviet fleet in the Indian Ocean in the late sixties (coupled with Britain's graduated withdrawal from its security commitments east of Suez), and growing isolation from a host of international cultural and sporting associations, these gains appeared negligible. Increasingly observers within and without the South African government viewed the persistent failure of the state to achieve its security aims as well as the concomitant growth of South African isolation from the West with alarm.[21]

For some, this was clear evidence that a dangerous and pernicious pattern was developing, one that sought to undervalue South Africa's strategic position and – utilizing specious arguments – misconstrue South Africa's domestic policies, thus effecting its isolation from the West. It was noted that even in those cases where South Africa moderated its policies to suit Western demands, such as Vorster's opening of 'multinational sport' in 1971, it only seemed to evoke further hostility from the international community. The source of South Africa's predicament was, according to this perspective, the Soviet Union which coveted control of the Cape route. It was argued that at the same time as this deliberate 'disinformation' campaign was being conducted, the Soviet Union, through its surrogates and with the assistance of misguided Western liberals, was providing support for revolutionary forces operating in neighbouring Rhodesia, South West Africa and the Portuguese colonies. Thus the Soviet Union, through this multi-dimensional campaign levelled against the Republic, was effecting the isolation of South Africa from the West while simultaneously laying the groundwork for the extension of its empire. Botha, the Minister of Defence, became the senior-most public official advocating this concept. He took up this theme of the multi-dimensional nature of the threat to South Africa in the House of Assembly debates in July 1970.

> It is operative in the economic sphere. It manifests itself in the form of incitement to boycotts and illegal strikes. It manifests itself in the sowing of confusion in govern-

ment ranks, such as by means of student unrest, etc. It manifests itself, consciously or unconsciously, in the news media of the world. It manifests itself through subversion, infiltration and the sowing of disorder, and in terrorism in its various forms . . . The military and economic fronts are but two of the ways in which that onslaught is being made on the Western World, but there are numerous others. Today, virtually every sphere of life is part of that overall strategy and that total onslaught on the free world and the people of the West.[22]

The Potgicter Commission Report on national security issues, which laid the groundwork for the establishment of the State Security Council, echoed this view. Published in 1971, the Report stated that the 'enemies' of the Republic were:

(A)ctive in many spheres . . . (including) (i) military; (ii) political; (iii) economic; (iv) social; (v) educational; (vi) psychological; (vii) subversive; (viii) terrorism; (ix) sabotage; (x) espionage . . . An onslaught may be made on the security of the State in each of these spheres . . .[23]

By 1973, the concept of total onslaught had become ensconced in embryonic form within the SADF's official lexicon. That year's White Paper on Defence and Armament Production, written by Botha, contains the following assessment of the threat to the state:

The RSA is a target for international communism and its cohorts – leftist activists, exaggerated humanism, permissiveness, materialism and related ideologies. In addition, the RSA has been singled out as a special target for the by-products of their ideologies, such as black radicalism, exaggerated individual freedom, one-man-one-vote, and a host of other slogans employed against us on the basis of double standards . . . (B)ecause the RSA holds a position of strategic importance, these ideological attacks on the RSA are progressively being converted into more tangible action in the form of sanctions, boycotts, isolation, demonstrations and the like. This renders us – and the Free World – the more vulnerable to the indirect strategy applied by the radical powers in the form of undermining

> activities and limited violence, whether employed openly or dissimulated behind ideological fronts. Geographically the RSA is a part of the Third World; in the military and cultural spheres it is a captive ally of the West, and ideologically a direct obstacle in the path of communism.[24]

The publication of the White Paper on Defence in 1973 placed total onslaught at the centre of the SADF's threat assessment. However, as articulated by Botha at that time, total onslaught appeared to be an unwieldy concept, still lacking the intellectual refinement upon which one could base the development of a comprehensive response. The preliminary effort to develop a response, based on French strategist André Beaufre's work, also received greater attention in that year's White Paper (see below). Only a few months after the release of the White Paper on Defence, events in Portugal were to set in motion a chain of events that threatened South Africa's pre-eminent position in the region. Within an alarmed South African military the result was the sharpening of the notion of total onslaught and, in particular, the acceleration of its efforts to develop an adequate response to this threat.

Total Onslaught and the New Military Doctrine

The sudden disintegration of Portugal's African Empire caught the South African government by surprise. Committed to his 'outward movement' policy – which was predicated on the establishment of cordial relations with African states as a means of easing Western hostility towards South Africa – Vorster discovered events had rendered his efforts obsolete. Faced with the evaporation of South Africa's *cordon sanitaire* and its replacement by potentially hostile governments in Mozambique and Angola, the Vorster administration prevaricated between accommodation and active intervention.

The initial thrust of Vorster's policy response to the dramatic shifts in the regional balance of power, emanating from the Departments of Foreign Affairs and Information, was the introduction of 'detente'.[25] Like its better-known namesake, Vorster's detente policy was in one respect a deliberate attempt at linkage and coexistence with African communist states – in the South African context, the focus was primarily Mozambique. The complexity of the situation in Angola, however, drew a very different response from the Vorster government where South African troops were sent in to provide direct support for anti-MPLA forces (see Chapter 1).

The Angolan intervention represented the definitive shift away from Vorster's detente policy and the eclipse of the Departments of Foreign Affairs and Information by that of Defence. Planned and coordinated without the knowledge of Foreign Affairs, the Angolan episode must have represented an unprecedented opportunity for the South African defence establishment. A cooperative military effort with the West could both demonstrate South Africa's strategic value and potentially serve as a catalyst for the long-sought formal alliance. Coming on the heels of the British Labour party's 6 June cancellation of the Simonstown Agreement – a devastating personal blow for Botha and one that left South Africa without any formal security links in a time of grave crisis – the prospect of a joint, or at least tacitly joint, covert campaign with the West would undoubtedly appear to South African officials to be a risk worth taking. It was the OAU's recognition of the MPLA government and condemnation of South African involvement, coming on the heels of the American withdrawal of support, which ultimately forced a reassessment of Pretoria's policy. By 22 January 1976, the SADF had pulled back to a narrow buffer zone along the Angolan/Namibian border.

In the wake of the recriminations over the Angolan intervention, one lesson in particular seems to have been drawn by the South African military establishment – that the West could not be relied upon, even in the face of direct Soviet military involvement, to come to the defence of South Africa. Defence Minister Botha, recounting the events in Angola over two years later, still spoke with bitterness.

> [W]e [intervened in Angola] with the approval and knowledge of the Americans. But they left us in the lurch. We are going to retell that story: The story must be told of how we, with their knowledge, went in there and operated in Angola with their knowledge, how they encouraged us to act and, when we had nearly reached the climax,

> we were ruthlessly left in the lurch by an undertaking that was broken . . .[26]

This disillusionment was to inform the government's decision to embark on a nuclear weapons programme (see Chapter 4).

The chorus of those individuals analysing events in terms of total onslaught grew in the months following the Angolan debacle.[27] Outside of the defence establishment, there was growing acceptance of the notion of a multi-dimensional campaign targeting South Africa. Most importantly, Vorster began utilizing the vocabulary of total onslaught to describe regional events. 'The nature of the onslaught on South Africa is not only going to be military. It also has a political side. A political onslaught will also be made on South Africa . . .'[28] In August, Vorster likened American pressure on Pretoria to that of communist subversion. 'In the one case, (the pressure on South Africa) will come about as a result of brute force. In the other case, it will be strangulation with finesse.'[29]

This concerted effort by members of the defence establishment to make total onslaught the central feature in South Africa's threat assessment bore fruit in 1977. As a vital part of the emergent strategic doctrine, Total National Strategy, total onslaught was defined in a concrete and systematized manner in that year's White Paper on Defence. This tightening of the amorphous formulations of the past assisted in the development of a threat perception upon which the SADF could base its strategic response.

The White Paper opened with an introduction of the concept of total onslaught, placing it in an historical context as well as describing its various manifestations:

> The process of ensuring and maintaining the sovereignty of a state's authority in a conflict situation has, through the evolution of warfare, shifted from purely military to an integrated national action . . . Up to and including the beginning of the 20th century, the successful resolution of a conflict situation was based purely upon the victory of one army over another. Since World War I, however, this type of warfare has made such excessive demands upon all resources of states that, due to the lack of co-ordinated national action, the result in many countries has been

> the total disruption of the national economy and the psychological disruption of the population. The resolution of a conflict in the times in which we now live demands an interdependent and co-ordinated action in all fields – military, psychological, economic, political, sociological, technological, diplomatic, ideological, cultural, etc. Germany had already realized this before World War II, and Russia has maintained a multi-dimensional campaign against the West since this war. Consequently we are today involved in a war, whether we wish to accept it or not.[30]

The White Paper went on to explicitly define the aims and strategies of Soviet communism and its allies towards South Africa:

> a. The expansion of Marxism by fomenting revolution in Southern Africa.
> b. The overthrow of the white regimes in Southern Africa so that the militant Africa bloc can realize its aspirations with regard to the destruction of so-called colonialism and racialism and the establishment of Pan-Africanism. In its desire to destroy alleged racism, the Arab bloc can, with certain exceptions, be regarded as the partner of the Africa bloc in its hostile actions as far as this serves its own purpose.
> c. The striving after an indirect strategy in order to unleash revolutionary warfare in Southern Africa and, by means of isolation, to force the RSA to change its domestic policy in favour of Pan-Africanism.[31]

With the publication of the 1977 White Paper on Defence, the comprehensive notion of total onslaught became fully embedded within the SADF's threat assessment.

Sources of Total Strategy: André Beaufre

To say that a nation's strategic doctrine is the product of a multiplicity of influences is to state a recognizable truth. Bureaucratic initiatives are seldom derived from a single source. Nonetheless, modern history does provide instances of individuals exerting an uncommon influence on the development of a nation's strategic doctrine – George Kennan and the American doctrine of containment is an outstanding example. So too, if less dramatically, in the case of General André Beaufre and South Africa's doctrine of Total National Strategy. The strategic writings of Beaufre, drawn from France's experiences with the brutal campaigns in colonial Indochina and Algeria, provided his South African counterparts with a comprehensive prescription for countering revolutionary warfare. Faced with a mounting unconventional threat – and, with the introduction of Cuban troops in Angola, a conventional one as well – to its security in the wake of the Portuguese coup, the SADF turned to Beaufre's theoretical work in formulating a response to the emergent total onslaught. This response became enshrined as the SADF's official strategic doctrine, Total National Strategy, in 1977.

The essence of Beaufre's work is to develop a rational approach to strategy that will successfully counter that of the totalitarian systems, particularly Leninist strategy. To do so effectively, Beaufre argues that the state must adopt a strategic approach to governance, one that embraces and coordinates actions in four principal areas: politics, economics, diplomacy and military affairs.[32] Calling this approach total strategy, Beaufre details the organizational structure that would accompany the adoption of this doctrine.

> Below the level of total strategy there must in each field (military, political, economic or diplomatic) be an overall strategy, the function of which is to allot tasks and co-ordinate the various forms of activity within the field concerned. It should be noted here that in the military field the notion of overall strategy already exists; its object is to co-ordinate action on land, in the air and on the sea. There is however no such thing as overall strategy in the political field (e.g. co-ordination of general political policy, internal policy, external policy and propaganda) nor in the economic field (e.g. co-ordination of production, financial policy and overseas trade) nor in the diplomatic field . . . Within each main field each branch of activity will have its own distinct category of strategy. This is the level at which concept and implementation meet . . . (Called operational strategy), [i]ts purpose is not only to harmonize the objectives laid down by overall strategy

> with the capabilities of the tactics and techniques in use in the branch concerned, but also to ensure that those tactics and techniques are developed in the directions which will best fit them to meet future strategic requirements . . .[33]

This outline, as will become apparent in subsequent sections, formed the basis of the SADF's doctrine of Total National Strategy.

Turning to Beaufre's ruminations on strategy, the twin influences of Hegelism and revolutionary warfare are immediately apparent. In *An Introduction to Strategy* Beaufre defines strategy as the 'art of the dialectic of two opposing wills using force to resolve their dispute.'[34] It is Beaufre's emphasis on the achievement of a psychological effect on the enemy, sapping his will to fight, that distinguishes the Beaufreian approach from other Western strategists. The concept of the manoeuvre is itself employed in conjunction with the two 'modes of action' available to the state: direct strategy, dominated by the military, or indirect strategy, which centres principally on non-military actions (i.e., in the political, economic, diplomatic fields). Given that the development of nuclear weapons has rendered the potential cost of direct strategy to prohibitive levels, Beaufre believes that indirect strategy has become the predominant mode of conflict in the post-war period.

This necessitates a strategic focus on the external environment, which Beaufre refers to as the 'exterior manoeuvre.' This entails the employment of an indirect strategy – again, with the ultimate object the opponent's psychological state – to the economic, diplomatic, political and, sometimes, even military fields so as to maximize one's freedom of action while paralysing the enemy through a system of multiple deterrents. Complementing this 'exterior manoeuvre' is what Beaufre calls the 'interior manoeuvre,' the implementation of a subtle coordination of indirect and direct strategy in the actual geographic area of contest (taking the form of Hitler's 'piecemeal' approach in pre-war Europe or that of protracted conflict – the so-called 'erosion' approach).

Another feature of the Beaufreian approach is the need to introduce domestic reforms concurrent with security measures to stem the tide of revolution. Beaufre states that through the implementation of 'thorough-going reforms we must cut the ground from under the feet of the malcontents.'[35] However, unlike others, Beaufre does not dwell on this significant component of counter-revolutionary warfare.

Contrary to the assumptions of many who have analysed Beaufreian strategy,[36] Beaufre is quite explicit in his delineation of the proper role of 'total strategy,' which he subordinates to that of 'high policy.' 'At the top of the pyramid and under direct control of the Government – i.e. political authority – is total strategy whose task is to define how total war should be conducted.'[37] The functional requirements of total strategy demand that the military play a role in conjunction with other governmental departments but there is clearly no room in total strategy for the dominance of the military side of the equation.[38] This insistence that the role of setting of the aims or goals of policy is solely the province of the highest offices of government permeates his entire work on strategy.

TOTAL STRATEGY AND THE SADF

The SADF of the mid-seventies was no stranger to Beaufre's work on total strategy. Strategists within the defence community had engaged in a debate centring on differing counter-insurgency approaches since the upsurge of guerrilla warfare in the region in the early sixties. The seminal event introducing Beaufre's work to the military was a series of lectures held in 1968 at SADF Headquarters by Professors Deon Fourie and Benjamin Cockram. (Fourie's 1968 publication, *War Potentials of the African States South of the Sahara*, is the first example of a South African's incorporation of Beaufre's work, albeit in a limited fashion.) The lectures themselves provided a general overview of the Beaufreian strategic approach.[39] Among the SADF officers in attendance was one Brigadier General Magnus Malan.[40]

Following this introduction, the debate within the South African defence establishment over the strategic direction that the SADF should take began in earnest. Individuals such as Lt.-General Fraser, Admiral Biermann and Professor Fourie were at the forefront of those seeking to educate the defence establishment as to the Beaufreian strategic approach.[41] Fourie, in a series of articles published in *Paratus* in 1971–2, outlined the development of Western strategy from its historical antecedents into the modern period. Accompanying his discussion of revolutionary warfare was an articulation of Beaufreian strategic concepts such as 'indirect strategy', 'direct strategy', 'interior manoeuvre', and 'exterior manoeuvre'. Fourie concludes this series by asking the rhetorical question 'Is there a lesson here for South Africa to learn?'[42]

These efforts found their most influential student in the person of the Minister of Defence. Under the tutelage of Lt.-General Fraser, Botha became an avid reader of strategy.[43] Beaufre's works made a particularly strong impact upon the Defence Minister during this period and the two men were to meet a number of times in the years preceding Beaufre's death.[44] One such visit, arranged by the Defence Attaché in Paris, brought the French General to lecture at the South African Defence War College in 1974.[45] As a result of this exposure, Botha became the foremost advocate of total strategy within the government.

Fuelling this debate on South Africa's strategic options was the growing belief in the multi-dimensional character of the onslaught on South Africa. As early as 1971, utilizing Beaufreian terminology, Botha was pressing for a strategic reorientation by the government to meet the threat.

> In all spheres (political, administrative, economic, psychological, and military) it has to be resisted. This indirect strategy is total in its scope and must be fought in a coordinated manner in every sphere . . . in the sphere of indirect strategy the free world as yet have [*sic*] no effective and total answer.[46]

By 1973, the Ministry of Defence had begun, in tentative fashion, to incorporate Beaufre's works into its official documents. The 1973 White Paper on Defence and Armaments Production, utilizing an elementary Beaufreian framework, stated that the government was in the process of developing a strategic policy that 'closely coordinated and integrated' internal, foreign and defence policy so as to meet the challenge of the 'present international climate which is typified by total strategy and which obliges us to face the onslaughts of monolithic organizations which are in absolute control of all the means available to their states'.[47] It was also noted that the case for South Africa's strategic importance was being threatened by the communist bloc's employment of the 'indirect strategy', another Beaufreian concept.

By 1975 the Ministry of Defence had moved closer to adopting total strategy. Botha, in his introduction to that year's White Paper on Defence, notes that 'all countries must, more than ever, muster all their activities – political, economic, diplomatic and military – for their defence. This, in fact, is the meaning of "total strategy"'.[48] This plea for the incorporation of the Beaufreian strategic approach was coupled with an acknowledgement that while military policy represents only one aspect of a comprehensive defence policy, it was nonetheless a vital part of such an overall policy approach.

1977 White Paper on Defence

South Africa's inability to effectively project power within the region, underlined by the Angolan intervention, demonstrated the weaknesses in the established governmental decision-making structures. These deficiencies stemmed, total strategy advocates contended, from the absence of an overall strategic and technocratic approach to the management of government affairs. To Botha and the strategists within the defence community, Beaufre's total strategy offered both a comprehensive organizational framework and series of strategic prescriptions that – if applied properly – could successfully counter the multi-dimensional threat confronting South Africa. With the Soviet Union and its allies massed in force in neighbouring Angola, the oft-spoken onslaught seemed to have been fully realized. No longer content merely to call for its adoption by the government, the Ministry of Defence appropriated Beaufre's total strategy – christening it Total National Strategy – and made it the SADF's official strategic doctrine. The White Paper on Defence of 1977 still stands as the most explicit summation of Total National Strategy.

Reviewing the contents of the White Paper, it declares that South Africa is facing a total onslaught from both the external and internal environment. Manifesting itself in the form of black unrest, Soviet and Cuban intervention in Angola, and an international campaign to isolate South Africa diplomatically, this total onslaught by nature requires a 'total response' on the part of the South African government in order to successfully combat its effects. The White Paper calls for the adoption of a Total National Strategy that will marshall all facets of South African society in a coordinated effort to thwart this externally-driven campaign to destroy the state.[49]

> Total strategy is . . . a comprehensive plan to utilize all the means available to a state according to an integrated pattern in order to achieve the national aims within the framework of the specific policies. A total national strategy is, therefore, not confined to a particular sphere, but is applicable at all levels and to all functions of the state structure.[50]

According to the White Paper, the fount of total strategy would lie within the State Security Council. It is there that total strategy would be formulated.[51] However, in order to accomplish these broad goals as set out in Beaufre's works, a range of government and non-government institutions would have to be brought into the process. Recognition of this led to the inclusion of an explicit outline of the scope of national security concerns and served notice that the interests managing those areas would, under Total National Strategy, need to coordinate their activities with the government.

> It is because of the complexity of this need [for a total national strategy by the government] . . . that co-ordination between government departments is of the utmost importance. There are few, if any government departments which are not concerned with one or other aspect of national security, or which do not contribute to the realization of national security . . . The aspects of national security which require attention on an inter-departmental basis are the following:
>
> — Political action
> — Military/para military action
> — Economic action
> — Psychological action

— Scientific and technological action
— Religious-cultural action
— Manpower services
— Intelligence services
— Security services
— National supplies, resources and production services
— Transport and distribution services
— Financial services
— Community services
— Telecommunication services

Together the above fields cover the whole spectrum of national security.[52]

In addition, a hierarchy of national aims, objectives and the concomitant policies developing out of these goals is listed.[53] Following Beaufreian imperatives, military objectives and policies are treated as a separate topic, subsumed beneath that of overall national policy concerns.

In keeping with the prescriptions of counter-revolutionary warfare, acknowledgement is made of the necessity to eliminate the sources of internal discontent that give rise to anti-government activity. 'Full and worthy opportunities in the economic, social and political spheres for all population groups in the RSA must be our aim; this can be achieved only by peaceful and evolutionary processes and without outside interference.'[54] This notion received further elaboration in another section of the White Paper. 'The internal policy (of South Africa) is . . . to follow a policy of independent development of all population groups.'[55] This included the promotion of self-governance and independence of the homelands and the establishment of separate self-governing institutions for the Coloured and Indian populations, as well as the establishment of a constitutional mechanism 'to serve matters and actions of communal interest.'[56] As will be demonstrated in subsequent chapters, this brief testament on constitutional affairs captures the essence of Botha's initiatives in the area of political reform.

The wholesale adoption of the Beaufreian framework in the Defence White Paper of 1977 was indicative of the fact that SADF had not fully integrated these concepts into the strategic environment of South Africa. Indeed, some defence establishment figures contend that the SADF latched onto Beaufreian strategy as a kind of panacea, without sufficient understanding of the actual intricacies and prescriptions of the strategy itself and that this would later manifest itself in a hesitant approach to the crises emerging out of the reform process.[57]

CONCLUSION

Was South Africa being confronted by a coordinated multidimensional threat orchestrated by the Soviet Union? Did South Africa actually occupy a central position in Soviet designs on the African continent? These questions, raised by hostile critics and sympathizers alike, bedevilled the Botha administration as it sought to justify the implementation of a plethora of policies predicated on combating the total onslaught. When confronted in the early eighties by evidence presented by the American CIA that the threat was not as menacing as it seemed, the South African intelligence service representatives came away thinking the CIA had gone 'soft on communism'.[58] Nevertheless, after weighing the evidence even critics of the Botha administration and its total onslaught thesis could say, 'Is the threat real? Definitely. But it is not total . . .'[59]

With the publication of the 1977 White Paper on Defence, the SADF had firmly committed itself to the concept of total onslaught and its solution in the form of total strategy. A few short months later, the Security Council of the United Nations – dominated as it was by the Western powers – passed a mandatory arms embargo against South Africa. This action, coming at a time of heightened insecurity within the South African government, further underlined the state's isolation from the West. For many white South Africans, the case for the existence of a multi-dimensional onslaught against the Republic had taken concrete form. Out of this quagmire emerged the military, relatively unscathed (Angola notwithstanding) by the shattered policies and initiatives promulgated under the Vorster government. Armed with a clear definition of the threat to South Africa and the requisite counter-response – Total National Strategy – the military establishment increasingly appeared to be the only governmental institution prepared to meet this national crisis. The unravelling of Vorster's position in the wake of the Information Scandal in 1977, an episode which further discredited his administration, gave Botha an opportunity to make a bid for the premiership. Narrowly selected to replace Vorster by the NP caucus in October, 1978, Botha found himself in a position to activate the Beaufreian prescriptions contained within Total National Strategy. It was through this process of implementation that the SADF's new strategic doctrine became transformed into a strategy for national reform.

3 From Military Doctrine to Reform Apartheid, 1978–80

Adapt or die. P.W. Botha addressing white South Africans in 1979.[1]

The Twelve Point Plan creates the guidelines for a total national strategy. P.W. Botha at the National Party Congress in September 1980.[2]

When P.W. Botha assumed the office of Prime Minister in 1978, he believed that he was inheriting a state under siege. Moving to address the crisis, Botha initially turned for guidance to the institution to which he had devoted over a decade of service as its chief minister: the South African military. Long cognizant of the potential threat facing white rule, the South African Defence Force (SADF) had by 1977 adopted a radical strategic doctrine and christened it Total National Strategy. This strategy called for the marshalling of all state resources to combat revolutionary warfare while simultaneously pursuing the aggressive introduction of substantive reforms designed to undercut the appeal of revolutionary action.

While the theoretical precepts of the security component of the strategy were already in place, Botha recognized that the reform component needed to be both formulated and, along with the recommendations for the institutionalization of a national security system, formalized within the government before he could embark on his national reform strategy. This he proceeded to do with the methodical thoroughness that was characteristic of his years in the Ministry of Defence.

Tackling the problematic issue of reform, Botha brought into his administration a generation of bureaucrats committed to restructuring the system in line with recommendations emanating from a series of government committees set to investigate state policy in economic, social and constitutional affairs. With the new military doctrine serving as inspiration, Botha introduced sweeping structural reforms of the executive branch that were designed to facilitate the formulation, implementation and coordination of his national reform strategy. Turning to the security side, Botha presided over the establishment of a comprehensive state apparatus for the management and coordination of government policy in the event of a national emergency, called the National Security Management System (NSMS). Held in abeyance by the Prime Minister, the NSMS acted as a guarantor that state control of the process of reform would be maintained should revolutionary forces ever present a genuine threat to governmental authority. These three initiatives, incorporated into the 'Twelve Point Plan' outlined by Botha in 1979, formed the basis of his response to the national crisis confronting the state. They were to guide the Botha administration as it plunged into the tumultuous decade ahead.

This chapter will examine the transformation of military strategic doctrine, with its twin imperatives of security and reform, into a national strategy for reform. First, the development of the reform side of national strategy will be examined, focusing on the role of committees of inquiry into economic, social and constitutional issues and their influence on the development of the Botha administration's approach to reform. Second, the establishment of the mechanism for the implementation of national reform strategy through the restructuring of the executive branch will be examined. Third, the formation of the security side of the national reform strategy, the NSMS, will receive attention. Finally, Botha's 'Twelve Point Plan' – the crystallization of the Prime Minister's programmatic approach to transforming the South African system – will be analysed.

THE DEVELOPMENT OF REFORM STRATEGY

The development of Botha's programmatic reform strategy had its roots in a series of government committees of inquiry established under his predecessor, Prime Minister Vorster. Socio-economic reform was first broached by the commissions of inquiry into labour and manpower utilization chaired by Nic Wiehahn and Pieter Riekert in 1977. Constitutional reform received its first official hearing at the Theron commission as early as 1973. None of their reports were spared some measure of government censure in the form of cabinet committee responses. Nevertheless, despite initial criticism, the Botha government utilized each of these three commissions as the basis for its reform initiatives carried out in the first half of the 1980s.

Blueprint for Socio-economic Reform: The Wiehahn and Riekert Commissions

Reformation of the subordinate socio-economic status of South Africa's black population instituted under Botha grew primarily out of the recommendations of two committees of inquiry established by Vorster. The Committee of Inquiry into Labour Legislation, commonly called the Wiehahn commission, and the Committee of Inquiry into Legislation Affecting the Utilisation of Manpower, known as the Riekert commission, together provided the framework for the series of government administered changes in socio-economic conditions affecting blacks. The central thrust of their recommendations was to reform the socio-economic circumstances of blacks in the urban districts by giving formal recognition to their permanent status in 'white' South Africa. The resultant easing of restrictions on employment, housing and related areas would – it was believed – meet the labour needs of state and industry while ameliorating the adverse conditions that gave rise to popular discontent. Concomitant with this approach was the maintenance of the 'homeland' system as both the vehicle for political expression of urbanized blacks and – in the eyes of government policy makers – the appropriate forum for the realization of social, economic and political aspirations of the majority of blacks in South Africa.

The Wiehahn Commission

South Africa's labour policy was intimately intertwined with the rise of white labour militancy in the twenties. White fears of being displaced by a mass of lower-paid black workers resulted in the establishment of a host of legislative acts by the Smuts government supporting the rights of 'civilized labour' (whites) to be guaranteed a job, a racially differentiated wage scale, and suppression of use of blacks in skilled and semi-skilled positions.[3] The NP drew some of its support during this period from the newly urbanized Afrikaner, who was in direct competition with urban blacks. This support of white labour interests was generally resisted by business interests in the country,[4] particularly as the economy grew in the post-war period; however, the election of the NP guaranteed that black labour would be relegated to a subservient position *vis-à-vis* white labour. As a result, the status of black employees in South Africa – poorly paid, occupying substandard housing, and working without fundamental legal protection – was nothing short of helots.

The outbreak of strikes of 1973 in Durban proved to be a watershed event in the drive towards official recognition of black labour rights. A growing consensus amongst government officials, segments of the business community, the media and the white public, encouraged Vorster to embark on a broad reform programme for industrial relations. With statutory discrimination as enshrined in the jobs reservation orders already being circumscribed with the complicity of the Ministry of Labour (almost 4700 exemptions to the jobs reservation orders were granted in 1972 alone),[5] the government took the step of introducing a new labour law governing black workers. Though severely limited in application, the Black Labour Relations Regulation Act of 1973 broke with past legislation by acknowledging the right of black workers to strike and send representatives to industrial council meetings. But the surest indication that the government was serious about its commitment to some measure of labour reform came with the appointment of the Commission of Inquiry into Labour Legislation in May 1977.

Under the guidance of Nic Wiehahn, the commission set about tackling the thorny issue of the status of black trade unionism. From the outset, it was clear that the Wiehahn commission intended to call for substantial changes in the existing legislation governing black workers. Shortly before his appointment to the commission, Wiehahn gave a public lecture in which he outlined the 'rights of labour', including the right to strike and the right to organize.[6] In following months – utilizing a carefully orchestrated campaign that depended upon press leaks, the floating of 'trial balloons' from Wiehahn's own labour relations institute, and the solicitation of advice from a range of prominent individuals and organizations – Wiehahn was able to develop a comprehensive plan of labour reform that met with the approval of most of the interested parties.[7]

In its first report issued in May 1979, the Wiehahn commission recommended that black trade unions be granted full recognition,[8] the job reservations orders be expunged or phased out, the maintenance of segregated facilities be waived (subject to the approval of employers and white unions), multi-racial 'workers councils' be established for purposes of bargaining, and even that limited rights for migrant workers be accepted.[9] Despite these substantive liberalizations, the newly recognized unions would still be subject to control by the government through the process of registration (the act of which put into effect the legal prohibition on union links with political organizations), the overview of a newly created National Manpower Commission, and recourse to the industrial court system.

The government's initial response to the commission's recommendations was released shortly after the Wiehahn commission report was made public. Its White Paper, while accepting many of the commission's recommendations, balked at allowing migratory workers to join black unions. A labour bill introduced into parliament a few weeks later went further by enhancing the power of the industrial court, banning multi-racial unions, preserving some job reservation orders, and imposing a fine on unions registering migratory employees. The resulting uproar and confusion led to a temporary stalling of the reform campaign, fuelled by a series of strikes by emergent black unions and the unexpectedly sympathetic rulings of the industrial court.

The passage of the Industrial Conciliation Amendment Act of 1979, followed by an array of legislative modifications, signalled the start of a long retreat by the government from its staunch adherence to the recommendations of its White Paper. Critical to this was the black unions' resistance to government's attempts to divide the black labour movement along migratory lines, bolstered by the opposition of liberal opinion in business circles. For the interim, the conflict over the status of urbanized 'insiders' and migratory 'outsiders' was to continue, played out in the battle over registration of organized labour.[10]

The Riekert Commission

Reforming South Africa's labour policies went only part way in ameliorating the condition of blacks in the urban areas. The raft of restrictive legislation that governed black life – from the 'influx control' laws of the Native (Urban Areas) Consolidation Acts of 1923 (amended in 1930) and 1945, to the Group Areas Act of 1950 forbidding blacks to reside permanently in designated white areas – placed immense hardship on the urbanized black population.[11] Separated from families (or unable to obtain permission for spouses to reside with them), relegated to crowded and substandard housing, subject to arbitrary arrest under the myriad of 'influx control' laws administered by the government's notorious Labour Bureaux, urbanized blacks lived in a shadow land of poverty and quasi-legality. Over the years, government and business recognition that black labour was crucial to the health of industry had resulted in the development of a convenient fiction to circumvent the exigencies of apartheid. Thus black workers in urban South Africa, though they might have lived in white areas for generations, were considered to be merely temporary sojourners.[12] Even those with the coveted 'Section 10' rights – which granted residency exemptions for blacks meeting its stringent criteria – were able to live only in designated townships, forswearing the possibility of ever possessing their own domicile. Restrictions on black business ownership within the townships acted as an additional affliction on the status and earning power of black residents.

The Commission of Inquiry into Legislation Affecting the Utilisation of Manpower was constituted against the background of growing labour unrest and the Soweto riots by the Vorster administration. Broadly charged with investigating socio-economic factors as they impacted on the utilization of black labour, the Riekert Commission (as it became known) came to focus the bulk of its attention on the question of 'influx control' and housing for black workers. In the course of the study, it sought to tread the narrow ground between outright censure of some of the legislative pillars of apartheid while tacitly justifying the maintenance of the basic outline of separate development.[13]

The Riekert Commission, submitting its report to the government in August 1978, recommended that blacks already established within the urban areas be granted substantial economic and social rights, that is the right to work and own housing in 'white' South Africa. In effect, it was suggesting that the government formalize the essential elements of the existing situation – the recognition of economic dependency on urban black and the accompanying need for a stable work force – while fracturing the black population between those with rights within South Africa and those residents of the 'homelands' without rights outside their polities. This approach coincided with the principle of 'insiders' and 'outsiders' underlying the recommendations on labour policy put forth by the Wiehahn Commission.[14] Additional proposals emanating from the Riekert report included the lifting of restrictions on black entrepreneurship through the limited introduction of 'free trade zones' and the elimination of legislation (such as the Masters and Servants Act 1924 of Transvaal and Natal) regarded as noxious or irrelevant under current conditions.

Significantly, the report did not call for concomitant political rights for blacks within the Republic. Urban blacks were to remain citizens of the 'homelands' and exercise their obligations as citizens in that particular forum. The report deemed it critical to the success of its recommendations that a genuine level of industrial development take place in the 'homelands' so as to curb the migratory trend to the big cities. 'Control over the migration of the population to urban areas is', according to Riekert, 'essential in order to obviate social problems'.[15] The question of economic viability of the 'homelands', a prerequisite of any scheme to stifle rural to urban migration, was left mute.

The government response to the Riekert Commission report came in the form of a White Paper produced by a cabinet committee devoted to reviewing the commission's work.[16] By accepting the majority of recommendations of the commission, the government signalled its intention to clear the way for modest change and a measure of reform – albeit within the confines of the black 'urban insider' and 'rural outsider' arrangement – of the existing socio-economic conditions for South African blacks.

Impetus for Constitutional Reform: The Theron Commission[17]

The roots of constitutional reform proposals lay in the debate over the position of the Coloured population within the South African polity.[18] As the product of miscegenation between whites and blacks, the Coloureds had long occupied an uncertain position in South African society. Having held limited political rights since the seventeenth century, the circumscribed voting rights for Coloureds were entrenched in the Act of Union in 1910, allowing the Cape and Natal provinces to retain a qualified Coloured franchise. This situation was deemed intolerable by the NP and, upon their coming to power, resulted in passage of the Separate Representation of Voters Act of 1951 which forced Coloureds onto a separate voters' roll.[19] This preliminary step was followed by the successful effort to force the exclusion of Coloureds from these same separate voting rolls in 1968, spearheaded by P.W. Botha, then Minister for Coloured Affairs.

With these changes completed, the government opened the debate as to the future of the Coloured people. The dictates of separate development required that each designated black population group exercise political rights within its own geographic area as defined by the white government; however, it was felt by NP pundits that the Coloured and Indian populations, while predominant in the Cape and Natal provinces, could not be said to have a traditional territorial bastion in which to conduct exclusive political affairs.[20] According to NP thinking, the Coloureds were to find their political expression through what was termed 'parallel development'.[21] However, the problem facing apologists for apartheid was the fact that 'parallel development' seemed ultimately to imply that Coloureds and Indians would have their own sovereign parliaments within the territorial confines of 'white' South Africa. None other than Vorster himself remarked on the occasion of the demise of the Coloured franchise that:

> We are going to be faced with a dilemma in this connection in future; we are going to create Parliaments for the Coloureds and the Indians and we are going to be faced with a dilemma that sovereign Parliaments cannot exist side by side in the same country.[22]

As the government sought to grapple with this dilemma, it chose to establish an interim body to accommodate Coloured political aspirations. The Coloured People's Representative Council (CRC), a partially elective and partially government appointed body that purported to represent the interests of the Coloured population, came into being in 1969.[23] A non-elective body – the South African Indian Council (SAIC) – was established in 1968 for the Indian population.[24] The shortcomings of these arrangements were highlighted by the persistently low electoral turnout and government actions to undermine the participation of any avowedly anti-apartheid figures in the process.

By the early seventies, Vorster and others within the NP were publically stating the need to rectify the situation of the Coloureds and Indians in a meaningful way. Vorster himself outlined his government's recognition of the need for a new dispensation for the Coloured people at the opening of the seventh session of the first council of the CRC in November 1974.

> The government . . . accepts that these aims [a new political dispensation for Coloureds] can only be achieved through a process of orderly constitutional evolution and not through artificial or abstract constitutional formulas that have no relation to existing political realities and proven practices . . . Furthermore, it must be accepted that orderly government is the only guarantee for progress or positive change in the economic, social and constitutional sphere . . . [T]he establishment of the Coloured Representative Council . . . is a beginning point, not an end point.[25]

The convening of the Theron Commission, the think tank on developing a new Coloured 'dispensation', was rooted in this debate on the status of the Coloured population which accompanied the community's disenfranchisement. Acting on the suggestions of an informal discussion group founded in 1966 at Stellenbosch University,[26] the government established an official commission in March 1973 to examine the status of the Coloured community over the last decade and submit proposals for the improvement of its situation.[27]

In keeping with its wide brief, the Theron Commission (the first multi-racial commission convened by a NP government) produced a host of recommendations with respect to the Coloured community, including the abolition of the Prohibition of Mixed Marriages Act and Section 16 of the Immorality Act as well as selective relaxation of the Separate Amenities Act and the Group Areas Act. However, the most influential of these points was on the subject of Coloured political rights. Acknowledging the Coloured community's resistance to the existing situation (as well as the concept of a Coloured 'homeland'), the commission noted that the CRC itself had proved to be an inadequate tool of political expression even on its own terms.[28] The commission then called on the government to make provisions:

> [F]or satisfactory forms of direct Coloured representation and a direct say for Coloureds at the various levels of government and on the various decision-making bodies . . . (W)ith a view to the implementation of the proposal above, a committee of experts be appointed to make more detailed proposals in regard to the organizational and statutory adjustments required . . .

This was followed by this keynote passage:

> [And] in the process of constitutional adjustment it will have to be accepted that the existing Westminster-founded system of government will have to be changed to adapt it to the specific requirements of the South African plural population structure.[29]

The Theron Commission's report, issued the day that the Soweto uprising began, is an important bellwether of the direction that the momentous changes in political affairs were soon to take. While the machinery of constitutional reform – a bevy of successive commissions and committees – examined the reforms originally proposed by the Theron Commission, the basic thrust of the commission's recommendations was retained. Specifically, the committee's underlying assumption that South African society was composed of fundamentally different and irreconcilable ethnic groups making it undesirable as well as unpractical to bring them together under one unitary political system became the starting point for all subsequent investigations. Secondly, the commission's assertion that the Westminster form of government, with its 'winner take all' system, was an inappropriate mechanism for any future South African constitution prompted the search for alternative governmental systems. The gravitation towards Arend Lipjhart's 'consociational' system became *de rigueur*, exercising a profound influence on all constitutional schemes.[30] Finally, thc call for a committee of experts to work out the details of a new constitutional dispensation was repeated by other commissions and ultimately given substance in the form of the President's Council.

The commission's recommendations received official consideration in a newly established Cabinet committee chaired by Botha.[31] Founded in August 1976, its task was to examine changes to the South African constitution that would permit the inclusion of the Coloured and Indian populations. Botha contacted constitutional expert Dr W.B. Vosloo in November of that year and asked him to draw up a draft constitution. Vosloo, who had authored the section of the Theron commission report devoted to constitutional affairs, composed two separate constitutions: one with a three-house parliament, corresponding to the three statutory population groups – whites, Coloureds and Indians; and a second with a four-house parliament, identical to the first save that it included a house for the African population. Both proposed systems had an executive consisting of a State President and a council of cabinets taken from each separate house of parliament.[32] These constitutional models were to serve as the starting point for subsequent proposals put forth by the NP government.

A White Paper was produced by the Cabinet committee and tabled in Parliament in April 1977. In it the committee rejected the Theron commission's call for direct Coloured representation in government, the abolition of the Prohibition of Mixed Marriages Act and the Immorality Act.[33] Instead, it pressed for the establishment of three separate parliaments for each population group with control over issues of group concern, coupled with a Council of Cabinets – constituted according to overall population ratios – that would legislate on issues of mutual concern. Replacing the office of Prime Minister would be that of an Executive President elected by an Electoral College, also composed in accordance with the population ratio. Augmenting this structure would be a Presidential Council, replacing the existing Senate, and the establishment of regional councils also based on population groups.[34] These recommendations were set before the four provincial branches of the party and overwhelmingly approved by August that same year.

Concurrently, the CRC and SAIC were given copies of the constitutional proposals to review. The outright rejection of these proposals by these representative bodies fomented a crisis in the political reform campaign.[35] Coupled with the burgeoning Information Scandal, the process of constitutional restructuring was temporarily called to a halt.[36]

The apparent culmination of this lengthy process was the submission of a draft bill on constitutional proposals to the House of Assembly on 3 April 1979. While the South African Constitution Bill never went beyond its first reading, its content reflected the influence of consociationalism by calling for the creation of three chambers (based on race) within a single parliament, the establishment of a State President elected by an Electoral College (drawn from the three chambers), the formulation of a President's Council to replace the Senate, and a Council of Cabinets that would consult and set policy on matters of mutual interest.

Under newly selected Prime Minister Botha, another commission of inquiry was established three months later to investigate constitutional reform.[37] A reaction to criticism that the 'new dispensation' was being formulated without adequate consultation and input from the Coloured, Indian and African populations, the Schlebusch commission renewed the search for a formula of constitutional re-structuring that would be acceptable to the established powers.[38] In its interim report issued on 6 May 1980, the commission called for the abolition of the Senate and its replacement by a multiracial President's Council.

The President's Council was created in January 1981, with

Alwyn Schlebusch as its head. Composed of 60 members of the white, Coloured, and Indian communities, this advisory body of notables replaced the moribund upper house of the South African parliament (which had largely been stripped of relevance through the machinations of the NP). A government plan to establish a separate appointed Advisory Council which would instruct the President's Council on issues directly relating to blacks was rejected by the homeland leaders.[39] Acting as the 'government's major constitutional think-tank'[40], through its five subcommittees the President's Council produced reports that were to serve as the basis of constitutional reform under Botha.

Conclusion

The Wiehahn and Riekert commissions, taken together, represent an effort to engage in modest reform of the state doctrine of separate development. Working in cooperation, the two commissions attempted to build into reform the concept of urbanized blacks with privileges unavailable to those blacks designated as 'outside' the system. Arguably the same basic assumption underlaid the Theron Commission recommendations on the status of the Coloured population – though it must be acknowledged that the Theron commission went further by calling for the abolition of the Prohibition on Mixed Marriages Act and the Immorality Act as well as direct Coloured representation in parliament – in that the 'multi-national' character of South African society was reaffirmed as a fundamental tenet of any reform contemplated of the system. This put all the proposed changes within the contours of Verwoerdian separate development or 'grand apartheid'.

At the same time, the reforms advanced by the commissions of inquiry – while eliciting a mixed reaction from the government in the form of various cabinet committee white papers – represented a significant break with certain central precepts of apartheid. Specifically, the principle that white South Africa was ultimately to be separate from that of the African, Coloured and Indian populations in economic, social and political terms was effectively discarded by the reports. The admission that at least *some* blacks in South

Africa were inextricably linked to the white polity meant that an effort to accommodate their aspirations within the context of the state was necessary.[41] The hobbled constitutional arrangement for Coloureds and Indians – which presaged the tricameral parliament's division between 'own' and 'group' affairs – epitomized the difficulties experienced by the government in harmonizing socio-economic realities with the introduction of legitizing political institutions as mandated by Verwoerdian separate development, all the while fulfilling the political imperative of maintaining white domination. In short, the Wiehahn, Riekert and Theron commissions were an attempt to set guidelines for the development of an institutional expression of this basic apostasy to separate development, while still seeking to reconcile these reforms with existing state doctrine.

THE ESTABLISHMENT OF THE MECHANISM FOR THE IMPLEMENTATION OF REFORM

The burgeoning administrative apparatus and unwieldy cabinet system presided over by Vorster was one of the major obstacles to reform inherited by Botha. The extent of this bureaucratic behemoth, revealed to the public through the Information Scandal, highlighted the administrative chaos that had characterized Vorster's personalized style of governance. Botha, determined to capitalize on the public censure surrounding his predecessor's administration, moved to refashion the centre of power both to reflect exigencies of Total National Strategy and to ensure personal control of the state bureaucracy.[42] Utilizing the recommendations of the Public Service Commission and that of the SADF doctrine of Total National Strategy, Botha instituted a broad reorganization of the executive while simultaneously reworking the structure of bureaucratic decision-making.

The Public Service Commission White Paper

The legislative basis for much of the structural changes initiated under Botha came out of the Public Service Commission recommendations. A long-established governmental institution, the Public Service Commission launched an investigation in late 1978 into government restructuring at the behest of the new Prime Minister. Speaking before parliament, Botha said that in addition to promoting 'clean' and efficient government, 'rationalization' itself was a practical and necessary step to counter the total strategy levelled against South Africa and which, with its full institutionalization, would give way to the abolition or consolidation of obsolete legislation. 'This is an essential step in the struggle against the onslaught which is being made on us.'[43]

The Public Service Commission's recommendations were tabled before Parliament in its White Paper on the Rationalisation of the Public Service and Related Institutions on 8 May 1980, resulting in the passage of the Public Service Amendment Bill. Empowered to reorganize government bureaucratic structures virtually at will, Botha embarked on a wholesale 'house cleaning' that involved the creation of new government departments, the shifting of departmental responsibilities, the establishment of clear lines of authority between departments and the formalization of bureaucratic procedures. Of particular importance was the expansion of executive authority in an enlarged Office of the Prime Minister.[44] Four permanent cabinet committees – Economic Affairs, Social Affairs, Constitutional Affairs and the already established State Security Council – were created to serve as centre of power and decision-making under the new government.[45] An effort was made to enhance organic links between departments by having the ministers heading up the four cabinet committees serve as chairmen of the four planning branches of the Office of the Prime Minister. Additional changes to the executive were the establishment of a cabinet secretariat and the founding of the Commission on Administration. On the security side, the Bureau of State Security (BOSS) was eliminated and replaced by the National Intelligence Service (NIS).[46] Coupled with this was the institutionalization of an extensive internal security apparatus – the National Security Management System – to be activated in emergency situations. (The structural changes in the security apparatus will be detailed in the next section.)

Another feature of the reorganization was the replacement of many of Vorster's hand-picked ministers and bureaucratic functionaries with Botha supporters. Given Botha's position as leader of the Cape provincial wing of the NP, he was vulnerable to the numerically stronger and more conservative Transvaal provincial wing of the party. To compensate, Botha put key figures from outside of the Transvaal provincial party hierarchy, such as Chris Heunis (Cape NP) and Alwyn Schlebusch (Orange Free State NP), into positions of power.[47] The schism of 1982 within NP ranks and the subsequent drift of intransigent apologists of apartheid to the newly formed Conservative party ensured that the reformist wing would henceforth dominate the NP.[48] A large number of persons brought on board by Botha to staff the bureaucratic apparatus for reform were drawn from the academic community or the private sector.[49] Distinctly *verligte* (enlightened) in their politics, Botha's bureaucrats represented a new generation of Afrikaners for whom the trials of the past, which had inspired their Verwoerdian predecessors, were mere history. The specialist skills of the new technocratic elite were harnessed by the government into a unit that consciously mirrored the contemporary British cabinet's Central Policy Review Staff.[50]

But 'rationalization' was more than just the fulfilment of a new administration's bureaucratic impulse to reorganize and, in the process, to staff government posts with Botha loyalists. 'The rationalization of the civil service and indeed also of top decision making structures is', as one contemporary observer noted, 'part and parcel of the total national strategy'.[51] The extent to which 'rationalization' was seen as flowing directly from the precepts of total strategy is captured in a statement by a former Director-General of the Office of the Prime Minister:

> The special circumstances in South Africa and the increasing sophistication of the 'onslaught' on the country on all levels of society, that is in the areas of politics, the economy, security and community life, requires a sophisticated scientifically planned and well coordinated policy framework.[52]

When weighing the administrative changes wrought under 'rationalization' against the prescriptions of Beaufreian strategy, it is clear that the French General's strategic approach exercised a guiding influence on the process. Beaufre's call for policy coordination in line with an established strategy to guide the state was heeded by Botha as he sought to stitch together the differing departments in an administrative web of consultation and interlocking responsibilities. Reflecting this was the constant reiteration of Beaufreian terminology, transformed into the dialectic of total onslaught, as an explanatory tool for the proposed structural changes. An attendant aspect of this movement was the rise of the South African technocrat, so much a feature of French administration, replacing the traditional picture of the Afrikaner bureaucrat who had secured his position through NP patronage.

Though much was done to alter governmental structures and a new clique of technocrats were brought into the process, the prominent ministerial and administrative figures who were a feature of Botha's earliest government remained in place throughout most of his tenure in office. Furthermore, while 'rationalization' was predicated on the need to eliminate a burdensome and ineffective bureaucracy, by the end of Botha's period of governance the South African public sector – principally due to the introduction of the tricameral parliament and the concept of 'own' and 'general' affairs – had become a mammoth institution in itself. And, though the basic structures that were to play such an important role in the reform process were not fully in place until 1982, the actual restructuring of governing edifices continued throughout the Botha era. This phenomenon was partially born out of the application of the incremental process of reform pursued by the government; but it was also a function of the need to remain flexible in light of the tenuous nature of programmatic reform. And, as elsewhere, some of the structural changes were purely a product of the politics of the day. This gradualist shift from a parliamentary form of government to a presidential one achieved its fulfilment with the introduction of the tricameral parliament in 1983.

ESTABLISHMENT OF THE MECHANISM FOR THE IMPLEMENTATION OF SECURITY

The National Security Management System (NSMS), implemented in conjunction with the host of bureaucratic reforms, represented the security side of Botha's programmatic approach to reform. As in the case of the reform programme, the security apparatus was the product of a variety of influences, ranging from Western counter-insurgency strategists to the Taiwanese national security system. Coupled with these theoretical inputs was a plethora of government commissions charged with resolving the seemingly intractable bureaucratic disputes that threatened the efficient management of South Africa's national security interests. These two strands converged in the turmoil that characterized the regional and domestic security situation in the late seventies and resulted in the establishment of the NSMS under the auspices of the Botha administration.

Influences on the NSMS

The strategic influences on the development of the NSMS were broad in scope. Principal among them were French strategist General André Beaufre, the American National Security Council, and the French national security system.[53] The Secretary of the SSC, Lt. General A. van Deventer, outlined the underlying theoretical tenets of the NSMS at a press briefing in 1983.

> The philosophy upon which the organization is based is that the Republic is confronted by a multi-dimensional threat – multi-dimensional in the sense that the Republic's enemies attack the constitutional, the economic, the social and the security bases in accordance with a co-ordinated plan or strategy. It is the conviction of the Government that this threat can only be met and turned back by the application of strategies using, in the same way as the enemy, the four main elements: constitutional, economic, social and security.[54]

Van Deventer's statement clearly echoes the Beaufreian strategic approach adopted in the SADF's strategic doctrine

Total National Strategy. General Magnus Malan, Chief of the Armed Forces and Defence Minister from 1980, reiterated this perspective in a speech before the Institute of Strategic Studies at the University of Pretoria.[55] His call for the integrated management of the state's 'four power bases' precisely parallels Beaufre's insistence that the state adopt a coordinated policy towards the management of politics, economics, diplomacy and military affairs.[56] According to one participant:

> [T]he underlying theme in the management of national security is joint management involving not only the security services and the intelligence services but also all the other government departments and organizations. These are brought together in the functions of management to ensure that all their energy and efforts are directed towards and focused upon the achievement of the national security goals set by the State.[57]

The Joint Management Centres (JMCs), a national system of regional and local management committees supporting the executive of the NSMS, were said to be inspired by the example of the French national security system. Van Deventer declared that France's decentralized system of security was viewed by the committee as an optimal example of balancing the government's need to have a 'security apparatus close to the Cabinet' with the government's desire to be 'close to the situation on the ground'.[58]

After the JMCs themselves were institutionalized, and with the advent of the cooperative relationship with fellow 'pariah state' Taiwan, the Taiwanese security system exercised a considerable influence over the introduction of various strategies to combating the threat of insurgency. Numerous SADF officers received specialized training in counter-revolutionary warfare at Taiwanese military colleges during the eighties, cementing the growing cooperative relationship in others spheres.[59]

Commissions and Committees

The debate over national security had raged within the government for a number of years. Cast principally in terms of competing institutions, the disputation hindered the effective conduct and management of a range of security-related initiatives.[60] The result was the establishment of a number of committees of inquiry into national security issues that sought to restructure the situation so as to place security considerations above those of a bureaucratic nature. It was through the mechanism of the commissions of inquiry that the organizational foundation for the future NSMS was laid.

The institutional rivalry between the SAP and the SADF, particularly in the area of intelligence-gathering, had been a matter of government concern during the sixties. Issues involving national security had originally been tabled in a cabinet committee on State Security but interdepartmental competition and irregular meetings rendered this forum moot.[61] By 1966, this committee was replaced by the State Security Advisory Council which in turn was eclipsed with the founding of the Bureau of State Security (BOSS) in 1969. The personal vehicle of General H.J. van den Bergh, BOSS virtually monopolized all aspects of the security and intelligence-gathering field, relegating the Ministry of Defence's efforts to that of a secondary status.[62]

Continuing problems resulted in the establishment of a commission of inquiry into matters relating to the security of the state in 1969. Known as the Potgieter Commission, it called for the establishment of:

> [A] council to be known as the State Security Council, under the chairmanship of the Prime Minister . . . it shall be the general function of the State Security Council to advise the Prime Minister in regard to the formulation of all aspects of national policy and strategy which relate to or may relate to the security of the State in order to make cooperation between Departments of State and Government authorities as efficient as possible . . .[63]

The Commission outlined the composition of the SSC, including the Prime Minister (as chairman) and five other ministers.[64] Acting on the recommendations of the Potgieter Commission, the Vorster government passed into law the Security Intelligence and State Security Council Act (64) in June 1972.

A second study, the Public Service Commission, was founded

in 1973 to analyse the capacity of the existing national security apparatus to successfully combat threats to the state.[65] In a classified Report on the National Security Situation, it called for the establishment of a national security management system with branches at the national, interdepartmental, departmental and subdepartmental levels of government. Coupled with these structures would be a permanent national security staff organization that would liaison with a series of regional committees so as to coordinate the implementation of security actions. The identification of security issues at every level of this broad network of departments and committees was deemed the crucial feature to the success of this system. This influential report laid the basis for the organizational structure that became known as the National Security Management System.[66]

The Vorster government responded to the report by establishing an interdepartmental committee chaired by the Deputy Director of Foreign Affairs to further investigate 'the question of the necessity for the formulation of strategy on the national level and the organizational structure required for this purpose.'[67] With the military's established knowledge and training in matters of strategy, it fell to the committee members from the SADF to provide the bulk of the work on formulating the committee's recommendations.[68] It did so by calling for the establishment of a work committee to assist the SSC to be staffed by senior members of the various Cabinet departments and the creation of a permanent secretariat within the SSC. In addition, it proposed that the government establish and coordinate an interdepartmental committee system in security-related areas.

The Structure of the National Security Management System

The NSMS was officially established by the Cabinet on 16 August 1979 at the same time that the rest of the government was undergoing reorganization. Utilizing the outline already presented by committees and commissions, the Botha administration established a five-tier structure for the management and coordination of national security. At the executive level, it consisted of the State Security Council (SSC), the Work Committee of the State Security Council, the Secretariat of the State Security Council, and the Interdepartmental Committees. Working in tandem with the executive level was a nation-wide system of regional management committees, or Joint Management Centres, that were further subdivided into local management committees.

State Security Council

The SSC was the heart of the revamped national security system. According to its enabling legislation, the SSC's functions were to advise the government as to:

> [T]he formulation of national policy and strategy in relation to the security of the Republic, and the manner in which such policy or strategy shall be implemented and be executed; a policy to combat any particular threat to the security of the Republic; to determine intelligence priorities.[69]

The legislation designated that the SSC be chaired by the Prime Minister, and include the senior minister in the Cabinet as well as the Ministers and Department Heads of Defence, Foreign Affairs, Justice, and Police. In addition, it was given the power to co-opt other ministers or heads of departments as it saw fit. The SSC met fortnightly, on the day before Cabinet meetings.[70] While the SSC was institutionalized in 1972, it did not contribute substantially to the coordination of national security policy until its status was enhanced under Botha after 1978.

Work Committee of the SSC

A vital component of the SSC was its Work Committee. Composed of the heads of the departments which are part of the SSC and the chairmen of other cabinet work committees, the SSC Work Committee's primary task was to set the agenda of the SSC as well as serve as an advisory body to the organization. According to a former Secretary of the SSC, the Work Committee met a few days before the SSC itself held its own fortnightly meetings, at which time any head of a government department could petition to put an issue on the Work Committee agenda – as a step towards getting the item placed on the SSC agenda – and then attend the relevant Work Committee meeting.[71]

Once the Work Committee had established the agenda for the SSC meeting, the SSC would meet to discuss in detail the various issues put before it and make specific recommendations. These recommendations would in turn be passed on to the Cabinet, which met two days after the SSC meeting, and its decisions would be conveyed back to the SSC. Generally speaking, the primary mode of action required from a Cabinet policy directive consisted of either communicating broad policy resolutions down to the lower levels of the NSMS structure or, if more than one governmental department was to be involved in the implementation process, seeing to it that the appropriate departments coordinated their respective inputs through the Interdepartmental Committee structure.[72]

It must be underlined that the process was not solely a 'top–down' affair, but involved to a considerable degree the transmission of local inputs through the mechanism of the JMCs and up to the SSC itself. For example, in the early eighties the local JMC in the Cape identified the black housing shortage in that area as constituting a potential security issue and forwarded that warning up to the SSC. After Cabinet review of the subject, the result was the marshalling of various departments – primarily the Ministry of Cooperation and Development – to provide the appropriate input to solve the housing problem in a manner consistent with government policy.[73]

Secretariat of the SSC

The Secretariat was a full-time institution presided over by the Secretary of the SSC, which provided the administrative support for the SSC and the Work Committee with a staff of approximately fifty employees.[74] In this capacity, it focused on the coordination of all security-related information from the various government departments and through the JMCs system and ensued that this material was directed to the Work Committee for consideration. In addition, it was the Secretariat's task to see to it that the overall strategies adopted at the Cabinet and SSC level were in fact carried out at the departmental level.[75]

The Secretariat consisted of four discrete sections – the Administrative, Strategic Communication, National Intelligence Interpretation, and Strategy. Of these, the latter two were the most important. The National Intelligence Interpretation branch was devoted to the interpretation of intelligence information supplied to it from other governmental departments (SADF, SAP, NIS, and DFA). It did not itself endeavour to procure raw intelligence but rather relied on the established security and intelligence structures to provide it with material.[76] The Strategy branch was the institution responsible for the development of governmental strategies and monitoring the implementation of such strategies by various government departments. Thus through its interaction with government departments – principally the Interdepartmental Committee system – the Strategy branch served as a critical link between SSC policy and actual implementation of that policy.

Discussion papers were produced by the Secretariat for the SSC meetings on specific issues. The majority of papers were concerned with strategies for combating various boycotts (both domestic and international), the stockpiling of strategic items, and regional foreign policy issues, and it was the task of the Secretariat to provide policy options for the SSC.[77]

Interdepartmental Committees

The Interdepartmental Committee structure served as the liaison between the executive of the NSMS and the other departments within the government as well as institutions outside of its ambit. There were 13 interdepartmental committees: Manpower, Security Services, Civil Defence, Transport, Security, National Supplies and Resources, Government Funding, National Economy, Telecommunications and Electrical Power Supply, Science and Technology, Community Services, Culture, and Political Affairs.[78] Composed of government and non-government officials with concerns in the above-designated fields, the interdepartmental committees were supposed to facilitate the coordination, planning and implementation of strategies emanating from the SSC and its subordinate institutions, as well as provide a forum in which these non-SSC institutions could voice their opinions.

Joint Management Centres

Supplementing the executive was a nation-wide system of 11 regional management committees called Joint Management Centres (JMCs). The task of the JMCs and their attendant subunits was to serve as a bridge between the central government and locally constituted bodies so as to facilitate the implementation of executive policy decisions in the areas of security, economic, social and political affairs. In addition, they were to serve as a source of intelligence on the status of local conditions, providing recommendations to the executive on everything from potential security threats to community infrastructural needs.

The JMCs were constituted in such a way that their administrative boundaries divided the country (including SWA/Namibia) into 11 areas, each centred around a major city, and corresponding to military areal command zones.[79] Serving as the JMC's administrative centre, the 11 cities – Johannesburg, Pretoria, Pietersburg, Nelspruit, Potchefstroom, Bloemfontein, Cape Town, Kimberley, Port Elizabeth, Durban, and Walvis Bay – represented the focal points of the NSMS structure.[80] Each JMC was itself divided geographically as well as administratively, with submanagement centres, mini-management centres, and local management centres corresponding roughly to the designated military command structure of that particular region.[81]

The JMCs were dominated in leadership terms by the security forces. While the chairmanship of the JMCs was open to all, the actual post was invariably occupied by members of the SADF or, to a lesser extent, the SAP.[82] Given the JMC's' dual mandate as a vehicle for coordination of policy between differing governmental departments and local bodies, as well as a source of intelligence on a variety of aspects of local conditions, it is not surprising that the security force – and in particular the military – came to play such an important role within the JMCs. According to JMC participants, SADF dominance of the JMC system was due to its prior training in the area of counter-revolutionary warfare as well as the existence of a sound command structure within the Defence Force – a requisite element for the rapid communication of intelligence.[83] However, it must be noted that domination did not necessarily mean that the JMCs were simply vehicles for the SADF or other security interests. The bureaucratic realities of the situation required that each JMC chairman, if he wished to have the cooperation of his counterparts in the various departments that participated in the JMCs, had to engage in a balancing of the different concerns operating within his jurisdiction. When security concerns dominated events within the JMC, the security forces played a pre-eminent role. Conversely, when the JMC was relatively quiescent, so-called welfare issues came to the fore and the appropriate departments dominated the work of the JMC.[84] A further factor inhibiting *any* department from dominating the JMC system was the fact that the JMCs did not have their own independent budget.[85]

In addition to the chairman, every JMC was staffed by approximately 50 personnel taken from 'all government institutions which may have [had] an interest in the activities of the Management Centres'.[86] Plenary meetings of the JMCs were held every two months[87] where 'formal presentations and . . . seminars whose aim it [was] to build up a consciousness of a "total" approach to Security Management' were conducted.[88]

The internal structure of the JMCs consisted of an Intelligence committee (Gesamentlike Inligtingskomitee, or GIK), a Security committee (Veiligheidskomitee, or VEIKOM), a Constitutional-Economic-Social committee (Staatkundige-Ekonomiese-en Maatskaplikekomitte, or SEMKOM) and a Communications committee (Kommunikasiekomitee, or KOMKOM). The JMC chairman presided over an executive board made up of the chairmen of the GIK, VEIKOM, SEMKOM and KOMKOM committees; as it was his task to report back to the Secretariat of the SSC, meetings were convened on a regular basis. Each of the four standing committees were said to meet ordinarily once every two weeks.[89] Intelligence briefings on the status of security within the region were a part of every plenary meeting; the GIK met a week in advance of such gatherings to review the security situation and establish recommendations for action.[90] A Secretariat carried out the administrative support necessary to each JMC's functioning. It was through these institutions that the JMCs were able to carry out their dual mandate of coordinating and monitoring the implementation of policy from above as well as identifying and setting local policy based on local conditions.

Within the regional boundaries of the JMCs were smaller committees called submanagement centres, of which there were 60.[91] Structurally, they mirrored the JMCs, containing an Intelligence committee, a Security committee, a Constitutional-Economic-Social committee and a Communications committee. The submanagement centres shifted the focus of their efforts – which was reflected in the changing composition of their membership – depending upon the specific situation faced in their area of authority. For example, when township violence flared up, the submanagement centre became dominated by security personnel; however, if the area was relatively quiescent, the 'welfare' components of the unit took the lead.[92]

Monitoring the progress and implementation of policy by the submanagement centres in times of crisis, as well as serving as an institutional linkage between the JMCs and the submanagement centres, were the Joint Operation Centres (Gesamentlike Operasiesentrum, or GOS/JOC). Activated during periods of unrest, the GOS/JOCs at times established their headquarters in the areas of disturbance themselves (townships for example) and from there coordinated security based operations such as the removal of radical leadership.[93] In addition to the GOS/JOCs, Joint Intelligence Centres (Gesamentlike Intelligensiesentrum, or GIS/JIC) provided both institutional support for the JMCs' Joint Intelligence Committee and linkage with the intelligence committees at the submanagement level. The GOS/JOCs were composed primarily of security personnel while the GIS/JICs were staffed principally by employees from the military and national intelligence services.[94]

The submanagement centres were themselves further subdivided into 354 mini-management centres.[95] The mini-management centres averaged 20 members, principally drawn from locally-constituted structures such as the Mayor's office and various departments within city or town government, local commanders of the security forces (SAP and SADF), and representatives of parastatals and businesses.[96] Finally, the smallest units of the JMC system were the local management centres. These were formed on an ad hoc basis to deal with specific issues and were staffed primarily by individuals outside of the government.[97] The ad hoc nature of the local management centres was also a feature of the joint liaison forums which were designed to provide linkages between the private sector and the NSMS. Joint liaison forums could be established at any level in the management system deemed appropriate.

Conclusion

In less than a decade the NSMS developed from the rudimentary coordinating mechanism that characterized the newly established SSC in the early seventies to the complex interlocking committee structure that managed the state of emergency in the late eighties. The expansion of its purview was a reflection of the perception within the Botha administration that government-inspired reform might induce revolutionary reaction. Incorporating the security and welfare functions called for by counter-revolutionary theorists, the NSMS was to be Botha's antidote – and one with the potential for surgical action at the local level – to any outbreak of violence that threatened state control. It is important to note that while the NSMS was legislated into existence in 1979, the formal JMC structure remained relatively dormant until the imposition of the full state of emergency in 1986. During this intervening period the JMCs served principally at the level of intelligence-gathering and supporting governmental socio-economic projects (see Chapter 4).

The degree to which the SSC came to play a pre-eminent role in the decision-making process under Botha was the subject of intense dispute amongst academics in the eighties. Some scholars have maintained that because of its legal status, the size of its secretariat (50 full-time employees versus five for the other three cabinet committees), its exclusive and high-powered membership, the SSC occupied a position of *primus inter pares* within the executive.[99] In this fashion, it was asserted that the SADF had become more than:

> simply an instrument for policy implementation . . . [b]ut an active participant in policymaking. Not merely in military matters, but in wider security issues, both domestic and external . . .[100]

Subsequent research has indicated that this scenario was over-drawn. Former government officials have pointed out that the centre of power in the Botha administration resided with the Office of the Prime Minister, not the SSC.[101] The strength of their contention has caused even former proponents of this theory to admit that 'these views have ignored the power, role and centrality of the State President and his office'.[102] Despite this overdue reassessment of the role of the SSC, it is important to recognize that the SSC would naturally serve as the instrument for 'crisis management'. Thus, ironically, much of what was said about the militarization of the South African government in the early eighties became reality only following the imposition of the full State of Emergency in 1986.

THE BLUEPRINT FOR REFORM APARTHEID: THE TWELVE-POINT PLAN

On 15 August 1979, the Prime Minister declared in a speech before an NP Congress in Natal that South Africa would henceforth be governed on the basis of a broad national strategy, one that would require the coordination of all departments of government, as well as the cooperation of business and the population as a whole. Reiterated at the other three provincial party congresses, the subject of journalistic and parliamentary debate, the Twelve Point Plan (as the speech came to be known) was the culmination of Botha's search for a programmatic approach to the issue of reform of the apartheid system. From 1979 and into 1986, the Twelve Point Plan acted as both a blueprint for national reform and as a guide to the parameters within which the reform process was to take place.

The Twelve Point Plan was the meridian of the Botha

government's efforts to transform the administrative, security and reform imperatives that characterized the SADF's Total National Strategy into a national reform strategy. Drafted in conjunction with future Minister of Constitutional Planning and Development, Chris Heunis,[103] the Twelve Point Plan is the seminal document for understanding the direction that Botha hoped to take the country as he mapped out its future.[104] And, remarkably, Botha stuck rather closely to the original intentions as stated in the declaration. The main points of the speech are duplicated below:

1. Recognition and acceptance of the existence of multinationalism and of minorities in the Republic of South Africa.
2. The acceptance of vertical differentiation with the built-in principle of self-determination at as many levels as possible.
3. The establishment of constitutional structures by the Black peoples to make possible the highest degree of self-government for them in States that have been consolidated as far as is practicable.
4. The division of powers amongst South African Whites, the South African Coloureds and the South African Indians, with a system of consultation and co-responsibility so far as common interests are concerned.
5. Acceptance of the principle that where at all possible each population group should have its own schools and live in its own community as a fundamental requirement for social contentment . . . The preparedness to consult as equals on matters of common interest with a sound balance between the rights of the individual and those of the community.
6. The removal of hurtful, unnecessary discriminatory measures.
7. The recognition of economic interdependence and the properly planned utilization of our manpower.
8. The pursuit of a peaceful constellation of Southern African States with respect for each other's cultures, traditions and ideals.
9. South Africa's firm determination to defend itself against interference from outside in every possible way.

10. As far as possible, a policy of neutrality in the conflicts between large superpowers and preference for South African interests.
11. Maintenance of effective decision-making by the State which rests on a strong Defence Force to guarantee orderly Government as well as efficient, clean administration.
12. The maintenance of free enterprise as a basis for our economic and financial policy.[105]

In analysing the Twelve Point Plan, it is clear that the proclamation is the distillation of the labour of the plethora of government-sponsored commissions of inquiry, cabinet committees and White Papers into aspects of reform and security that had multiplied under Vorster and Botha. Placing the emphasis on the domestic environment, Botha underlines both the priorities and the limitations of his programmatic approach to reform. The first two parts of Botha's proclamation restate his administration's ideological commitment to the basic precepts of separate development: multi-nationalism and vertical differentiation. The constitutional components of the reform programme are captured in points three and four. Particularly notable is the reiteration of the government's commitment to go forward with the 'homelands' scheme for blacks and power-sharing – implicitly based on 'own' and 'group' affairs – between white, Coloured and Indian populations (point four). The focus of points five, six and seven are socio-economic affairs, with point five highlighting the government's continued adherence to the physical separation of ethnic communities and the maintenance of Christian Nationalism as the basis of the education system.[106] Points six and seven are a direct adaptation of the commission and committee recommendations into the government's urban and labour policies.

Turning away from the realm of reform and the domestic environment, the proclamation outlines the Botha administration's foreign policy objectives. Point eight highlights the government's long-standing desire to establish a regional economic and political organisation formalizing links between countries in Southern Africa. Point nine is, in essence, a warning to states both inside and outside the region that the government would use any means possible to counter interference in its domestic affairs. The statement of South African neutrality contained in point ten is an outgrowth of the Republic's growing isolation from the West and represents the continuing effort to find a new security arrangement in a hostile world.

The eleventh point sets out the parameters within which the reform programme can take place, that is to say, the government considers the maintenance of control as a *sine qua non* of the reform process. The military and the police force are to serve as 'guarantors' of government control, though no direct reference to the establishment of a vast domestic security apparatus (the NSMS) is made. The allusion to 'efficient, clean administration', duplicating Botha's statement upon taking office on 28 September 1978, served as a justification for the introduction of the sweeping 'rationalization' programme. And, finally, the last point is a declaration of the government's commitment to the free market system, both as a statement of principle and, presumably, a spur to the South African business community to support the Botha initiatives.

Two observations must be made with respect to the strategic implications of the Twelve Point Plan. First, Botha's restatement of the NP creed in points one, two and five is an effort to place his policies on the firm footing of NP doctrine while at the same time sifting out or diluting certain policies of his predecessors that did not fit into the Botha vision of reform. In a very real sense, Botha hoped to appropriate a truncated version of the NP creed, with the approval of the party stalwarts, to serve the needs of his reform programme. At the same time, Botha's need to maintain the unity of Afrikanerdom, even after the split with key conservative parliamentarians in 1982, remained crucial to understanding his entire reform programme. The measure of Botha's belief in these prescriptions was to be reflected in his inability, in the latter part of his administration, to take steps that would represent an actual break from these fundamental tenets. Reflecting upon this years later, Botha insisted that Afrikaner unity was a fundamental concern of his throughout his administration.[107] In fact, this attitude may have been responsible for the policy vacillations which were to characterize the government's approach to reform in subsequent years (and would ultimately act as a brake on the process).

The second observation is that the Twelve Point Plan is a remarkably vague document. The ambiguity that shrouds many of the proclamation's key points, particularly those devoted to domestic reform, confounded both supporters and critics alike. On the one hand, this ambiguity reflected the lack of consensus within the Botha administration as to the actual scope of the reform programme, something that was to become apparent in subsequent years. According to one of its co-authors, 'At that stage we had no clear vision of actual structures (of reform) but we had a clear vision of the *need* for structures.'[108] On the other hand, the Twelve Point Plan was a product of Botha's desire to retain the support of the traditional constituency of the NP, the farmer and the working-class Afrikaner. Fundamentally, the fact that it was open to a variety of interpretations suited Botha's interests. Secure in the knowledge that the NP congresses had given the programme its approval, the reformers within his administration hoped to gradually redefine the limits of some of the more controversial points as they embarked on further substantive reforms.[109]

CONCLUSION

The realization of the need for significant reform of the apartheid system was grasped by the leadership of the NP as early as the mid-seventies. With the riots in Soweto acting as a spur to reform, the government established a series of commissions of inquiry to assist in the development of an ad hoc reform programme that would be acceptable to both the party's white constituency and the country's black majority. With the ascension of P.W. Botha to the premiership, the search for a way out of the crisis engendered by apartheid took on a new form as Botha sought to graft the preliminary reform initiatives broached by his predecessor onto the SADF's strategic doctrine, Total National Strategy. The result was the development of a programmatic reform strategy that attempted to balance the state's security concerns and the requisite reform imperatives called for by counter-revolutionary strategy. With the institutionalization of Total National Strategy virtually complete through the restructuring of the government bureaucracy, the focus shifted to the implementation of programmatic reform. In this area, Botha's elucidation of his programme in the Twelve Point Plan indicated that he intended to follow the cautionary approach to reform adopted by the NP at the close of the seventies. Two astute observers of South African politics, Adam and Giliomee, analysed the content of this method of reform.

> First, it is accepted by the leadership that for the sake of party unity no such reforms should be presented as a break with the past. Second, it is a firm conviction that any public declaration of the intention to institute far-reaching reforms will only harm the cause of reform: To have publicly announced five years ahead that the government was committed to mixed sport on club level, the abolition of job reservation, and the desegregation of theaters countrywide would have raised such an outcry in the party that any reforms would have been suppressed. Third, the ministers have adopted the practice of assembling the leaders in a particular field in confidential meetings where they argue the case for reform. After consensus has been established, everyone is bound to these decisions. Fourth, the press was persuaded not to publicize the gradual implementation of reforms . . . Fifth, the caucus was confronted with the *fait accompli* of these reforms but assured that control would continue to be exercised by way of permits. Existing legislation has rarely been repealed: It is the administration, not the law, that has been changed.[110]

While the efficacy of this 'stealthful' strategy of reform had remained essentially unchallenged within *verligte* circles for a number of years, by the early eighties two cataclysmic events demonstrated the inherent weaknesses in this strategy. The first was the split within the NP over the introduction of limited power sharing in the form of the tricameral parliament, which culminated in the formation of the Conservative party. The second was the emergence of popular resistance – particularly amongst the black population – to the truncated constitutional reforms represented by the tricameral parliament and related legislation. Each of these events was to pose severe challenges to Botha's cautionary strategy of reform and each in its own way, as will be demonstrated in subsequent chapters, contributed to a shift in strategy by the Botha administration.

4 The Security State and the Implementation of Reform Apartheid, 1979–84

Though committed to the process of constitutional development and change the Government is not prepared to take any steps that may in any way jeopardize . . . order and stability in this country. Chris Heunis 1983[1]

With the twin pillars of reform and security in place by the early 1980s, the stage was set for the implementation of Botha's broad strategy of reform for South Africa as outlined in the Twelve Point Plan. On the socio-economic front, the government initiated an uneven programme of change in the laws governing industrial relations and social status of urbanized Africans in the country. The linchpin of the reform strategy at this particular juncture, the development of a new constitutional dispensation for the Coloured and Indian populations coupled with the creation of governmental structures at the local level for urbanized Africans, was cautiously introduced by the newly formed Department of Constitutional Development and Planning (DCDP). The South African security establishment supported these domestic reform initiatives by taking an activist role in what it deemed to be fomenting a stable internal environment and a favourable external environment in which domestic change could transpire. This period between the onset of the implementation of Botha's reform programme in 1979 and the implementation of the tricameral parliament in 1984 represented the high water mark of Botha's national reform strategy. It was the outbreak of protest in the Eastern Cape, rippling across the black townships and developing into a full-fledged insurrection by 1985, that was to pose the severest challenge to this process of state-led reform.

This chapter will examine the operationalization of Botha's strategy for reform of the South African state between 1980 and 1985. First, the government's bid to secure an electoral mandate from the white community for the reform programme embodied in the Twelve Point Plan will be examined. Second, the conduct of the security side of strategy will be investigated by looking at the role of the security forces in internal and external environments. Third, the reformist initiatives in the socio-economic area will receive attention. Finally, the introduction of constitutional reforms – epitomized by the Black Local Authorities Act 1982, the establishment of the tricameral parliament and the Regional Services Councils Bill – will be examined.

SEEKING A MANDATE FOR CHANGE: THE ELECTION OF 1981

The winning of an electoral mandate from the white community for the proposed reforms was a critical component of the Botha administration's plans. In order to bring across the necessity of substantive change as outlined in the Twelve Point Plan, Botha turned to the same analytical constructs – total onslaught – which had informed his decision to embark upon a reformist course. Coupled with this was the need to tie conservative members of the NP, whose hostility towards the proposed changes was palpable, to the government reform programme.

The unprecedented success of the right-wing Herstigte Nasionale Party (HNP) in securing over 40 per cent of the vote in by-elections held in October 1979 served as a warning to the newly installed Prime Minister. Against the background of this erosion of support for the NP amongst its traditional constituency of working-class and land-holding Afrikaners, coupled with the in-fighting within elite circles of the NP over the proposed reform programme, Botha called for a general election in January 1981.

The election itself was contentious from the start. In addition to the HNP and New Conservative party challenge, the conservative faction of the NP, centred in the numerically dominant Transvaal provincial branch, hoped to win enough support from incoming MPs to form a substantive opposition to the Botha programme. In some cases conservative candidates, over the objections of the NP apparatus, garnered enough local support to unseat existing MPs; in other instances, protests were lodged by party stalwarts against the party's imposition of reformist candidates.[2]

To combat the drift away from the reformist agenda envisioned in his Twelve Point Plan, Botha launched an aggressive campaign that centred around the spectre of a 'total onslaught' levelled against the Republic. Hammering on themes of the communist threat to the survival of the state, Botha hoped to educate a reluctant electorate into the vital necessity of embracing reform much as he and the military had been convinced. An indication of the importance Botha placed upon securing the mandate for reform was the government's use of illegal methods, in the form of military-inspired 'psych-ops' campaigns, in support of his campaign. In the end, the NP did retain 131 seats (losing seats in four districts) but with substantially reduced margins amongst its traditional constituencies.[3] A further restraint on any positive interpretation of the election results was the increased support for the conservative perspective within the NP itself, particularly pronounced in the all-important Transvaal provincial branch. This dampened any notion within reformist circles of the government that the white electorate would give unequivocal support to reform.

The election did, however, accomplish a key objective set out by the Botha administration as the majority of whites voiced approval for the incremental reform programme which the Botha administration was about to embark upon. Unfortunately for the Botha administration, the equivocal nature of the white community's support for the Twelve Point Plan, demonstrated by the growing support for the right wing, clearly showed the limited parameters within which Botha and the reformers in his government had to work. Wedded to the belief that unity within Afrikanerdom was of paramount importance, by gaining an incomplete mandate for change from the electorate the Botha administration felt forced to approach the proposed reform programme with utmost caution. This had the effect of slowing the introduction of reforms and, consequently, dampening the expectations raised by the Botha administration.

The only area in which Botha was unable to secure longlasting gains was in staving off the ideological split within the NP itself. Led by Dr Andries Treurnicht, whose discomfort with the proposed reform programme was manifest, NP conservatives continued to raise strident objections to Botha's proposed reforms. Within little more than a year after the election the conservative faction of the NP felt strong enough to make a bid for control of the party (see below). Their ousting from party ranks was critical in clearing the way for further changes in the political landscape.

SECURITY

Between 1979 and 1984, the South African security establishment engaged in extensive preparation at home and activism abroad. While the pace of ANC infiltration increased, coupled with the development of a higher profile for the South African military and the extension of security-oriented legislation, the internal environment remained essentially quiescent during this period. Government confidence was reflected in its unwillingness to fully activate the extensive domestic powers embodied in the structure of the National Security Management System. Externally, an activist approach was adopted by the SADF to combat the perceived growth in the Soviet-inspired threat to the country. This took the form of a 'destabilization' campaign in neighbouring states evincing open hostility to established South African interests, focusing particularly on Zimbabwe, Mozambique and Angola. By 1984, the SADF's policy had produced concrete results as South Africa secured a series of non-aggression pacts which effectively gave recognition to its pre-eminent position within the region.

Security: the Internal Dimension

Overall, the internal security scenario looked more stable in the first years of the Botha administration than that of the external environment. Despite the growing influx of ANC cadres, coupled with a rise in acts of sabotage and terrorism within South Africa itself, the domestic environment remained fundamentally undisturbed during this period. This was a reflection of the relatively apoliticized nature of the mass of South Africans, the strategic and institutional weaknesses of the liberation movements and the success of the SADF's 'destabilization' campaign directed against ANC bases in neighbouring states.

Revolutionary Strategy and the Threat to the State

Since the security clampdown of the early sixties, South Africa had been devoid of any overt sign of dissent originating from exiled organizations such as the ANC or its rival the PAC. Following the failure to extend guerrilla operations based in Lesotho, the PAC effectively resigned itself to playing the role of an exile movement.[4] For its own part, following the Rivonia Trials of 1963, the ANC attempted to salvage its crippled revolutionary campaign within South Africa from its distant headquarters in Lusaka.[5] An abortive foray into Rhodesia in the late sixties, the outgrowth of an alliance with the Zimbabwean National People's Union, ended in disaster; so too, promised international support on the introduction of further punitive sanctions against South Africa was slow to materialize.

Despite these disappointments, with the establishment of sympathetic governments in Mozambique and Angola the prospects for reigniting the armed struggle improved dramatically. A joint ANC-SACP mission was sent to the Democratic Republic of Vietnam to garner information from their experience in defeating the French and the Americans. Building on the changes instituted at the Mogorogo Conference held in Tanzania in 1969 which saw a significant strengthening of the relationship between the ANC and SACP, the mission identified the need for the implementation of political mobilization and institution-building to complement the coming military campaign.[6]

In strategic terms, the ANC's newly formed Political–Military Strategy Commission adopted the classic four-stage path of revolutionary war utilized in Vietnam.[7] Locating the South African situation between stage one and stage two of the revolutionary typology – 'internal political reconstruction' (political mobilization) and 'armed propaganda' (sabotage and terrorism) – the Commission placed particular emphasis on the creation of a broad front of anti-apartheid organizations which would serve as a wellspring for the development of an internal dimension of the movement.[8] Aligned to the ANC symbolically at first, this front organization would, as far as possible, articulate ANC goals as well as provide potential recruits for the underground structures. The Commission was adamant that the connection between the ANC and this front should at least initially remain obscured.

> The guiding hand of our liberation movement did not always have to be seen publicly or acknowledged. Our work had to proceed in a way which could not unnecessarily expose the legal and semi-legal organizations to more intense enemy harassment and provide the excuse to destroy these public bodies. This required, among other things, an intelligent assessment of how far such bodies could be expected to go in publicly associating themselves with some of our more long-term and radical policies.[9]

In pursuit of this goal, the Commission recommended providing support to existing anti-apartheid organizations, promoting the development of civic organizations and trade unions, and the calling for the establishment of youth and women's detachments.[10] These organizations would be encouraged to launch a series of campaigns within South Africa, amongst them one centred on releasing Nelson Mandela and another repopularizing the Freedom Charter, the latter designed to provide a counterpoint to the government's enhanced local authorities structures and would in turn lay the basis for activism against these bodies. Identifying the forthcoming elections to the South African Indian Council as an appropriate target, the Commission declared that boycott campaigns of these elections and institutions should culminate in the 'permanent destruction' of government structures.[11] In addition to all of this, significantly, the Commission report called for the development of a strategic approach to the homelands, a heretofore neglected feature of ANC policy.[12] Concurrent with the active promotion of an anti-apartheid front organization, the Commission advocated the systematic building of an underground structure which, drawing in the most promising of individuals to the ANC, would serve as the nucleus both for the development of alternative political structures and the establishment of an internal military force.[13] Confident that this new strategic outlook would usher in successes denied in the past, ANC policy-makers operated with the expectation that a three-year application of this approach would lay the foundation for movement to the next stage in the revolution: the instigation of a 'people's war' (guerrilla warfare).[14]

The launching of the ANC's newly redirected political and military campaign soon provided tangible results. Overall, incidents of sabotage and armed attacks rose steadily, from thirteen in 1978 to fifty-six in 1983.[15] The most dramatic act of sabotage conducted by the revitalized ANC was the destruction of SASOL (South Africa's national synfuel programme) storage tanks on 1 June 1980, causing an estimated R58 million worth of damage.[16] Coming on the heels of this action was the attack in July 1981 on power stations in the eastern Transvaal. A rocket attack on Pretoria's military base, Voortrekkerhoogte, in August 1981 was followed by the explosion of four limpet mines at the Koeberg nuclear power plant in Cape Town over a year later. Attacks on police stations, transport facilities and a variety of government offices increased in frequency and sophistication during this period, demonstrating that the ANC was capable of functioning despite government efforts to curb revolutionary activities.[17]

While the ANC initially had a stated policy of avoiding civilian casualties, underscored by its signing of the Geneva Protocols in 1980, this approach was partially disavowed by the leadership in August 1981.[18] The outcome of this decision was an increase in ANC inspired attacks on so-called 'soft targets', including a bomb attack on South African Air Force Headquarters, killing 19 people and injuring 217 on 19 May 1983. Assassinations of ANC-designated informers or collaborators rose during this period as well.[19] In spite of this, by 1983 only 47 civilian casualties were directly attributable to revolutionary action.[20]

While MK conducted its 'armed propaganda' campaign, the arduous task of building up the organization within the country was being undertaken by cadres infiltrated into or recruited in South Africa. In the aftermath of the Soweto riots, the ANC attempted both to influence the activist student organizations emerging out of the Black Consciousness movement, such as the Soweto Students Representative

Council, and to develop its own front organizations, of which the Black Parents Association was alleged to be one.[21] The infiltration of established institutions as well as the support and creation of its own organizations became a vital component of the political mobilization strategy. Modelled on the Soweto Civic Association (SCA) and the Port Elizabeth Black Civic Organization (Pebco), which were established in September and October 1979 respectively, a plethora of similar organizations took root in various communities across the country. These were to join together in August 1983, creating a national body – the United Democratic Front – which was to pose the most serious challenge to the South African government to date (see Chapter 5).

Counter-revolutionary Measures

With the formal establishment of the NSMS in August 1979, the institutional foundations of one of the most crucial elements of the government's counter-revolutionary strategy were laid. The early eighties were devoted to transforming this embryonic NSMS structure, whose basis was found in the SADF areal command edifice, into an instrument of counter-revolutionary strategy.

As early as 1977 a rudimentary version of JMCs was in place in most areal commands in South Africa. It consisted of the SADF commanding officer in charge of the area, the top police official and the local 'native affairs' officer.[22] The inclusion of the civilian officials in charge of matters pertaining to the African population reflected the domestic concerns of the South African security establishment up to that time. With the exception of reacting to the occasional ANC-inspired incident, the bulk of the security work was devoted to assisting in such actions as the removal of African populations from 'white areas' to designated homelands, customary po-licing actions and providing general support for infrastructural development. Regular meetings of these top officials took place relatively infrequently: one former commanding officer of an areal command put the number of meetings at once every three months.[23] The absence of matching administrative boundaries within civilian departments inhibited cooperation with civilian officials on a range of issues as SADF commanding officers found themselves having to approach several civilian counterparts from the same department (all of whom, by virtue of their overlapping administrative sectors within the areal command, could lay claim to authority over an issue) in order to address any particular problem.[24] This cumbersome situation acted as a brake on the development of the JMC system beyond the existing structures described above.

The turning-point in the transformation of the NSMS from its mere formal status to operational status came in 1983. That year, the Minister for Constitutional Development and Planning, Lt.-General C. Lloyd and other senior civilian and military officials devised a plan to redraw the military's areal commands to coincide with the DCDP's proposed nine development regions (see below). In doing so, the government elected to place a premium on the rationality of administering *civilian* functions over that of security functions.[25] This decision reflected the growing belief in government circles, championed by individuals like General Lloyd, that it was the employment of a counter-revolutionary strategy which was needed to combat the threat of revolutionary violence. This allowed the JMCs to directly overlap with the executive committees of the Provincial Councils and, as such, facilitated the coordinating functions that the JMCs were designed to achieve. As a result, some areal commands like that of the Northern Transvaal were carved up into three smaller areas (Far North, Northern Transvaal and Eastern Transvaal).[26]

At this stage in the development of the NSMS, the primary task of the newly instated chairmen of the 11 JMCs was to extend the management centre system down to the local level of government.[27] To accomplish this, the JMC chairmen were obliged to recruit local bureaucrats from the civilian departments to serve on the JMCs or their attendant subunits (principally the submanagement centres and mini-management centres). Businessmen operating in the area were also brought into the process through the institution of joint liaison forums.[28] A crucial objective of top JMC officials at this juncture was to educate and accustom these newly co-opted individuals into approaching the issues which constituted their respective fields in terms of the broader strategic implications.[29] Linked to this was the institutionalization of this process through the development of the range of coordinated decision-making mechanisms inherent in the JMC structures.

Concurrently, the SADF embarked on a preliminary Civic Action programme in the rural areas of South Africa. Mirroring in certain aspects the programme instituted in Namibia, the Civic Action campaign within the various JMC areas was at this stage more an expansion of the duties traditionally performed by the SADF than an outright application of a key tenet of counter-revolutionary strategy. National servicemen, many of whom were selected specifically for their professional interests or skills, were the primary instruments of this programme.[30] Utilizing their skills as teachers and medical personnel, the SADF sent conscripts into remote villages which hitherto had been out of reach to provincial authorities, to engage in such tasks as education and the administration of health vaccines.[31]

In keeping with the precepts of counter-revolutionary theory, the Botha administration moved to create a covert capacity that would engineer 'dirty tricks' campaigns against its enemies. According to observers, some time in 1979–80 the State Security Council approved a secret plan to establish special units to conduct a range of sensitive operations which would remain outside of normal government channels. Entitled 'Institutions and Functions of Special Forces', the programme made provisions for covert recruitment, management and funding of special teams of operatives and also outlined a range of destabilization techniques open to these units, including assassination. The target areas were to be outside of the country, though in practice this distinction was to blur by the mid-eighties. Drawn from the SAP, the SADF and other government agencies, this programme was to spawn the SADF's elite Delta 40 unit which in turn later evolved into the government's notorious Civilian Cooperation Bureau.[32]

Finally, anticipating an upsurge in revolutionary action and unrest, the government introduced in the early eighties a battery of security-related legislation that sought to more fully integrate the country into the precepts of Total National Strategy. Among the most important laws promulgated was the National Key Points Act of 1980 which gave the Minister of Defence the power to identify industrial sites as critical to the economic well-being of the state and mandate that companies introduce security measures to prevent 'terrorist actions'. The legislation authorized the establishment of a National Key Points committee, headed by the Chief Director of Operations in the SADF and assisted by relevant military and civilian authorities, to carry out the identification process. By 1985, the committee had designated some 337 industries, airports, and other areas as 'key points'.[33]

To combat the flight of white farmers from their land on the South Africa's borders, Parliament passed the Density of Population in Designated Areas Act in 1979, which provided for financial credits to white farmers living on property which the government recognized as important to state security. A three-year delay in drawing up the guidelines for the programme did nothing to stem the flight of whites, driven from the border regions as much by financial distress as by security considerations.[34] By 1982, an estimated 40 per cent of the farms on the border with Mozambique and Botswana had absentee landlords. Coupled with this legislation was the setting up of border fences and a radio network modelled on Rhodesian and Namibian programmes, linking together farms in security-risk areas.

An additional step was the extension of the rules guiding compulsory military service for white males. Required to serve alongside the Permanent Force for two years, national servicemen's post-service obligations to the Citizen Force were amended in 1982 from 30 days per year over eight years to 30 days per year over 12 years.[35]

Security: the External Dimension

The security environment external to South Africa in 1979 could hardly have encouraged the government's military observers. To the north-east, Angola housed the threat of an estimated 20 000 Cuban troops, supplemented by Soviet and East European advisers.[36] In addition, Swapo guerrilla forces bent on dislodging the South Africans from Namibia had gained a base of operations in the Angolan hinterland from which to launch assaults. After years of debilitating warfare, the guerrilla war in Rhodesia seemed poised for a negotiated settlement, yet there was always the threat that talks would break down. Neighbouring Mozambique, initially cooperative in its relations with South Africa, had not only become a base of support for the ANC, but had gone so far as to sign a security pact with the Soviet Union in 1977. Even the international environment – while always a perennial source of criticism – had taken on a new level of active hostility towards South Africa with the introduction of military sanctions in the United Nations, the cancellation of French arms contracts, and the pointed criticism of the Carter administration in Washington. Despite these adverse circumstances, within a few months of the announcement of the Twelve Point Plan, foreign developments would shatter even this tenuous situation.

It was against this background that the Botha administration developed its security and foreign policies. Drawing upon the strategic imperatives of total strategy, the government sought to employ the full range of means at its disposal – diplomatic, economic, political and military – to support the interests of the South African state. These were brought to bear upon targeted states or organizations through the skilful calibration of incentives, such as technical and financial assistance, and disincentives, such as economic sabotage and support for anti-government forces. The particular 'tactical mix' of incentives and disincentives employed at any given time by the South African government was dependent upon its perceptions of a given situation.[37] These were introduced through the medium of direct and indirect strategies or, as Beaufre called them, direct and indirect 'modes of action'. The direct mode was dominated by military means while the indirect mode consisted of both military and non-military activities. Total strategy as rendered by South African strategists, was implemented in three broad theatres: Namibia/Angola, the Southern African region, and the international environment. A fourth area, that of nuclear strategy, became a growing – if clandestine – feature of total strategy.

Namibia and Angola

South Africa's continued occupation of the former League of Nations mandate, South West Africa, posed a host of problems for Pretoria. Namibia, as the territory came to be known, held a unique position in the South African government's view both because it was geographically contiguous and because it had long-standing ties of a political, economic and cultural nature with South Africa. The initiation of guerrilla warfare in 1966 in the northernmost region of the territory by the South West African Peoples Organization (Swapo), coupled with a sustained effort by the international community to deny the legality of South African administration of the territory, continually raised the costs the South African involvement. The collapse of colonialism in Angola in 1974 and the intervention of the superpowers in that country's civil war marked the elevation of the Namibian question to that of a regional conflict with global security dimensions.

The passage of Security Council Resolution 385 in 1977, which called for elections supervised by the UN and the withdrawal of the South African presence, set the parameters for international acceptance of Namibian independence. Intermittent discussions, sponsored by the Western Contact Group[38] between South Africa, Angola, Swapo and the Front Line States continued to take place. A more specific set of proposals emerged out of these talks, embodied in Security Council Resolution 435, to which Prime Minister Vorster gave his tacit assent in April 1978. In anticipation of the resolution of the Namibian question, the South African government supported the emergence of the Democratic Turnhalle Alliance (DTA), a coalition of moderate ethnically-based parties whose election would ensure a cooperative non-communist government in Windhoek. Calling for the establishment of a confederal system of government incorporating the homelands in an independent Namibia, this initiative marked the high water mark of South African optimism that the electoral process could produce a moderate and pliant government in a neighbouring state.[39]

The change in government in South Africa in 1978, putting P.W. Botha at the helm, saw a shift in government policy towards the Namibian situation. While the South African government continued to pursue a two-track approach based on the implementation of counter-revolutionary strategy in the territory while simultaneously engaging in negotiations with the international community, under Botha there was a willingness to put the military option to greater use.[40] South African strategy came to consist of three basic components: a counter-insurgency programme, a civic action programme and a restructuring of the political system. Coupled with this was the utilization by Pretoria of the tools of direct and indirect strategy against Swapo's host government, Angola.

The counter-insurgency programme implemented by the SADF incorporated the classic elements of counter-revolutionary strategy (see Chapter 6). These included the development of local military capabilities, relieving some of the burden of defence shouldered by the SADF, the creation of special units specifically trained for counter-insurgency activities, the establishment of a security zone on the Angolan border and the granting of emergency powers to security forces. With an estimated 80 000 SADF troops operating on the border in 1981 at a cost that continued to spiral upwards,[41] the South African government had compelling reasons to broaden local participation in defence of its interests in Namibia. To this end the government increased local recruitment into the South West African Territorial Forces (SWATF) as well as turned over nominal control of the SWATF to the newly elected local authorities in Windhoek in 1980.[42] In addition to extending the local commitment, Pretoria introduced crack counter-insurgency units to combat Swapo guerrillas. The 201 Battalion and 32 Battalion, both highly trained in counter-insurgency methods, operated on the border intercepting Swapo guerrillas and pursuing them into Angola.[43] Coupled with this was the founding of a police unit, Koevoet ('Crowbar'), whose successes won it praise within military circles while earning it a notoriety amongst the Namibian population. Finally, a buffer zone one kilometre in width, backed by a security fence running the length of the border, was established to thwart further Swapo infiltrations. All of these steps were supported by the introduction of emergency regulations in the northern districts of Namibia, enabling security forces to operate with fewer legal constraints.

Complementing the counter-insurgency programme was the establishment of an extensive civic action programme. Based upon the Rhodesian experience and informed by American strategist J.J. McCuen, the civic action programme was initially employed in the contentious region of the Caprivi strip where it met with success.[44] Introducing the winning hearts and minds strategy (WHAM, as it was known) to the populace, the civic action programme hoped to undercut the appeal of revolutionary forces through the alleviation of the sources of grievances which fed discontent against the government. Aimed primarily at the rural areas, it was administered by the SADF, who provided national servicemen for a variety of tasks, from medical services to educational activities.

Reforming the political system within the territory was the third feature of the South African government's plan to engineer a favourable transformation of the Namibian situation. The first step taken by Botha was to put into place an internal solution, along the lines of earlier Rhodesian efforts, through the sponsorship of elections in December 1978. Conducted without the participation of Swapo (whose internal legal wing boycotted the process), the results of the elections were considered suspect by the international community. Nevertheless, with the DTA winning 41 of 50 seats in the Constituent Assembly (soon to be granted legislative powers), Pretoria handed over substantial control of the territory to the governing Council of Ministers in Windhoek. Shifts in South African government policy with respect to political reform, undercutting efforts by reformist Administrator-General Marthinus Steyn to abrogate apartheid laws, ended up dividing the fragile coalition of moderate parties which had participated in the elections. The result was the emergence of a right-wing opposition amongst Namibian whites, which forged links with their confrères in South Africa, and complicated Botha's efforts in Namibia.

The utilization of direct strategy against the Angolan government, entailing military operations into that country, was a major component of the Botha government's efforts to secure a favourable outcome to the Namibian question. Following the SADF's intervention in Angola in 1975, the border region had settled into a period of tension marked by increasing skirmishes between SADF and Swapo forces.[45] The declaration of a state of emergency in the northernmost provinces in early 1976 and the subsequent removal a year later of Ovambo tribesmen from a kilometre-wide strip of land along the border, as well as the construction of a security fence, did not seem to stem the tide of Swapo infiltrations. In fact, by 1977 the SADF said that interceptions of Swapo guerrillas were occurring at a rate of 100 times a month and three years later annual SADF casualties were up to 100.[46] In addition to the threat posed by Swapo, the SADF believed that the build-up of thousands of Cuban troops in Angola was the harbinger of a conventional assault upon South African forces.

The South African military took steps to counter these threats through the maintenance of an occupied security zone in southern Angola, periodic military incursions into Angola and support for anti-MPLA guerrilla forces. A series of military operations deep into southern Angola struck out at Swapo (and later Fapla) forces encamped in the bush. Among the biggest SADF actions was Operation Protea, launched in August 1981, against a newly installed ground-to-air missile system. Two South African armoured columns moved 120 miles north into the Angolan bush, occupying territory and towns in the country for several weeks and eliminating the Angolan defence capability.[47] The result of these pre-emptive strikes was to confine Swapo bases to northern Namibia, thus significantly hampering its ability to operate in the territory. Concurrent with the demise of the insurgency threat was the increase in Cuban and Fapla troop strength in the south, a development which caused concern amongst South African military planners.[48]

Indirect strategy, brought into operation to encourage policy shifts amongst South Africa's antagonists to the north, was applied by the South African government through the support of Unita. With the assistance of the SADF, Unita was able to sustain campaigns of sabotage and terror aimed against the MPLA government in Luanda. The vital Benguela railway, linking the copper mines of Zaire and Zambia with the

Angolan coastal ports, was effectively rendered inoperable much of the time by Unita.

While employing counter-revolutionary strategy in Namibia, as part of the two-track approach the South African government continued to participate in the negotiation process sponsored by members of the international community. Critical to the Botha administration's approach to Namibia and Angola was the introduction of the Reagan administration's policy of 'constructive engagement'.[49] Coupled with the implementation of the Reagan Doctrine, it marked a significant shift in American policy towards the Namibian question from that of the Carter presidency. Imbued with a strong sense of anti-communism, the Reagan administration viewed the Soviet, Cuban and Eastern Bloc presence in Angola to be a major international security issue. An explicit policy of American support for Unita in southern Angola developed as did an acceptance of the linkage of a Namibian settlement with that of a withdrawal of Cuban forces in Angola. Informing the American position was a belief that it was necessary to meet South Africa's security concerns if a settlement was to be achieved. Dogged diplomatic efforts by the Americans resulted in an agreement in July 1982 by South Africa and Angola to all components (save the actual conduct of elections) of Security Council Resolution 435, but the talks continued to falter over the issue of the linking the withdrawal of 25 000 Cuban troops to the implementation of the UN-sponsored plan.[50]

By the end of 1983 the South African government was ready to seriously negotiate a mutual withdrawal of forces in southern Angola. With the annual cost of the South African presence estimated to be over $US1bn and shrinking support amongst Namibians for the DTA, a negotiated truce seemed to offer tangible benefits to the Botha administration; at the same time, the Angolan government found that, despite the opprobrium of dealing with the South African government, it would be in their interest to reduce the exorbitant costs of involvement in the conflict, which were estimated to run to $US1.5bn annually.[51] The result was the signing of the Lusaka Agreement 16 February 1984, implementing a cease-fire as a first step towards a settlement of the Namibian question.[52] Despite violations, the cease-fire was to hold for over a year. Born of its aggressive persecution of total strategy and, ironically, the rising costs of pursuing that approach, this uneasy truce between adversaries afforded the Botha administration with a regional diplomatic triumph rivalled only by the Nkomati Accord with Mozambique.

Regional Policy in Southern Africa

The Botha administration's approach towards Southern Africa, as outlined in the government's seminal policy statement – the Twelve Point Plan – centred on one fundamental theme. That was the achievement of institutional recognition of South Africa's economic and political pre-eminence in the region and, flowing from such recognition, the attainment of security for the state while it embarked on its domestic reform programme. This objective was to devolve into two basic approaches. The first was to take the form of a call for a loosely defined economic community of states in the region. The second was the procurement of non-aggression pacts from neighbouring states which would serve to deny or nullify the effect of revolutionary movements gaining territorial sanctuary adjoining South Africa. To realize these objectives, the Botha administration employed a blend of incentives and disincentives, mediated through the application of direct and indirect strategies which shifted as circumstances dictated.

Regional Policy in Southern Africa: Consas

In November 1979 the Botha administration issued a call to black leaders in Southern Africa to participate in the establishment of a regional confederation. Championed by the Foreign Minister, R.F. (Pik) Botha, the Constellation of Southern African States (Consas) was to incorporate a range of black-ruled states from Zimbabwe-Rhodesia (as the country was called at the time) to the north to neighbouring Mozambique, and the BLS (Botswana, Lesotho and Swaziland) countries as well as the 'independent' homelands and the territory of Southwest Africa/Namibia. While the organization's *raison d'être* was to be economic cooperation, the South African government plainly stated its hope that Consas's focus would one day include the development of 'a common approach in the security field . . . even the political field'.[53]

The key to the proposed scheme was the active participation of Zimbabwe. Situated at the geographic crossroads of Southern Africa, Zimbabwe was economically the most developed state in the region outside of South Africa itself and, as a result, would act as a magnet to neighbouring states. A climate of optimism had pervaded the Department of Foreign Affairs over the durability of 'internal' solutions to perennial South African fears of black majority rule in the region, bolstered by the electoral win of Bishop Abel Muzorewa in Zimbabwe in April 1979 and that of the Democratic Turnhalle Alliance in Namibia in December 1979. Operating under the assumption that at the upcoming Lancaster House sponsored elections 'moderate' black forces would win the day (with the covert support of the South African government), the South African government boldly anticipated both the outcome of the election and Zimbabwe's adherence to the constellation project.[54] This confidence was shattered by the unexpected victory of avowed radical Robert Mugabe in April 1980. The impact of Mugabe's explicit repudiation of the Consas scheme was exacerbated by his leading role in the formulation of a regional organization – the Southern African Development Co-ordination Conference (SADCC) – specifically designed to reduce regional dependency upon South Africa. With the acquiescence of nine states in the region to SADCC, including those already formally linked to the Republic through the Southern African Customs Union (Botswana, Lesotho and Swaziland), the constellation project disintegrated.

The collapse of its envisioned supra-regional organization forced the South African government to scale back on its regional ambitions. A rump version of the constellation scheme took form, with the independent homelands serving as the solitary formal participants in the economic confederation. At the same time, throughout the rest of the eighties the government retained the basic thrust of the project as it sought to tie the states of the region to the essential elements of Consas through the establishment of bilateral agreements in the economic and security fields.

Regional Policy in Southern Africa: Zimbabwe

Under Botha, South African policy towards Zimbabwe was a complex affair befitting the complicated nature of the relationship between the two neighbours. Two distinct phases in Pretoria's approach to Zimbabwe can be discerned during the early part of the eighties, the first predicated on cooperation and the second, emerging out of the failure of the initial approach, based on coercion. The apparent divergence between the two phases notwithstanding, it was the enduring economic links between the two states that set parameters within which South African and Zimbabwean policies were to be formulated and implemented.

The first phase of the Botha administration's policy towards Zimbabwe was characterized by an effort to both woo and stamp its imprint on the emerging state (see above). Much to the dismay of South African officials, Mugabe's Zanu party trounced both Muzorewa and rival nationalist Joshua Nkomo in the British-sponsored elections of 1980. With Mugabe's announcement of the formation of SADCC, the contentious relationship between the two states crystallized. The Zimbabwean government's subsequent downgrading of diplomatic relations in September, coupled with its decision to restrict the repatriation of profits, a move which was directed at South African firms, fuelled the growing hostility.[55] Furthermore, his reputation as a Marxist seemed to harbinger both a radical restructuring of the Zimbabwean economy and a reorientation of the country's foreign policy to one of direct support for liberation movements. Nevertheless, the ousting of ANC guerrilla forces which had infiltrated Zimbabwe on the eve of elections,[56] taken along with assurances of support for white farmers and businessmen, served as a signal to Pretoria that despite its often vitriolic rhetoric against South Africa the new Zimbabwean government fundamentally wished to retain correct relations with its neighbour.

Mugabe's pragmatism notwithstanding, there were key areas of disagreement over regional policy which were to remain a bone of contention between the two states. Specifically, Zimbabwe's active sponsorship and pursuit of its economic de-linkage scheme was anathema to the Botha administration's larger regional objectives. Given Zimbabwe's central position in SADCC, the South African government felt bound to exert pressure on that country's efforts to circumvent the economic ties and transportation networks which had become particularly pronounced since the advent of UDI and the subsequent closing of the port of Beira to Rhodesian traffic. Further aggravating relations between the two states was the Zimbabwean government's crucial role in mustering of international support for sanctions against South Africa.

With the patent failure of Pretoria's efforts to tie an independent Zimbabwe to South African interests, the second phase of South African policy took shape. Its objective was to effect a change in the policy of the government in Harare from one which pursued a course of action that was antithetical to the South African government's interests to one which at least implicitly accepted the veracity of these interests.[57] This approach was predicated upon the calibrated use of techniques drawn from indirect strategy. The methods employed included everything from economic measures to those of unconventional warfare. Underlying the entire venture was a recognition of the limitations imposed by the complicated relationship between the two states.

The first manifestation of conflict in the economic realm was the South African decision in March 1981 to revoke a long-standing preferential trade agreement between the two countries. While Pretoria ultimately backed down on this issue, it refused to sign any new agreement without direct ministerial participation on the part of the Zimbabwean government (implying recognition of the South African government). The withdrawal of 25 locomotives on loan to the Zimbabweans in April 1981, coming at a critical point in the maize harvest, caused disruptions that cost the country $Z7 million a week.[58] The turnaround time on rail traffic originating from Zimbabwe at South African ports increased, slowing the delivery of critical goods, including diesel fuel. And finally, the exorbitant cost of economic sabotage in neighbouring Mozambique had a drastic effect on the economy of land-locked Zimbabwe.

The employment of unconventional warfare took three basic forms. The first two were the use of sabotage and assassination in Zimbabwe itself. Largely carried out by ex-Rhodesians, the acts of sabotage were directed against key economic, military and political targets within Zimbabwe. Amongst the most spectacular was the demolition in August 1981 of over $US36 million worth of military hardware housed in barracks outside Harare. This was followed by the destruction of a quarter of the Zimbabwean air force on 25 July 1982.[59] Coupled with this was a spate of assassinations of senior ANC officials based in Harare, beginning with the death of Joe Gquabi on 3 August 1981. The premature detonation of a bomb planted in Zanu party headquarters in advance of a meeting of the central committee was another indication of the tactics employed by the SADF.[60] Direct incursions into Zimbabwean territory also featured at this time as the interception of SADF Special Forces units testified.[61] Overall, these actions served to knock out key installations in the country, eliminate and terrorize the ANC, and demonstrate Zimbabwe's vulnerability in the face of South African regional designs.

The second form of unconventional warfare utilized by the South African government was that of support for anti-government forces both within Zimbabwe and neighbouring Mozambique. Taking advantage of the serious post-independence upheavals in Matabeleland (which commenced in November 1980 and flared up again in February 1981), where dissident elements of Joshua Nkomo's Zapu movement were fomenting anti-government activities, the South African government began to supply the insurgents with a wide variety of armaments some time in 1982.[62] According to the testimony of captured dissident guerrillas, an estimated 5000 Zapu guerrillas (so-called Super-Zapu) received training with the SADF in the northern Transvaal.[63] Added to this was the establishment of a clandestine radio station which started broadcasting anti-Zanu propaganda in March 1983.[64] All in all, the Zimbabwean government tabulated over 7000 incidents of Super-Zapu 'banditry' between 1982 and 1986.[65]

But the principal theatre of insurgent activity was on Mozambique's Beira corridor. There, the SADF unleashed the refurbished Renamo guerrillas upon the already enervated Mozambican state. Their campaign of sabotage and violence, ambushing both the rail and road traffic on the Beira corridor, rendered this vital transport link virtually inoperative for large portions of the year. The Mutare to Beira pipeline which supplied Zimbabwe with its fuel needs was destroyed on the eve of its rehabilitation in October 1981. The end result of this activity in Mozambique was to oblige Zimbabwe to utilize South African rail and road transport which connected to the port of Maputo via the undamaged Chicualcuala route, undermining the fundamental objective of the entire SADCC project. With the commencement of Renamo attacks on the Chicualcuala railway in the aftermath of the Nkomati Accord, coupled with the introduction of higher tariffs on the South African portion of the railroad,[66] Zimbabwe was faced with having no viable transport alternative to direct links through South Africa.

The reaction to this blizzard of incidents directed against the newly independent Zimbabwean state was swift. To quell the incipient rebellion in Matabeleland, the Zimbabwean government resorted to a ruthless campaign of terror against the Matabele people. With the backing of the North Korean-trained 5th Brigade and the elite One Commando Battalion, the Zimbabwean government uncovered arms caches, burned villages, rooted out the dissidents and their supporters, and killed hundreds of Zimbabweans in Matabeleland.[67] In neighbouring Mozambique, Mugabe sent in the first of thousands of Zimbabwean troops to guard the Beira corridor in late 1982. Their superior training and expertise over that of the Frelimo troops enabled them to be more effective in protecting the Beira corridor and routing Renamo guerrillas. Despite these steps by the Zimbabwean government, the threat of South African intervention, whether direct or indirect, was sufficiently alarming to stifle any actions explicitly directed against Pretoria's interests.[68]

Regional Policy in Southern Africa: Mozambique

In neighbouring Mozambique, South African policy-makers sought to build upon the perceived shortcomings of Vorster's informal 'detente' policy towards the Marxist state. As in the case of Zimbabwe, the government's approach was characterized by efforts to maintain a semblance of cordial relations with its neighbour to the east. With the abandonment of this approach, forsaken due to ideological differences which manifested themselves in Mozambique's unremitting support for the anti-Apartheid struggle, the South African government turned to a twofold coercive strategy based on the application of incentives and disincentives. This involved undertaking direct action in the form of pre-emptive strikes against targets within Mozambique. The second approach sought to utilize the range of options available through the employment of indirect strategy, such as economic actions against the state and providing support for the counter-revolutionary movement Renamo, to effect policy changes in Maputo.

Despite the appearance of relatively congenial relations between the two neighbours in the late seventies, there were a number of fundamental areas of disagreement which obviated any lasting rapprochement. Firstly, the Mozambican state espoused an ideology, Marxist-Leninism, which was as inimical to the South African government as apartheid was to Maputo. Flowing from this obvious ideological conflict was the build-up of a significant ANC presence in Mozambique. This became an increasingly contentious issue between the two states, particularly as ANC infiltrations and acts of sabotage began to have a direct impact.[69] Linked to this was the growing presence of Eastern Bloc military advisers, numbering 3000 by the mid-eighties, whose involvement centred on the establishment of the state security apparatuses. Finally, President Samora Machel's unmitigated support for the development of the SADCC project, which sought to sever the ties of economic dependency that bound the states of the region to South Africa, posed a blatant challenge to the Republic's pre-eminent position in the region. Mozambican adherence to SADCC was crucial to the success of the venture, as its transportation system offered land-locked countries of the interior – particularly Zimbabwe – the only viable alternative route to that of South Africa.

At the same time that the Mozambican government was giving policy content to their ideological predilections, the South African government was also embarking on a second policy 'track'. Through the Military Intelligence Directorate, the SADF began in 1979 to develop contacts with the Rhodesian sponsored MNR[70] and provide the organization with an estimated $1 million of supplies by the year's end.[71] As Zimbabwean independence loomed closer, a deal was struck between the Rhodesian Central Intelligence Organization and Military Intelligence to transfer all 'compromised' units, including the MNR and the Selous Scouts, to South Africa. Within days of Mugabe's electoral victory, the entire MNR operation was shifted southward to bases outside of the Kruger National Park where the organization received further recruits and training. By late 1980 the MNR had grown from a force estimated at the time of the Zimbabwean elections to be 1800 personnel to approximately 7000 trained fighters.[72]

It appears that the brief springtime of reconciliation which characterized South African–Mozambican relations from 1978 to 1980 was merely posturing as the states consciously pursued policies that were fundamentally inimical to each other's vital interests. By late 1980 relations between the two states were headed on a collision course, with each government professing opposing ideologies, pursuing different regional economic agendas, and giving support to insurgency movements dedicated to the overthrow of their neighbour's governments. It was the South African government which, utilizing the strategic 'tools' inherent in its total strategy, gave indisputable and overt expression to the latent hostility between the two states.

The first application of total strategy's direct approach was the military attack levelled against the Mozambican capitol itself. Launched on 31 January 1981, the SADF engineered a lightning strike at a series of ANC offices and 'safe houses' in the suburbs of Maputo, killing thirteen members of the organization. The elimination of the Solomon Mahlangu Squad (attached to the Special Operations Section of MK) was, according to South African intelligence sources, the key objective of the mission.[73] This action was followed in August 1982 by another SADF operation into Mozambique hitting six targets identified as ANC bastions of support.[74] Again in October 1983, an SADF commando struck out at an ANC office in Maputo.

Despite these instances of direct military involvement in Mozambique, the primary means of effecting policy changes in the Mozambican government was through the application of indirect strategy. This took on two major forms: the first being the flexing of South Africa's considerable economic muscle through such steps as the reduction of traditional sources of vital foreign exchange earnings; the second being the activation of the counter-revolutionary movement, the Resistençia Naçional Moçambicana (or Renamo, as the MNR came to be called). This included everything from logistics and training to joint covert operations with the SADF.

As noted above, economic relations between South Africa and Mozambique remained correct, fortified by the notion held in both Pretoria and Maputo that Mozambique's economy was dependent upon the South African mining industry and port revenues. Nonetheless, South Africa's utilization of Maputo's port facilities dropped steadily during this period as did its recruitment of Mozambican mineworkers. In fact, by 1983 South African traffic to the port of Maputo was reportedly half that of the previous year and 16 per cent of the traffic in 1973.[75] During this period, the overall number of Mozambican miners employed in South Africa fell from 118 030 in 1975 to 45 491 in 1983. The cost in lost miners' remittances was estimated to be US$568 million.[76] All of these factors were to have a crippling effect on an economy so dependent upon South Africa.

The counter-insurgency force initially fostered by the Rhodesian government in its struggle against Zanu guerrillas became the other pillar of South Africa's indirect strategy against Mozambique. Renamo unleased a ruthless campaign of intimidation and violence in the countryside, immobilizing government security forces and crippling the already debilitated Mozambican economy. Schools, health centres, Frelimo party offices and government officials themselves were targeted by the guerrillas. Key economic sites were also singled out by Renamo. Transport routes and in particular the Beira corridor became the object of continual assaults by the anti-government movement. Covert operations by SADF in conjunction with Renamo forces, such as the destruction of 34 oil storage tanks worth $40 million in Beira on 9 December 1982, took out vital components of the already strapped Mozambican economy.[77] By late 1982, the situation in Mozambique had deteriorated to the point where Zimbabwean troops were brought in to protect the vital Beira corridor.

Reeling under the impact of South Africa's destabilization

campaign, President Samora Machel recognized that Mozambique could no longer sustain its current position. A succession of secret meetings between Mozambican and South African officials were held in 1983, culminating in the highly-publicized Nkomati Accord. Signed on 16 March 1984, the Accord called for the closing of ANC offices and curbing of ANC activities within Mozambique in exchange for the suspension of South African support for the Renamo guerrillas.[78] A month later, the Mozambican government began to conduct raids on ANC houses in the country. By October, over 800 ANC members had been forcibly expelled from their former sanctuaries.[79] On the South African side, within a few weeks of signing the Nkomati Accord, three Renamo training bases were closed down as was the movement's radio station.[80] However, Renamo forces were permitted to cross over to Mozambique with their military equipment intact and, according to some sources, were the beneficiaries of a huge resupplying effort conducted by the South African navy later that year.

The process inaugurated at Nkomati did not stop with the ousting of the ANC cadres. In October 1985, the South African government attempted to broker a peace settlement between Frelimo and Renamo. After a meeting presided over by South African security personnel and Foreign Affairs, representatives of the two opposing forces discussed the possibility of bringing the conflict to an end. A declaration of principles was publicly endorsed by all parties to the negotiations, only to be renounced hours later.[81] With Renamo insurgents pouring into the Zambezia, Tete and Gaza provinces, bringing with them the rapacious brutality for which they had become infamous, it became apparent that what was a major diplomatic triumph for the Botha administration was an unmitigated disaster for the Mozambican government.

Regional Policy in Southern Africa: Botswana, Lesotho and Swaziland

Of all the front line states, only the precarious situation of Botswana, Lesotho and Swaziland *vis-à-vis* their neighbour invoked the appellate 'captive states'.[82] Integrally linked to the South African economy through such vehicles as the

Southern African Customs Union (SACU), the BLS countries' vulnerability strongly militated against pursuing any policy directly antithetical to South African interests. In spite of these factors, all three countries attempted in one fashion or another to assert their independence from South African domination. The most dramatic manifestation of this was the BLS countries participation in the SADCC project. Recognizing that formal adherence to Consas was not in the offing, Pretoria nevertheless sought to tie the BLS countries to the economic and political goals embodied in the Consas project through bilateral economic and security agreements as well as neutralize their role as a sanctuary for ANC support. As the BLS countries took tentative steps which went against professed South African interests, the Botha administration turned to the use of the coercive tools of indirect and direct strategy to modify their behavior.

Botswana, bolstered by a thriving economy based on diamond mining and stock ranching, had traditionally pursued a cautious policy towards its neighbour to the South. This approach was manifested in Botswana's unwillingness to allow the ANC to use its vast expanses as an infiltration point. With the Botswanan government actively employing its defence forces to thwart ANC cadres crossing over from Zambia, a South African security official could state in June 1985:

> There is no allegation of bad faith by South Africa against Botswana. We believe Botswana is doing everything it can. But we are dealing with a sophisticated terrorist organization . . . [which] is not, perhaps, in the experience of a small Third World country's intelligence organization and police force.[83]

At the same time, the government in Gaborone did allow South African refugees to take up residence in Botswana, although there was no official support for the ANC as such, and a significant exile community did establish itself. And, despite the professed efforts of the Botswana Defence Force and the SADF both the ANC and the PAC admitted using Botswana as a transit point at one time or another.[84]

Botswana's friendly stance towards South Africa notwithstanding, the Botha administration remained committed to gaining adherence to a security agreement and an extension of the existing regional economic cooperative agreement (SACU) so as to garner tacit recognition for the 'independent' homelands. Pressure was brought to bear upon the government through diplomatic, economic and military means. With the signing of the Nkomati Accord with Mozambique, the South African government went so far as to present Gaborone with a similar document for its signature. The South African government also attempted to exert pressure on Botswana through SACU and the withholding of requisite South African capital for development projects. Finally, the tactics of direct strategy were utilized against the ANC exile community in Botswana in June 1985 when the SADF launched an attack on ANC targets. While Botswana refused to go along with Pretoria's plans, verbal assurances were given by Botswanan officials which amounted to acceptance of the conditions of the non-aggression pact.[85] Thus a fig-leaf of independence, allowing the government to claim a kind of neutrality in the struggle to the south, covered Botswana's capitulation to the terms of a security accord with South Africa.[86]

Lesotho, surrounded geographically by South Africa and utterly dependent upon remittances from Basotho miners in the Republic, was the most vulnerable of the three states. Despite this condition, the government of Lesotho had since the sixties allowed their country to become a safe haven for South Africans seeking asylum. By 1982, 11 500 South Africans – many of whom were ANC members or supporters – lived in the tiny mountain state.[87] Lesotho's leader Chief Leabua Jonathan, who came to power in 1970 allegedly with the covert support of the South African government, had by 1976 begun to shift his government's previously submissive stance towards South Africa to one which gave increasing support to anti-apartheid forces in the region. This included the failure to give diplomatic recognition to the newly 'independent' homelands and Lesotho's tacit support of radical politics as espoused in Mozambique, as well as the continual housing of the growing ANC exile community.

With respect to incentives to cooperation, the South African government held out the possibility of a joint hydroelectric project based in Lesotho which had the potential to earn the impoverished state substantive foreign exchange.

There were indications that the South African government was willing to trade territory – in this case the nearby homeland enclave of Qwa Qwa – for some form of support or concessions on Lesotho's part. However, faced with the series of potentially dangerous deviations by the government in Maseru, the Botha administration elected to employ the tactics of direct and indirect strategy, including the use of economic means and support for anti-government forces, to engineer a change in Lesotho's policies.

Indirect strategy took the form of economic pressure, to which Lesotho was highly susceptible, and support for the anti-government forces of the Lesotho Liberation Army (LLA). The LLA, formed by dissident members of Chief Jonathan's governing party, began to receive covert support from the South African government and in May 1979 launched a campaign of terror and sabotage. The destruction of bridges, postal and telegraph facilities and attacks on police stations, came to a halt after Chief Jonathan met publicly with Prime Minister Botha in August 1980.[88] However, this respite was brief. Following the rise in sabotage actions within South Africa, in early 1981 the LLA renewed its attacks on the government through sabotage and the assassination of political figures.

Economic coercion was employed through such instruments as the South African dominated Southern African Customs Union as a means of getting Lesotho to grant recognition to the 'independent' homelands. The periodic institution of strict border checks, done in the wake of terrorist incidents within South Africa, had the effect of imposing a limited economic blockade on Lesotho. Sabotage of economic targets also placed a financial burden on the already impoverished country. Finally, in December 1985, the South African government instituted a blockade which apparently precipitated a coup against Chief Jonathan's government.

The direct approach employed by the South African government took the form of a number of raids against ANC targets in Lesotho. The SADF struck on 9 December 1982 at ANC safe houses in Lesotho's capitol, killing 30 members of the organization.[89] After the raid, Lesotho broke openly with Pretoria, establishing diplomatic missions with the Soviet Union and other eastern bloc countries. Three years later another cross-border raid into Maseru killed six ANC cadres and, coupled with the application of an economic blockade against the country a few days later, led to the overthrow of the government.

As in the case of the two other 'captive states', Swaziland was highly dependent upon South Africa. The reluctance of the Swazi government to jeopardize the economic welfare and position of the state spawned a relatively high degree of overt cooperation with Pretoria.[90] This attitude naturally found favour within official South African circles and may have contributed to the still-born land-exchange scheme – revolving around the transfer of the homeland of KaNgwane to Swaziland – that was floated for a time in the early eighties.[91] Concurrently, however, the Swazi government continued to give sanctuary to South African refugees and allow the ANC to operate in a limited fashion within the country. In fact, by the late seventies, Swaziland had become the ANC's primary conduit for internally bound financial support and served as a contact point for recruits coming out of South Africa.[92]

South African concern over the proximity of the ANC, heightened by the emergence of a sabotage campaign within the country, caused the Minister of Defence to issue a warning in October 1981 to the Swazi government that continued support for the ANC would result in military incursions into its territory by the SADF. A crackdown on ANC officials followed, resulting in general harassment and the ousting of over 100 members of the organization. This action was bolstered by the conclusion of the first of the non-aggression pacts between South Africa and its neighbours. Signed secretly on 17 February 1982, the Swazi–South African Agreement Relating to Security Matters called on both parties to disallow 'any activities within their respective territories directed towards the commission of any act which involves a threat or use of force against each other's territorial integrity'. The agreement also called upon the signatories to refrain from allowing 'foreign military units' to operate in their respective territories.[93]

The International Environment

The UN Security Council's passage of a mandatory arms embargo in 1977 was, as it turned out, to be the apogee of collective action in that forum against South Africa. Attempts to extend mandatory sanctions, as in the case of the still-born Security Council resolution of April 1981 (linking the failure to withdrawal from Namibia to the sanctions issue), came up against a recalcitrant Western bloc.[94] Unwilling to jeopardize business interests and conscious that once imposed by the Security Council sanctions would be difficult to lift, the Western leadership blocked further resolutions designed to introduce economic sanctions against South Africa. Faced with this dilemma, the anti-apartheid movement shifted its energy away from obtaining collective action in the UN to that of achieving the same aims through other forums. Chief among these were the Commonwealth, the European Community and individual countries themselves.

The initial results of this shift in strategy were meagre as the key Western states – notably Britain and the United States – came under new conservative administrations that were reluctant to challenge the Botha administration's incremental reform programme at this juncture.[95] And while within both the Commonwealth and the European Community sentiment was growing for the imposition of sanctions there nevertheless remained enough significant opposition in these organizations to stifle concrete action.

Two events were to revolutionize the international sanctions campaign. The first was the product of South Africa's destabilization campaign which forced neighbouring states to oust the ANC from their territory. Stripped of the ability to operate effectively through the use of territorial sanctuaries and threatened by growing internal dissension within its military wing, the ANC had to fall back upon alternative strategies such as securing the imposition of international sanctions.[96] But the second event which acted as a catalyst to the sanctions campaign was the development of a sustained uprising in the black townships in 1985. Though not directly attributed to the ANC, the rebellion convincingly demonstrated that Botha's reform programme – and in particular the tricameral parliament – was unacceptable to the majority of South Africans. This gave dramatic impetus to the ANC's efforts to isolate South Africa, as the Western community could no longer effectively argue for patience with the Botha reform programme or the virtues of 'constructive engagement'. The result was to lay the foundation for the introduction of economic sanctions against South Africa on an unprecedented scale.

South Africa's Nuclear Programme

The turmoil in Angola, demonstrating unequivocally South Africa's military isolation even in the face of Soviet intervention in the region, proved to be the final impetus needed to embark upon South Africa's own nuclear weapons programme.[97] Since the fifties, South Africa had served as a major supplier of uranium to the West and, during that time, benefited from the expertise of American, German, French and Israeli nuclear technicians in the construction of two nuclear reactors completed in 1965 and 1967. In the late sixties, discussions were held by top government officials about the possibility of developing a South African bomb. While never directly initiated at this stage, the government clearly sought to retain its options through continued financial support of its nuclear programme.[98] In the wake of Angola, a decision was taken in 1974 by the Vorster government to develop a nuclear device and a testing site was established in the Kalahari desert the same year (following its disclosure in 1977 and the combined pressure of Washington and Moscow, it was mothballed). After 1975, the 'Valindaba' and 'Pelindaba' plants in the Pretoria region, which had been built to supply existing reactors with fuel, began to produce weapons-grade uranium for the construction of an atomic bomb.[99] South African scientists, in conjunction with their Israeli counterparts, were able to build six devices (though the Atomic Energy Agency estimates that up to 25 bombs could have been developed) each with approximately the same destructive power as the bomb which struck Hiroshima.[100] The South African Air Force, armed with the Mirage and its own Cheetah aircraft, along with its world-renowned G-6 artillery, was capable of delivering the bombs over a target in the field. On 22 September 1979 American satellites detected the flash of a nuclear explosion well out from the South African coast and, despite ardent denials by Pretoria, the world assumed that South Africa had joined the nuclear club.

Under the Botha government, the South African nuclear weapons programme continued to receive strong support. In the early eighties Armscor announced that it had engineered an intermediate-range missile system based on the French Exocet missile. This was followed by statements which suggested that a military site in northern Natal had been used for the development of long-range missiles.[101] It was only in July 1989 that the South African government officially announced that it had successfully conducted a ballistic missile test.[102]

Throughout this period, the strategy of the Botha government was to neither confirm nor deny its possession of a nuclear capability. With respect to the actual usage of a nuclear device, it would appear that the South African government viewed the possession of an atomic bomb as a means of drawing in Western support – and in particular American support – for South Africa in the event of a direct Soviet threat to the state.[103] At its heart, this approach reflected an acknowledgement that its regional opponent, the Soviet Union, had immensely greater nuclear and conventional resources to throw into any conflict between the two. South African deterrent strategy – much like that of Ian Smith's Rhodesia and its use of 'hot pursuit' into Mozambique in the final years of its existence – believed that the West could be blackmailed into abandoning its anti-apartheid stance and provide the nuclear guarantees against the Soviet threat (or that of its proxies) which the state sought. Thus, the government pursued a policy of calibrated hints verging on disclosures as a means of both communicating the seriousness with which it viewed its security situation and, at the same time, securing Western assistance in its struggle.

Conclusion

The government's stated prerequisites for the successful introduction of its reform programme, the maintenance of domestic tranquillity and the fostering of a favourable regional environment, underlaid the pursuit of its security policy.

Informed by the tenets of total strategy, the Botha administration had embarked on an aggressive foreign policy towards the region, the fruits of which were evident by 1984 with the creation of both a formal and informal network of non-aggression pacts with states in the region. A dangerous component of this approach was the development of an independent nuclear capability which was designed, in the eyes of South African strategists, to draw in Western support for the embattled regime. This situation was complemented domestically through the development of the state's capacity to counter internal security threats such as the revolutionary activities of the outlawed ANC. While Swapo infiltrations in Namibia and ANC actions in the Republic continued to be a concern of the South African government, by the mid-eighties it appeared that the security establishment had successfully created the breathing-space necessary for the introduction of Botha's incremental reform programme. This assumption was soon to be challenged by the tide of sustained unrest sweeping the country in the months following the implementation of the government's programme for political reform.

SOCIO-ECONOMIC POLICY

The haphazard implementation of socio-economic reform, one of the pillars of Botha's programme, belied even the limited expectations raised by the Wiehahn and Riekert commissions. The government's grudging extension of full rights for black trade unions was accompanied by a struggle to elevate the socio-economic status of those urbanized blacks recognized by the government as 'insiders'. Legislation designed to institutionalize these reforms stalled over the unresolved debate within the government bureaucracy as to both the direction and the scope of change. Further exacerbating these problems was the government's commitment to a range of policies in other areas such as 'homeland' independence that necessarily contradicted the thrust of some of the socio-economic reform legislation. The resultant confusion led to a growing frustration amongst reform-minded allies of Botha's programme both inside and outside South Africa.

Labour Policy and the African Trade Union Movement

The expansion of African labour rights which followed the release of the Wiehahn reports did not see a concomitant rise in political activism amongst the nascent African unions. Throughout the early eighties, African trade unions focused their energies on extending the scope of their hard-earned labour rights, increasing their membership and building their respective organizations. The closest the African trade union movement came to engaging directly in politics of the day was to defy the government's attempts to define worker eligibility for unions in terms of the Wiehahn/Riekert 'urban insider' and 'migrant outsider' categories utilized to officially register unions.[104]

At the beginning of 1979, a series of strikes jolted South African industry starting with the Fattis and Monis action in Cape Town and followed by the lengthy Ford Motor Company strike in Port Elizabeth and finally moving up to the Witwatersrand area in the early 1980s.[105] As unions tested their new-found strength and the efficacy of the collective bargaining structure put into place by the Department of Manpower, the government and business for the most part sought to resist the changing realities of the workplace. Acting against the background of growing labour unrest, the government attempted to reclaim the initiative through the introduction of the Labour Relations Bill in 1981 but, after stiff resistance from the trade unions, abandoned the effort.

By the end of 1982, the struggle between the African trade unions and the government had fundamentally been decided in favour of the trade union movement as the Botha administration conceded the rights of African labour on virtually all fronts. One observer writes: '[T]he authorities were no longer trying to prevent unions gaining rights – but they did want them to win them inside the system.'[106] Concurrently, the African trade unions had managed to double their membership between 1981 and 1985, and were able to successfully build a solid labour structure across industries and the country as a whole.[107] The ability of the Federation of South African Trade Unions (Fosatu), the super-union formed in 1979, and other trade unions to mobilize over 100 000 workers in two short days to protest the death in detention of labour activist Neil Aggett in 1982 spoke to the level of sophistication the African trade union movement had achieved in the span of three years.

Socio-Economic Reform Initiatives and Legislation

The enduring influence of the recommendations of a number of government commissions – chief among them the Riekert commission – on socio-economic issues was felt in the President's Council, the recalcitrant Department of Cooperation and Development (DCD) and, following its establishment in August 1982, the reformist DCDP. Pressing for the improvement of conditions and rights for urbanized Africans, the work of these commissions was recast in Botha's Twelve Point Plan as a call for the repeal of 'hurtful, unnecessary discriminatory measures . . . [and the] recognition of economic interdependence and the properly planned utilization of our manpower'.

The Constitutional and Economic Affairs Committees of the President's Council broached the contentious issue of racial segregation in its report in 1981. By calling for the establishment of joint decision-making structures between the racially defined institutions of local government, the President's Council challenged some of the underlying precepts of such apartheid legislation as the Separate Amenities Act (see below). With the completion of this report in 1982, and the concomitant establishment of the DCDP in August that same year, socio-economic issues became directly linked to the general constitutional restructuring programme.

Reforming the raft of legislation governing interracial social relations that had cropped up under apartheid put government officials in a paradoxical situation. On the one hand, abolishing laws like the Mixed Marriages Act – long considered to be one of the cornerstones of apartheid legislation – was virtually cost-free in the sense that abolition did not necessitate or imply a concomitant government commitment to redress imbalances resulting from this legislation. On the other hand, the political costs associated with taking such a step could be very high for the NP as many of its supporters had come to view the legal separation of racial groups within the country to be sacrosanct. To minimize the political costs of such actions, the NP government increasingly turned to non-enforcement of apartheid legislation and the provision of localized decision-making on such matters. As always, the concerns of the NP's natural constituency – the Afrikaner – weighed most heavily into any such decision taken by government officials, whether on a local or national level.[108]

The result of the government's predicament was the simultaneous declaration and implementation of two contradictory streams of policy. On a national level, Botha himself continued to reiterate his government's commitment to established social segregation. At the same time, various government ministers proclaimed on separate occasions either their adherence to 'petty apartheid' or their unwillingness to sanction such measures. Irrespective of the contradictory nature of stated government policy, officials monitoring local-level developments continued to issue exemptions in an assortment of areas including entertainment facilities, hotels and sports. Despite these actions, the failure to realize the promised eradication of 'hurtful' features of government policy, leaving the major legislative pillars restricting social contact between the races on the statute books, went a long way towards damaging the Botha administration's reformist credentials.

Turning to the government's reform policy towards African urbanization, the contradictions which plagued the proposed elimination of 'petty apartheid' were even more apparent. While the government moved to introduce new contentious legislation on African urbanization (see below), the DCD continued to administer its policy of forced removals of Africans residing in 'white' South Africa. This policy was dramatized by events in the Western Cape, where tens of thousands of illegal migrants residing in the Cape Flats area outside of Cape Town were forcibly taken to designated homeland areas.

On the legislative side of government policy, the first initiative which followed in the wake of the government's acceptance of the Riekert report was the publication of three bills in October 1980. Products of the 'apartheid bureaucracy' ensconced within the DCD, the Orderly Movement and Settlement of Black Persons Bill, the Black Communities

Development Bill and the Black Local Authorities Bill provoked a storm of controversy across the country. Among other things, the proposed legislation abolished Section 10 rights and replaced the existing system of influx control with a much harsher regime than before. According to some observers, the 'Koornhof Bills' were actually 'designed by the minister's recalcitrant servants to bamboozle him and sabotage Government plans'.[109]

Under censure from all sides, the proposed legislation was withdrawn from consideration and subsequently reintroduced in a substantially revised form under the influence of DCDP officials. After much debate the Black Local Authorities Act became law in 1982, while the Black Community Development Act became law in 1984. The last bill, the Orderly Movement and Settlement of Black Persons Bill, aroused additional controversy when it was submitted to Parliament in May 1982. Cast in much the same terms as in its previous incarnation, the Bill was viewed as no more than another attempt at tightening up influx control. With the advent of the new constitutional dispensation and concomitant changes in local and regional government in the pipeline, the Orderly Movement and Settlement of Black Persons Bill was jettisoned.

The collapse of this last legislative initiative corresponded with the demise of the DCD itself. As the DCDP began to assert its authority beyond that of constitutional issues affecting the white, Coloured and Indian population, the DCD concurrently lost its prerogatives in matters governing the lives of the African population. Thereafter, incremental reform in the socio-economic area moved at a quicker pace. The Coloured labour preference policy, which had enforced the hiring of Coloureds over that of blacks in the Cape province, was officially abandoned in 1984. Coupled with this announcement was the extension of 99-year leasehold rights – which had been introduced in 1978 – to blacks in selected townships in the Cape. In 1985, the Black Consolidation Act was amended to alleviate some of the more flagrant aspects of the law on influx control.[110] By the end of 1985, the government position had shifted still further. The Minister of Constitutional Development and Planning declared that those blacks who qualified for the 99-year leasehold rights in township areas would henceforth be allowed to own their own homes in township areas.[111]

These preliminary breaches in the Riekert framework were soon to be eclipsed by more substantial violations. Reporting September 1985, the President's Council proposed that the government abandon much of the current influx control legislation in favour of a non-discriminatory urban policy which centred on the acceptance of rural-to-urban migration (see Chapter 5).[112] At the heart of the report's recommendations was a shift away from the 'insider/outsider' dichotomy which had characterized the approach adopted by the Riekert commission. With the formation of the DCDP, socio-economic issues were increasingly drawn directly into the constitutional development process itself.

Conclusion

Reform in South Africa's socio-economic policy suffered from a number of defects. Wedded to the Riekert strategy and, with it, the maintenance of the homeland structures, the government too often presented a picture of verbal renunciation of the past on the one hand while on the other hand carrying out measures, such as forced removals, that were vintage apartheid. Exacerbating the situation was the divisive role played by the 'apartheid bureaucracy' in the DCD, whose actions served to cast further doubt on the direction of the Botha administration's reform programme. Still, even judged in terms of the limited reforms envisioned by Riekert, one observer was able to point out that:

> by 1985 little had been done to implement the proposals of the Riekert commission and the two parliamentary select committees to which subsequent Bills were referred.[113]

In dramatic contrast with the aspects of socio-economic change described above, reform in the field of African labour relations had moved substantially by 1985. The critical element in the overturning of the Botha administration's initial approach to African trade unionism, based on the Riekert/Wiehahn formula, was the rapid growth of the labour movement. Faced with a mobilized opposition in the form of the new African trade unions, the Botha administration's determination to implement the Wiehahn commission's recommendations to their fullest extent wavered and with it the government's commitment to the whole 'insider/outsider' formulation. This crack in the Riekert/Wiehahn facade was eventually to spill over into all aspects of the government's policy towards African urbanization and culminated in the development of a new urbanization strategy contained in the government White Paper on Urbanization of 1986.

POLITICAL REFORM POLICY

Of the many aspects of reform contemplated by the Botha administration, political change was the most daunting. Unlike reforms in the socio-economic area – which could be effected through deliberate government oversight or by issuing exemptions – political reform was by its very nature a public manifestation of relative power that the white minority government was chary of broaching. For the Botha administration, the task of restructuring the political system at all three tiers of government – local, provincial and national – was coupled with a desire to transform South Africa's relations within the region through the introduction of a confederal arrangement amongst neighbouring states. Government policy regarding these often contentious constitutional issues was debated in three forums: the President's Council, the Office of the Prime Minister, and the DCDP. A fourth forum, the DCD, was to play a divisive (though diminishing) role as the process of reform gathered momentum. The major legislative initiatives emerging out of these institutions during this period – the Black Local Authorities Act, the establishment of the tricameral Parliament and the Regional Services Councils – reflected the government's basic concern with extending differing degrees of consultative powers to the Coloured, Indian and African peoples while simultaneously preserving white political pre-eminence.

The Institutions of Political Reform

The President's Council and the DCDP were the central mechanisms of constitutional reform in the Botha administration. While the blueprints for structural changes were originally products of the President's Council, the establishment of the DCDP corresponded with a shift in the centre of policy-making in constitutional affairs into the hands of the newly created ministry. Of the two forums established by the government to set the policy agenda on political reform issues, it was the DCDP which came to occupy a central position in the policy development and administration of the government's political reform programme. Led by Botha's trusted colleague Chris Heunis, the DCDP attempted to guide government policy through the political morass that threatened both the NP's monopoly on power and the South African state's long-term viability.

The DCDP had its origins in the five planning branches of the Office of the Prime Minister that were established through the 'rationalization' scheme undertaken in 1980. In August 1982 these branches were transferred and formed into chief directorates of a new separate ministry, dubbed the DCDP, and put under Heunis. A 'close liaison' developed between the committees of the President's Council and their planning section counterparts in the DCDP.[114] Three policy initiatives in particular emerged out of this ministry: the restructuring of local and regional government; the scrapping of the provincial administrations; and the introduction of the tricameral Parliament.

In contrast to these newly formed institutions stood the DCD, whose purview included virtually all aspects of relations with the African population. This bastion of apartheid bureaucracy had a vested interest in the maintenance of the old order which clashed with the reforms envisioned by strategists within the President's Council and the DCDP. The newly established DCDP set about stripping of responsibilities from the DCD and absorbing its powers into the reformist fold. As one academic observes:

> The transition in roles was not a smooth one, reflecting the tensions inherent in the process of converting a well

> developed repressive apparatus into a more facilitative mould. It became clear that a hard-fought struggle was being waged within the state apparatus itself between its various branches; and that the 'reformist' wing led by the Department of Constitutional Development and Planning was set upon dismembering the once-powerful Department of Co-operation and Development.[115]

This acrimonious process was not to be complete until the official dismantling of the DCD in 1985, by which time the damage to the Botha administration's reformist credentials amongst the black population was virtually irreparable.

Political Reform Initiatives and Legislation

The foundation of Botha's political reform policy, as outlined in the Twelve Point Plan, was that of the extension of political rights to Coloured and Indians on the basis of the maintenance of South African society's statutory populations while, concurrently, pursuing the expansion of limited political rights to urban Africans and the political development of the 'homeland' system. This guiding principle was to be the common thread running through all of the DCDP's proposed political changes. It was to be given effect through the creation of a distinction between those areas which 'especially or differentially affect a population group in the maintenance of its identity and the upholding and furtherance of its way of life, culture, traditions and customs', known as 'own affairs', and those areas which were considered to be within the purview of common concerns, known as 'general affairs'.[116] Legislation developed on the basis of this division and was given content in local and regional restructuring and at the national level. Political reform at the supra-national level, centring on the 'homeland' system, moved hesitantly towards a restructuring of the country into nine economic regions which, alongside the more ambitious Consas scheme, would reconstitute South Africa on a confederal basis.

At the same time that the principle of the retention of South Africa's group identity was being promulgated through the government's reform programme, there developed a contradictory trend within the political reform process. Within the evolving political structures introduced by the government, which were grounded on this group basis, the necessity of intra-group decision-making on matters of 'general affairs' acted as an incentive to cooperation on multi-racial terms at a level never before experienced in official South Africa. This paradoxical situation was acknowledged by officials within the DCDP and, in the case of some senior figures, represented the conscious fulfilment of an objective to transform by stealth the very institutions created in the wake of the Botha reform programme from segregationist to integrationist.[117]

Reform Initiatives at the Local and Regional Level

The initiatives for restructuring local and regional government originally came, as in the case of other reforms, from a series of government-sponsored committees. These committees, building upon each other's work, played an important role in the formulation of the new policy towards government at the local and regional levels. All of these various initiatives in constitutional restructuring were ultimately to culminate in a radical departure from traditional NP policy: the institutionalization of multi-racial authorities at the local and regional level – albeit conforming to the dictates of being founded on the basis of group identity – in the form of the new Regional Services Councils and the revamped Provincial authorities.

Over the years, the situation confronting African, Coloured and Indian municipalities had varied as each statutory population group underwent a different historical experience. With respect to the African population, African municipalities were traditionally administered by neighbouring white municipalities. Following the Soweto riots in 1976, responsibilities for administering African affairs were divided between the white Administration Boards and newly created Community Councils. The Community Councils continued the policy of providing little effective executive powers to the Africans sitting it. As such, Councillors, though elected, came under direct criticism from township residents who perceived them to be merely agents of the Administration Boards. By 1980, with some of the preliminary improvements called for by the Riekert Commission report in place, 224 Community Councils had been established across the country.[118]

The situation for the Coloured and Indian populations differed from that of the Africans. The coming of NP rule brought with it both further restrictions on local autonomy and political restructuring in keeping with the dictates of apartheid. An amendment to the Group Areas Act in 1962 removed the Coloured and Indian communities from the direct control of white local authorities and put in its place a system of local consultative committees for each racially constituted community. An evolutionary process was envisioned, such that consultative committees with purely advisory powers would evolve into management committees with limited executive powers. This process was to ultimately culminate in the creation of local authorities for Coloureds and Indians with an independent municipal status. By 1982, while 158 management committees had been founded for the Coloured community and seven for the Indian community, none had evolved into the autonomous local authorities called for by the legislation.[119]

The continual failure of white local and provincial authorities to fully implement the provisions called for in the amendment to the Group Areas Act prompted the government to appoint a number of committees of inquiry into the matter.[120] The essence of all of the findings was that an adequate mechanism for financing of any local structures must be linked to their establishment and that opportunities for the joint utilization of services between municipalities did in fact exist.[121]

Concurrently, the President's Council's issued a report on local and regional management systems on 12 May 1982 with the call 'at the level of local government, (for) the principle of maximum devolution of authority and decentralization of administration to be accepted as a matter of policy.'[122] Adequate provisions for financing African local authorities would be necessary, and the report called for an increase in the tax base through property and sales taxes.[123] At the same time, it recommended the establishment of a multiracial liaison mechanism, or 'joint services committees', that would 'be regarded as forerunners to the metropolitan/regional authorities' to administer bulk services to communities.

Local and Regional Reform: the Establishment of Local Authorities for Africans, Coloureds and Indians

With multi-racial management of local and regional government advocated by a plethora of government-sanctioned commissions, the question remained as to how Botha would reconcile this principle with the retention of white power. The legislation promulgated towards reform of local and regional government during the early eighties was done so in a manner which conformed to the government plan of dividing the African population between urban insider and rural outsider while bolstering the institutional standing of the Coloured and Indian communities to put them on par with the white community (but without the concomitant power to overturn white interests). In particular, two legislative acts – the Black Local Authorities Act of 1982 and the Black Community Development Act of 1984 – epitomized the government's constitution strategy for the urbanized African population in this initial period. In the meantime, a series of new laws were promulgated enhancing the status of local governing structures for Coloureds and Indians in line with the emerging tricameral parliament. However, as was to become evident by the middle of the decade, the reformists within the Botha administration sought a further transformation of local and regional government which featured the institutionalization of joint decision-making between statutory racial communities.

The Black Local Authorities Act of 1982 was to be the linchpin in the new system governing African political participation. Under its provisions, the myriad of black Community Councils (of which there were 232 in the 299 African townships within 'white' South Africa) would be phased out and supplanted by town or village councils. These would be elective bodies with both a measure of autonomy and some of the executive powers formerly vested in the Administration Boards.[124] A Director of Local Management, under the jurisdiction of DCD, would oversee these local authorities. By allowing African communities to elect African officials to the local councils, as well as give them the authority to set and administer policy for these areas, the Botha administration hoped to confer legitimacy to their overall plan to decentralize authoritative political structures.

Linked to the Black Local Authorities Act was the passage of the Black Communities Development Act of 1984. This act redefined the administrative boundaries of the institutions governing Africans residing outside of the homeland structures. In effect, the old Administrative Boards were reconstituted as Development Boards and brought under the control of the DCD. Under the terms of the Act, the Department's wide-ranging powers over the establishment of regulations for housing, land acquisition and the setting of the developmental agenda within the African townships was reaffirmed. Significantly, the legislation envisaged the gradual devolution of responsibilities *away* from the Development Boards and to the emerging African town councils. This was not to occur without serious conflict between the officials of the DCD and local African authorities.

As was to become evident, the failure to provide a stable and significant source of financial outlays for these reinvigorated political units proved to be a critical weak point in the new dispensation. The newly formed Development Boards, saddled with growing fiscal responsibilities but lacking a sound mechanism for financing development projects, soon floundered under the weight of their deficit.[125] The Local Authorities Loan Fund Act of 1984, growing out of recommendations by the Croeser working group, represented a limited attempt to meet this concern by easing the securing of loans from previously established local sources.[126] Despite this effort, the government's inability to put the black local authorities on a sound fiscal footing was to be a major contributing cause of the uprising of the mid-eighties.

The situation of Coloured and Indian communities differed substantially from that of the Africans under the political restructuring programme instituted by the Botha administration. As a key feature of the building of the tricameral parliamentary system, the government sought to bring into being revitalized local authorities for Coloureds and Indians. To achieve this, it would first require the shifting of responsibilities for the overall administration of Coloured and Indian governmental structures away from provincial authorities and to that of the DCDP. Secondly, the DCDP would need to accelerate the development of autonomous local authorities in order to put Coloured and

Indian politics on an equal (albeit in a juristic sense) footing with that of white politics. These combined steps would lay the groundwork for the government's long-term plan of establishing joint decision-making between the statutory racial communities on all levels within an enlarged and decentralized confederal system.

With the encouragement of the DCDP, regional committees drawn from the white, Coloured and Indian communities were established on an informal basis to discuss local government issues.[127] This in turn gave rise in 1982 to a non-statutory forum, the National Interim Liaison Committee, whose purpose was to bring these regional committees together on a bi-annual basis. According to the former Minister of Constitutional Development and Planning, these preliminary multi-racial forums performed an important function as they 'provided the main element lacking up till then – trust between [community] leaders'.[128] Anxious to build upon this achievement, the government decided to formalize these preliminary multi-racial forums through the institutionalization of a Council for the Coordination of Local Government Affairs (or Coordinating Council) for all of the white, Coloured and Indian municipalities. The creation of the Coordinating Council and the Municipal Development Boards were the key features of the Promotion of Local Government Affairs Act passed into law in July 1983.[129]

Established in January 1984, the Coordinating Council's primary function was to advise the government on those issues deemed to be 'general affairs' under the lexicon of the tricameral parliament. This all-important body, in effect, gave Coloured and Indian leaders an opportunity to participate to an unprecedented degree (though still subject to DCDP review) in influencing the central government's reform programme as it affected their communities. Concurrently, the Coordinating Council allowed the DCDP to vet ideas for reform with the different community leaders and, through that process, legitimize the government's undertaking in the area of political reform. At the first meeting of this new body, six committees were appointed to investigate specific issues falling under the rubric of 'general affairs' ranging from municipal franchise qualifications to the joint rendering of services.

The DCDP also moved to establish Municipal Development Boards which were designed to provide financial assistance and advice to local authorities. Oriented towards building and expanding the functional capacity of local authorities, these boards were directly linked with the regional offices of the DCDP. Notably, all of the actions growing out of the Promotion of Local Government Affairs Act were a further step towards emasculating the authority of the exclusively white provincial councils.

Reacting to the recommendations of the President's Council and the Coordinating Council, the government introduced the Local Government Franchise Act of 1984. This piece of legislation instituted a uniform set of voting requirements for the three statutory population groups for the election of the newly established local authorities. In a bid to strengthen the hand of property owners over that of non-property holders, the Act designated owners of businesses ('juristic persons') additional votes based on their proprietary status. Registration of voters was to continue along statutory population group lines.

This was followed by the Promotion of Local Government Affairs Amendment Act of 1985 which sought to accelerate the establishment of a single system of local government for whites, Coloureds and Indians by empowering the Minister of Constitutional Development and Planning to define the criteria for the conditions and extent of power of local governing authorities.[130] Coupled with this was a clause extending membership of the Coordinating Council to authorities within the newly established tricameral parliamentary system, members of the African municipality organization UCASA (Urban Councils Association of South Africa) and representatives of African local authorities.[131] This was to be an important first in extending the Botha reforms beyond the tricameral structure.

Local and Regional Reform: the Demise of the Provincial Councils

The Provincial Councils as constituted were an obstacle to the larger restructuring aims of the Botha administration's reform programme. In particular, these all-white institutions stood in the way of the implementation of the principles of 'general' and 'own' affairs which underlaid the new tricameral parliamentary system and were to be given content through the Regional Services Councils. As such, the curtailment of their authority was essential to the success of the constitutional reform process. With the publication of the President's Council report on local and regional government in 1982, which took aim at the provincial councils, the foundation was laid for the development of an alternative system.[132]

The Minister of Constitutional Development and Planning announced on 5 May 1985 that the provincial councils would be reworked in order to fit them into the substantial and ongoing structural changes at other tiers of government as well as the wider social changes sweeping the country.[133] The result was the abolition of the existing provincial councils, to take effect between April 1986 and June 1986, and their replacement by a new system that featured provincial administrators and an executive committee with statutory legislative and executive powers appointed by the State President and answerable to parliament. Unlike the provincial councils of old, the new authoritative provincial institutions would be multi-racial (whites, Coloureds and Indians) in composition and their focus would be in the area of 'general affairs' only (the minister's councils of the separate chambers of the tricameral parliament would rule on 'own affairs'). The creation of a series of advisory councils, 'linked to' the electorate (but not elected), was also envisioned by the Minister. Finally, Heunis enigmatically noted that while provincial boundaries would remain unchanged, 'new regional dispensations might in due course develop within provincial boundaries'.[134] This apparently included the possibility of subdividing the Cape and Transvaal provinces into smaller units with their own administrators and executive committees.[135]

With respect to African participation in the new provincial system of government, Botha administration officials categorically stated that this was an issue which was under consideration by the Special Cabinet Committee investigating the constitutional position of the African population.[136] After hinting at the accommodation of African political aspirations at the provincial level in October 1985,[137] four months later Heunis was calling for direct participation in provincial government by representatives of the African population.[138]

Local and Regional Reform: the Regional Services Councils

The Regional Services Councils (RSCs) were inextricably linked to the main elements of the tricameral parliamentary system. That is to say, 'power-sharing' in the proposed RSCs was to take place between statutory racial communities through the newly established governmental structures which were deemed to be on a parallel or equal footing with those of the white community. At the same time, in keeping with the dictates of tricameralism, such power-sharing was to be limited to those areas designated as 'general affairs'.

Picking up where the Department of Finance and the President's Council left off, the newly formed Coordinating Council put forth recommendations for the establishment of a regionally based body for the administration of bulk services.[139] The product of these deliberations was incorporated into the RSC Bill which was put before Parliament in September 1984. The essence of the Bill was the establishment of joint provision of bulk services (water, electricity and other infrastructural areas) through the mechanism of a racially mixed representative council made up of whites, Coloureds and Indians. Tackling the long-standing problem of financing costs amongst the black municipalities, the RSCs proposed to secure revenue through taxation of businesses.[140] Representatives to the RSCs would be drawn from participating local authorities who were apportioned voting rights on the council based upon their financial contribution to meeting the costs of service but were limited to 50 per cent of the allotted votes on the RSC executive committee.[141]

By this time, the DCDP had been empowered through legislative fiat to redraw the territorial and administrative boundaries of local authorities to suit its configuration for a radical restructuring of local and regional government. Intriguingly, Heunis signalled at this early stage his intention to bring in the African municipalities by stating on the eve of the introduction of the RSC Bill that the new African local governmental structures would 'open up the possibility of coordination with adjacent structures in the Republic, and, where practicably possible, also the self-governing and independent national states.'[142]

An initial version of the RSC Bill was withdrawn from full parliamentary consideration and returned to the parliamentary standing committee on constitutional affairs where a significant alteration was made. After consultation with the newly elected black councillors – who were desperately seeking additional sources of revenue – Heunis announced in December that the new African town councils were to be included in the RSC arrangement.[143] In the new version of the Bill presented for consideration in June 1985, representatives of African local authorities were to participate as full members of the RSCs.

The RSC Act passed by the newly seated tricameral parliament later that same year. A target date for the establishment of RSCs country-wide by 1 January 1986 was set in August by the DCDP. The black councillors, struggling under the fiscal constraints imposed by previous legislation (not to mention the township rebellion) by and large supported the legislation. Any qualms that the councillors may have had over the distribution of voting power in the RSCs was apparently shelved in light of the fiscal benefits to be gained through the arrangement. Strong resistance to the arrangement came from the South African business community, which felt that the additional financial burden in a period of economic recession was unfair, resulted in a delay in the introduction of the financial levies outlined in the Act until June 1986. This, coupled with resistance from white municipalities and provincial authorities, caused the government to put off the actual implementation of the Act for close on two years.

Reform at the National Level: The Tricameral Parliament

The specific initiatives for political reform at the national level came from the constitutional committee of the President's Council. Drawing upon the work done by previous committees, the constitutional committee was able to put forth a proposal for the restructuring of the national government that incorporated elements of the consociational model within the framework of a truncated Westminster-style system.[144]

Tabled on 12 May 1982, the President's Council's recommendations formed the basis for the government's proposed constitution unveiled at a special federal congress of the NP held later that year.[145] At the heart of the constitutional proposals was the maintenance of statutory population group identities as the basis upon which the political system was to be restructured, coupled with the division of responsibilities along the lines of 'own affairs', which would fall under the purview of each respective chamber, and 'general affairs', which would require cooperation and consultation between the three chambers. The new proposals brought the different groups together into three houses of parliament under one titular head, the State President. The State President was to be selected by an electoral college made up of members of all three houses selected on the basis of proportional representation (50 whites, 25 Coloureds and 13 Indians). In his role as both head of state and head of the government, the State President was empowered to rule on whether issues were of a 'general' nature or rather the province of 'own affairs'. If the State President could not resolve a dispute over 'general affairs', he could turn this matter over to the President's Council for a definitive ruling.[146] He also had the authority to dissolve parliament and curtail debate on the budget, as well as a range of appointive powers within the government.

The parliament itself was divided into three houses. The House of Assembly was to consist of 178 representatives of the white community, the House of Representatives was to consist of 85 members of the Coloured community, and the House of Delegates was to consist of 45 members of the Indian community. The ratio of 4:2:1, reflecting the population spread between the three racial groups, was such that the Houses of Representatives and Delegates would not alone or together be in a position to dominate the House of Assembly.

Rather than a Council of Cabinets envisioned by the 1977 proposals, the new constitution created a multi-racial cabinet to deal with matters of general concern to the country and three separate ministers' councils within each parliament to deal with 'own affairs'. The State President appointed all ministers to the cabinet and ministers' councils. A series of Joint Standing Committees, consisting of members drawn from each of the houses of parliament, were established to consider legislation of a general nature before bringing it to the separate houses for debate.

As for the black population, both the Constitutional Committee of the President's Council and the government argued for the continuation of the policy of bringing the homeland system to independence while concurrently promoting a confederal arrangement.

Cognizant of the criticism surrounding the 1977 constitutional proposals, which were scuttled due to the complete absence of consultation with the Coloured and Indian population, the DCDP undertook to confer with officially recognized leaders in those communities. In addition to the fact of the multi-racial character of the President's Council itself, Heunis's department held protracted discussions with figures in the Coloured and Indian communities about the proposed constitution – talks which actually preceded a formal presentation to the NP's caucus.[147] In the end, government consultation paid off as political leaders of these two communities agreed to participate in the new constitutional dispensation, thereby giving some measure of legitimacy to the process of political reform.[148] And finally, at a meeting of the NP caucus, Botha secured the acquiescence of party stalwarts to an eight-point resolution supporting the constitution which included a promise of the maintenance of separate voting rolls and the integrity of the white parliament.[149]

The move towards implementation of the constitutional proposals sparked a traumatic split in the much vaunted unity of Afrikanerdom. Defections began in 1981 from the Afrikaner secret society, the Broederbond, signalling the degree of opposition amongst conservative elements within the Afrikaner elite towards direction of the government's reform programme. But the turning point came at a meeting of the parliamentary caucus of the NP on 24 February 1982 in which conservative members of the party openly objected to the use of the term 'power sharing' in an official NP publication.[150] Prodded into a confrontation by reformists, 22 MPs refused to support a motion of confidence in the Prime Minister. After a week-long stand-off, 16 of the MPs (all save two from the Transvaal wing of the NP) were expelled from the party. Led by Dr Andries Treurnicht, the rebel MPs formed a new political organization, the Conservative party, which was to contest the NP for the soul of Afrikanerdom in coming years. This challenge was not an idle one, as within five years of its formation, the Conservative party was able to win approximately 50 per cent of the Afrikaner vote.[151] As one political observer noted: 'The ethnic glue of Afrikanerdom has finally dissolved.'[152]

The constitutional proposals went on to be officially unveiled by the Prime Minister at the NP congress for its consideration on 30 July 1982. With Treurnicht and other hard line segregationists out of the party, Botha's task of winning the support of party stalwarts was made all the easier. Thus, after minimal discussion, the constitution was accepted by the delegates of all four provincial wings of the NP. With the crucial assent of the Labour party to participation in the new constitutional structure given at its annual congress in January 1983, the Botha administration seemed well on the way to establishing its tricameral parliament.

Reform Legislation at the National Level

The constitutional proposals were introduced to Parliament on 5 May 1983 and provoked a lengthy debate which the government utlimately curtailed on 31 August. The government position, articulated by Heunis, was that the proposed constitution was:

> A serious and bona fide endeavour by this Government to make progress on the road towards realizing the general constitutional objective as far as Whites, Coloureds and Indians are concerned. But let it immediately be added and stressed that this Bill does not provide the total answer for all times to come and for all our constitutional problems . . . There are mainly two reasons for this. Firstly, the Bill as such does not address the problems regarding Black constitutional development. Secondly, it is a political fact of life that steps being taken on an evolutionary constitutional path form part of a process – they are not final solutions – and should be regarded as such. If they

are regarded as being final, I believe that we have left the road of orderly, stable constitutional development.[153]

Following the passage of the Republic of South Africa Constitution Act, the Prime Minister announced that a referendum was to be put before the white community on 2 November 1983. It asked the question: 'Are you in favour of the implementation of the Republic of South Africa Constitution Act, 1983, as approved by parliament?' In an atmosphere of intense debate fuelled by some degree of confusion over the actual proposal itself, 76 per cent of the white electorate went to the polls to register their views and 66 per cent of these gave their support to the new constitution.[154]

Fearful of the implications to the reform process should it obtain a 'no' vote on the planned constitutional referendum from the Coloured and Indian communities, the government dropped a promised referendum on the subject. Support for this step came from self-styled moderate leaders in the Coloured community and, to a lesser degree, the Indian community.[155] In its stead, the Botha administration went straight to an election campaign which was conducted in August 1984 under conditions of strong pressure from the newly formed United Democratic Front (see Chapter 5). The result was the election of an overwhelming majority of Labour party members to the House of Representatives on the basis of participation by (according to official estimates) 30.9 per cent of the electorate. In the case of the House of Deputies, the seats were divided between the National People's party and the Solidarity party, with an estimated (according to official statistics) 20.29 per cent of the electorate participating.[156]

The new constitution came into operation on 3 September 1984 and the members were sworn in the next day. As expected, the electoral college unanimously supported the nomination of the former Prime Minister for the position of acting State President. On 14 September, against a background of growing violence on the Reef, P.W. Botha became the first State President under the new constitution. He formally opened the three houses of the new tricameral parliament at a joint sitting on 18 September calling on its members to exercise:

> self control and mutual respect to lay the foundations for sustained economic prosperity and further constitutional development . . . Means will have to be found to enable African communities outside the national states to participate in political decision-making in matters affecting their interests.[157]

Reform at the Supra-Regional Level: The Regional Development Strategy and the Homeland System

The Botha administration's policy towards the patchwork of nominally independent or self-governing states was marked by contradiction. The first strand of government policy as stated in the Twelve Point Plan sought the further development and consolidation of the Verwoerdian 'grand apartheid' scheme 'as far as is practicable'. This approach was predicated on giving effect to the Riekert Commission's division of the African community between urban insider and rural (i.e. homeland dweller) outsider. Balancing this policy was the government's adoption of a regional development strategy which sought not only to give institutional recognition to the abiding economic linkages between the homelands and South Africa but to channel economic growth into nine designated regions so as to promote decentralization within the country. In so doing, the government hoped to promote its broader goals of regional political decentralization and lay the foundation for a future confederal system in South Africa.

Homeland Policy

Under the terms of the Promotion of Bantu Self-Government Act of 1959, Verwoerd had set the homelands on a course towards nominal political separation from the Republic that was to culminate in the granting of independence. Comprising approximately 13 per cent of the total area in South Africa and fragmented into dozens of non-congruous pieces, the ten homelands were assailed by the scourges of poor economic infrastructure, inept or corrupt management, and a weak resource base. Under the tutelage of Vorster, the government's policy was to accelerate moves towards 'independence' for the self-governing homelands.[158] Nonetheless, international support for recognition for the independence in 1976 of the Transkei, an enclave on the Indian Ocean, followed the next year by the fragmented state of Bophuthatswana was not forthcoming. And, despite these changes, the homelands – whether nominally independent or self-governing – remained by and large highly dependent upon South African largesse for their economic and political survival.

The first step taken by the Botha administration on homeland policy was to establish a commission to review the issues surrounding consolidation of the homelands in 1979. Initially, it seemed that the van der Walt commission's brief entailed a further round of consolidation including the granting of additional territory to the fragmented homelands. The bestowing of 'independence' of Venda in September 1979 followed by that of Ciskei in 1981 gave further evidence of the government's determination to carry on with separate development. However, by 1980 it became clear that government attitudes towards homeland consolidation had begun to change. In a speech to the Associated Chambers of Commerce in October that year Botha indicated that geographic consolidation alone could not make the homelands workable.[159] This was seconded by the DCD which issued a policy statement signalling a shift away from territorial consolidation along geographic lines in favour of regional economic cooperation. According to the statement, further territorial alterations would only take place if the land would contribute to the development of a homeland, would be utilized productively and if white landowners were allowed to retain title to the land.

The van der Walt Commission finally tabled its report before the Cabinet in July 1982. On the one hand, it urged that the consolidation proposals approved by Parliament in 1975, which called for the fulfilment of territorial separate development schemes within the context of the Native Trust and Land Act 1936, be continued. This, however, was balanced with a shift in emphasis by declaring that any such consolidation should take place within the context of building economic cooperation on a regional and supra-regional basis. The commission's report was seconded by the President's

Council report of the same year in which the Constitutional committee reaffirmed the government's intention to carry out the confederal scheme of bringing the homelands to independence while recognizing their links with the South African economy through the Consas arrangement. On the basis of this 'two track' policy towards the homelands, the DCD moved forward with its efforts to consolidate the disparate holdings of KaNgwane, Gazankulu and Lebowa.

Regional Decentralization Strategy

At the second major meeting between top government officials and the business community held in Cape Town in 1981, the Prime Minister unveiled his administration's proposals for the establishment of a 'coordinated regional development strategy' for South Africa and the homelands. By April 1982 the new regional development strategy had been hammered out in detail, calling for the decentralization of industry through the introduction of a coordinated development policy taking aim at regional inequities, employment concerns and wasteful duplication of effort by the myriad of political authorities operating in these areas. In order to achieve this, the government proposed to divide the country into nine development regions that cut across provincial and homeland boundaries. Within each region, policy makers would focus on promoting development in three zones: metropolitan areas, deconcentration points and industrial development points. The metropolitan areas were already recognized as highly developed and as such were subject to restricted growth through fiscal measures. At the same time, the improvement of living conditions in the urban areas would be a primary goal. The deconcentration points were located near existing metropolitan areas and to benefit from some fiscal incentives. The industrial development points, such as portions of the homeland territories, were the prime target of the new regional development strategy and consequently the beneficiary of a host of attractive financial inducements.[160]

To facilitate their common purpose, the government and the business community established a development bank in 1983 to serve as the primary financial vehicle for development in the territory. With a projected annual expenditure of R650 million, the Southern African Development Bank hoped to play the role of a catalyst in economic growth along the lines projected by the new regional development strategy.[161] Significantly, the institution's charter left open the possibility of countries outside of South Africa and the independent homelands applying for associate membership.[162]

It is worth noting that, in many respects, this new regional development strategy mirrors the basic thrust of policies emerging out of separate development. For instance, the emphasis on decentralization of industry through such mechanisms as legal prohibitions on businesses operating in urban areas and fiscal incentives for industries in rural areas – all stemming from a desire to curb African rural to urban migration – remained a prominent feature of the Botha administration's new approach to development. Nevertheless, the focus had edged away from the overt segregationist notions of separate development (and the explicit political implications that accompanied them) towards the more familiar developmental dilemma of rapid urbanization. That this shift was not totally at odds with the traditional NP project of seeking means of avoiding the political domination of the white community by an African majority through geographic and political fragmentation was recognized and used by senior government officials to quell potential dissent within the party. Echoing this notion, Heunis disingenuously told a NP audience in 1985 that economic decentralization was an effort to 'carry out the policy of separate development to its logical conclusion'.[163] However, unlike separate development, this new geographic fragmentation of the South African population was predicated upon an open acknowledgement of the economic realities governing the situation. These in turn were to be reflected in the changing attitudes within NP circles towards viable political reform.

With the passage of the new constitution in 1983, the government's plans for reintegration of the homelands through a confederalist arrangement began to take shape. The forum for this process was the newly formed Special Cabinet Committee on the Constitution which took up its mandate to investigate further reforms of the South African polity. To this end, a working liaison committee was established with the homeland leaders in 1984. It was here within the Cabinet Committee on the Constitution that the next stage of reform at the supra-national level was debated and formulated.

CONCLUSION

The government's reworking of the political structures of the state was an explicitly acknowledged intermediary step towards the resolution of the political dilemma facing the NP. Constructed along lines envisioned in the Twelve Point Plan, incremental reform of the apartheid system sought to introduce preliminary reforms at the three levels of government – local and regional, national, and supra-national – as the first phase towards refashioning the polity into a confederal system with a high degree of autonomy for its respective components. At the local and regional level, the reform programme accomplished the establishment of local political bodies for blacks with, for the first time, a degree of autonomy and local control. The stalling of the government's experiments in limited multi-racial management – embodied by the RSCs – at this level was a worrying setback for DCDP reformists. At the national level, the introduction of the multi-racial tricameral parliament ironically represented both a break with apartheid and, concurrently, the fulfilment of aspects of that vilified system. And at the supra-national level, after policy vacillations by the government, the groundwork was laid for a radically restructured confederation of regions constituted principally on economic criteria. Guiding the entire reform programme was the government's overriding imperative, to be accomplished through the introduction into the new political system of the construct of 'own' and 'general' affairs, that the racio-cultural identity of South Africans be maintained.

While the institutionalization of these changes in the South African political system represented a significant break from concepts which had served as the foundation of 'grand apartheid', there remained much in the government approach that was informed by the discredited policies of the past. Perhaps the most obvious, beyond that of the Botha administration's clinging to the maintenance of racially constituted political structures, was the failure to incorporate the African majority into political reforms at the national level. Another anomaly was the growing centralization of power in the hands of the government, which had declared its intentions to develop strong autonomous political units at the local and regional levels. These facts, coupled with the deliberately slow pace of political change, were responsible for the erosion of even tacit support for the Botha administration's reform programme amongst many black South Africans.

Five years after introducing the programmatic strategy for incremental reform as outlined in the Twelve Point Plan, the Botha administration could look back upon the course of events with satisfaction and even cautious optimism. The security situation, particularly at a regional level, had improved dramatically with the application of total strategy. The signing of non-aggression pacts, coupled with the curtailment of ANC activities in neighbouring states, had been effected without significant opposition by the international community. Domestically, preparatory steps to combat ANC infiltrations – while by no means eliminating the threat – seemed to be on the way to containing it. Despite the obstacles presented by recalcitrant members of the South African community to socio-economic reforms, changes in the socio-economic milieu were – with varying degrees of commitment to the process – nonetheless beginning to be actually implemented. And, the preliminary structures of political reform – the introduction of more inclusive and enhanced representative government at the national, provincial and local level for blacks – were being put into place, albeit not without a measure of censure both at home and abroad. Perhaps the most critical boost for the reform process came in the wake of the splintering of Afrikanerdom into two main political parties. Shorn of the need to cater to the conservative wing of the NP after 1982 (though ever careful not to alienate the Afrikaner voter), the Botha administration's reform programme entered into a new phase of development with the bureaucrats at the DCDP taking a leading role. Thus, for his supporters, Botha appeared at the end of 1984 to be in the position of simultaneously providing concrete solutions to the internal political problems that had bedevilled the South African state since the late fifties and effecting the breakdown of South African isolation from Africa and the West.

It was this triumphantalist atmosphere which pervaded as the newly sworn-in State President embarked on tour of Europe in June 1984. Unprecedented for a NP leader, Botha's visit to eight European countries was very much the fruit of his administration's policies in the realm of reform and security and, as such, a unique opportunity to personally win over foreign sceptics of his reform programme. To this end, the State President presented his European audience with the ultimate goals of his incremental reform strategy:

> What is certain is that we are on a road leading to the extension of democracy in South Africa. What is evolving in South Africa today is a devolution of power. We are working towards a form of confederation.[164]

Linked to winning European support for his government's approach to reform was the securing of European acceptance of South Africa's position as a regional power and, as a feature of this acknowledgement, its recognition of the South African perspective on vital regional questions such as Namibia. Addressing this point to the West German community, Botha stated:

> The Republic of South Africa is a major force in the subcontinent and we do not apologize for our industrial and military strength . . . South Africa recently signed a non-aggression pact with Mozambique which sets a new course in the history of the sub-continent. We have thereby signalled to the world that countries with different socio-political and economic systems can live together in peace and harmony . . . [With respect to Namibian independence it] is also our view that the outstanding obstacles to the implementation of a settlement have been resolved with the exception of the continued presence of approximately 30,000 Cuban troops in Angola.[165]

However, the success of the South African government's strategy, predicated on the careful introduction of limited reforms coupled with the maintenance of security concerns, was to be illusory. In late 1984, a chorus of protest against Botha's reforms rose in black townships across the country, jeopardizing the fledgling institutions upon which the state had based its programme. With the rebellion spiralling out of control, the leadership of the South African security state equivocated, seemingly caught between the necessity of deepening the reform process and the temptation to unleash the full force of its repressive powers.

5 Reform Apartheid in the Eye of the Storm, 1984–86

> *Three little words, words that express so eloquently our seriousness in this struggle. We want all our rights, we want them here and we want them now.* Reverend Alan Boesak, addressing the affiliates to the United Democratic Front in August 1983.[1]

> *I am not prepared to lead White South Africans and other minority groups on a road to abdication and suicide . . . My Government and I are determined to press ahead with our reform programme, and to those who prefer revolution to reform, I say they will not succeed.* State President P.W. Botha, August 1985.[2]

The explosion of township violence in September 1984 erupted throughout the country in the next year and a half. Led by the United Democratic Front and the National Forum, South African blacks registered their opposition to the political changes engineered by the Botha administration. Within ten months of the outbreak of unrest, the new State President was forced to declare a state of emergency in 36 magisterial districts in the country in an effort to contain the incipient rebellion. Though the incrementalist strategy of reform employed by the Botha administration came under fire at home and abroad, the South African government continued to pursue that approach through the measured introduction of socio-economic and political reforms. With the imposition of a full state of emergency the following year, brought about in the face of unabated political violence, the process of state managed reform initiated by Botha neared a crisis point.

This chapter will examine the outbreak of revolutionary unrest which challenged the process of reform and change inaugurated under the Botha administration and the government's reaction to this challenge. First, the rise of organized and sustained opposition to the state's reform programme will be investigated. Second, the state's response to the challenge posed by this outbreak of revolutionary unrest will be reviewed. Finally, the government's continuing programme of reform in the socio-economic and political spheres will be examined in light of the changing circumstances engendered by the township rebellion.

REVOLUTION

The political side of Botha's reform strategy – the new tricameral parliament and the creation of black local authorities – was born under the gathering storm clouds of country-wide protest. Spearheaded by the newly established United Democratic Front and the National Forum, black dissent quickly evolved from scattered protest focused on localized issues to that of a national campaign against the government's reform initiatives. With the rising tide of protest, even the formerly recalcitrant black trade union movement adopted a more overtly political stance towards politics of the day. The result was the formation and consolidation of a loose domestic alliance of anti-apartheid forces that threatened to undermine the carefully calibrated government reform programme.

The Rise of Black Opposition to the Reform Programme: Cracks in the Reformist Approach

The reform programme embarked upon by the Botha administration in the early eighties came under sustained attack from the very community it sought to win over. Opposition to Botha's reforms within the black community was principally focused on two areas: specifically, the inadequacies of the newly established black local authorities and, more generally, the problems associated with introducing an incremental reform programme in an increasingly revolutionary climate. Viewed against the background of economic deprivation for the majority of township residents (those in the volatile Vaal Triangle and Soweto experienced a drop in per capita income from the mid-seventies through the mid-eighties), the escalation of rents and services represented a significant hardship.[3] These factors, when wedded to the organizational skills of the national anti-apartheid movement, presented an unprecedented challenge to the government's authority.

Black Local Authorities

The shortcomings of the newly formed black local authorities were to be a major source of discontent amongst the black communities in which these structures were established. Principal among the complaints was the raising of rents for township dwellers, the majority of whom had only minimal financial means at their disposal.[4] While in the past the white local authorities, coupled with the provincial and national government, all provided a limited measure of financial support to the rudimentary black political structures, under the new system the burden of raising revenue was placed squarely on the shoulders of the local authorities themselves.[5] The government's privatization of liquor sales and the elimination of employment levies on businesses hiring blacks, both significant sources of income for township administration in the past, drastically reduced the fiscal options available to the new black town councils. Its continuing commitment to the maintenance of administrative self-sufficiency for the councils, despite warnings from internal governmental sources (see Chapter 4) caused these authorities to raise rents, as the principal remaining source of revenue, substantially in order to finance both administrative costs and fund any new projects.[6]

These major structural flaws in the local government system placed an immediate and pressing handicap on black officials elected to administer the town councils. Saddled with both enhanced authority and expectations under the government's new law, the black councillors faced a myriad of intractable developmental problems that fuelled doubts about their legitimacy within black communities already sceptical of their credentials. The meagre electoral turnout of 21 per cent for the 29 statutorily upgraded community councils, held in November and December 1982 in the wake of the passage of the Black Local Authorities Act, was indicative of the precarious position that the councils occupied within the townships.[7]

The structural problems associated with the black local authorities was seconded by the lack of input on the actual development of these structures from legitimate leaders drawn from the black communities. With organizations such as the ANC illegal, the pool of recognized leaders within the black community was limited to those who had elected to participate directly in the apartheid system, such as the town councillors, and those whose anti-apartheid politics placed them on the periphery of legality, such as leaders of churches, community organizations and some labour activists. The latter were loath to take part in any restructuring schemes which implied even tacit recognition of Pretoria's role as reformist of the apartheid system.

Problems with Incremental Reform

Botha and the reformist wing of the NP had taken as their lodestar an incrementalist approach to major structural reform of the South African system. In adopting this approach, they were attempting to steer a middle passage between what was perceived to be the untenable position of the right and the unacceptable propositions of the left, all the while seeking a solution which sought to retain the NP's control over the process of reform. At the same time, Botha remained extremely sensitive to the opinions of the Afrikaans-speaking electorate and worked to retain the overall support of that community as he embarked upon his administration's programme of change. Hence the government took the step of conducting elections at critical junctures in the reform process to secure a mandate from the whites, and in particular the Afrikaans-speaking community, for any proposed reforms. Recourse to democratic procedures within this constituency influenced the cautious approach to the restructuring of the apartheid bureaucracy by reformers in the DCDP, slowing the already deliberate pace of reform.

The difficulty with using this tack was to be made manifest by the mid-eighties. In essence, by speaking the language of reform in the early part of his administration Botha raised expectations within the black community that significant changes were in the offing. The gradual introduction of these proposed reforms, coupled with the rise in material prosperity for the nascent African middle class, translated into further dissatisfaction with the status quo amongst politically-minded black South Africans.[8] In the words of one scholar: 'Urban reform and promises of reforms by the authorities . . . have raised expectations without providing . . . results and outcomes.'[9] This classic formulation of the revolution of rising expectations, identified by political observers from de Toqueville to Gurr, has historically contributed to conditions of dissatisfaction which can translate into outright revolution.[10] The sensitivity on the part of the government to white – in particular Afrikaner – sensibilities was matched by its relative to total insensitivity towards black aspirations. Coupled with this were the continuing structural constraints on blacks such as the pass laws which were a demeaning reminder of the second-class status of blacks in South Africa. These merely highlighted:

> [t]he inability of blacks to aspire beyond the 'township', both socially, residentially and politically. The framework of local government has been perceived as an impediment to the real aspirations of the rising middle class and to the political idealism of the leadership of voluntary organizations.[11]

In the South African case, it was left to the emergent anti-apartheid organizations to give sustained political direction to these frustrations experienced by the black majority.

The Rise of Black Opposition to the Reform Programme: Political Organizations

The national anti-apartheid movements which came to dominate the mid-eighties were formed against the background of a developing, though localized, political consciousness within the black community that took hold in the aftermath of the Soweto uprisings. This consciousness was manifested in everything from intermittent student protests to the proliferation of locally based civic associations concerned with community affairs. While primarily attentive to local issues, these different organizations served as a counterpoint to the introduction of state-sponsored instruments of local government and, as such, were a direct challenge to a crucial portion of the overall reformist programme envisioned by the Botha administration.

Grievances with South Africa's segregated education system – with its ill-qualified teachers, poor facilities and inadequate teaching materials – was the source of a mounting campaign of protests amongst black students. Starting in February 1980, protests conducted by the Congress of South African Students (Cosas) brought Coloured education in the Western Cape to a standstill.[12] With an estimated 25 000 students boycotting classes in the Cape, the focus shifted in April to the north where Cosas led Coloured students on a series of marches that were broken up by police. Despite government efforts to defuse the crisis, including everything from meeting with protesters to detaining suspected agitators, classroom disruptions spread to communities in other parts of the country. Emboldened by the support of the newly formed civic organizations like Pebco and the Parents' Action Committee in Cape Town (see below), the students succeeded in forcing the closure of over 70 secondary schools and reopening the debate on black education at the highest levels of government.[13]

Newly established civic organizations took up issues of a local nature, such as gaining provisions for better housing, that were of direct import to the black communities in which they operated. Typical of these was the creation of the Soweto Civic Association (SCA) founded in September 1979 to mobilize opposition to rent increases by the newly elected Soweto Council. According to a contemporary analyst of the SCA:

> It was intended that the [newly founded] SCA would take up local community issues. Since then the SCA and branches have responded and taken the lead in such matters as the recent bus disaster, bus fare increases, rent increases and the boycott of proposed community council elections.[14]

Within a year, the SCA had adopted a more consciously political stance with its chairman pressing for the release of imprisoned ANC leader Nelson Mandela and negotiations with the government based upon the principle of majority rule.[15]

Soon other civic associations sprang up across the urban townships of South Africa, several organized specifically to oppose the government's new black local authorities.[16] In Port Elizabeth, one of the most overtly radical of the civic associations was established by residents of neighbouring townships.[17] The Port Elizabeth Black Civic Organization (Pebco), founded in October 1979, took as its main point of departure opposition to the community councils which were said to 'represent attempts [by the government] to link africans [*sic*] in urban areas to the "homelands" system'.[18] Its chairperson, a former school teacher and employee of the Ford Motor Company named Thozamile Botha, called on the government to release Nelson Mandela and provide Africans with freeholder rights within 'white' South Africa.[19] Within a month Pebco had not only taken it upon itself to establish branches in the neighbouring townships of Port Elizabeth but had actively promoted the formation of civic associations across the Eastern Cape region. Its call for a national movement of civic associations, bringing Pebco further prominence in South Africa, was given substance through the establishment of formal links between it and the SCA.[20] While the civic association's meteoric rise was cut short with the banning and detention of its leadership in January 1980, Pebco helped lay the foundation for the establishment of civic associations in the townships and the promotion of cooperation between such organizations.

As these community-based organizations grew in numbers and sophistication, the ideological divisions which separated both their members and different organizations began to make themselves manifest. While it was the black consciousness movement which inspired the formation of most of the initial community-based organizations, the subsequent exposure to ANC doctrine and cadres exercised an increasing degree of influence over the character and direction of these organizations.[21] It was the competing influences of the black consciousness movement and the revitalized ANC which gave rise to the rival national anti-apartheid organizations, the United Democratic Front and the National Forum.

The Establishment of the United Democratic Front and the National Forum

The UDF was launched on 20 August 1983 at a meeting outside Cape Town. Twelve thousand people, representing over 560 anti-apartheid organizations, listened as speaker after speaker denounced the government reform programme as a travesty. A UDF pamphlet produced at the time outlines the goals of the organization.

> The main organizational focus of the UDF campaign would be at the local and regional levels. Organizations affiliated to the UDF will run campaigns around certain aspects of the new Constitution that affect their membership in a direct way. This is to ensure that the UDF does not simply become a political protest group, but is able to build and strengthen nonracial democratic organizations as an alternative to apartheid itself.[22]

The seminal event in the formation of the UDF was the successful boycott of elections for the South African Indian Council (SAIC) in 1981. Faced with the prospect of government-sponsored elections to the SAIC, members of the Indian Management Committee of Lenasia (Johannesburg) and the Natal Indian Congress decided as early as October 1977 to organize a boycott.[23] The anti-SAIC movement launched a campaign to halt participation in the SAIC elections to be conducted in November 1981. This decision followed on the heels of a successful boycott of Republic Day by a coalition of interests drawn from the Indian community, which had utilized the ANC's Freedom Charter as its rallying point. The elections, held under a cloud of violence and accusations of intimidation by both sides, saw a voter turn-out of a paltry 11 per cent. With this meagre showing as a measure of community support, the SAIC was effectively rendered inoperative.

The positive response to the electoral boycott from the Indian community generated enthusiasm for like-minded ventures amongst anti-apartheid activists. Alan Boesak (then president of the World Alliance of Reformed Churches) speaking at a meeting of the Transvaal anti-SAIC organization in January 1983, encouraged the extension of the boycott to cover other government initiatives such as the so-called Koornhof bills (see Chapter 4) and the new constitutional proposals. Following the establishment of committees devoted to this proposition in three of South Africa's four provinces, the delegates came together in Cape Town to formally inaugurate the UDF.

In structural terms, the UDF operated as an umbrella organization for a variety of anti-apartheid entities which would coordinate activities and serve as a spokesperson for the member affiliates. The leadership was drawn from these ranks, and consisted of newly released political prisoners from the rebellion of the early sixties, leaders from the Indian community's Congress tradition, and the black consciousness generation of the late seventies.[24] Members of the UDF were asked (though not obliged) to declare their adherence to the principles contained in the ANC's Freedom Charter. This was a deliberate policy to encourage the participation of as many anti-government groups as possible.[25]

The initial phase of UDF activity focused on fulfilling Boesak's promise to combat the Koornhof bills and the proposed constitution. Under the slogan 'Apartheid Divides, UDF Unites', the organization launched a campaign to boycott the upcoming elections for the newly established black local authorities and the Coloured management committees. With the voter turn-out in the African local elections in November and December 1982 averaging 21 per cent and in the Coloured local elections on the Cape peninsula held in September 1982 averaging 1–11 per cent, the UDF declared their strategy to be a success.[26] The follow-up to the election boycott was a door-to-door campaign to secure one million signatures of those opposed to apartheid, affording the UDF an opportunity to establish itself in the townships at the grassroots level. Emerging out of this action was, particularly in the case of the Eastern Cape region, a solid community organization structure which would later form the base of the alternative structures called for in the wake of the township rebellion.[27]

As noted in the previous chapter, the formation or infiltration of local organizations at the community level was a stated policy of the ANC. Thus, it was no surprise that the UDF found amongst its members many ANC sympathizers if not actual members of the banned organization. The formal adherence by many of the affiliates to the UDF to the ANC's Freedom Charter, as well as the recognition given on an official level to ANC stalwarts like Nelson Mandela, gave additional credence to the notion that the UDF served as merely a front for the exiled movement. The leadership of the UDF maintained that it was a separate entity from that of the ANC, with no formal links to the organization.[28]

Alongside the formation of the UDF was the establishment of a rival grouping of anti-apartheid activists drawn from the black consciousness tradition. The founding of the National Forum (NF) on 11 June 1983 represented a continuation of the trend toward bifurcation in the history of black politics in South Africa. The NF, an umbrella organization for over two hundred black consciousness groups, was the direct heir to the black consciousness movement of the seventies which strove for solidarity amongst black peoples (Coloured, Indian and African) and promoted a policy of non-collaboration with white liberals and overtly non-racist organizations.[29] In terms of ideology, the NF was committed to a socialist programme of radical redistribution and general opposition to the white presence in the country.[30] While cooperation between the UDF and the NF did at times occur, the instances of hostility and even conflict multiplied as time passed.[31]

The Rise of Black Opposition to the Reform Programme: the Township Rebellion

Like the proverbial drought-striken prairie, the townships in the early eighties needed only a well-placed spark to set them ablaze. In the areas of education and the politics of government-sponsored institutions for blacks the rising tide of discontent and protest was finally transformed into violent confrontation in September 1984. In examining the period, two phases of the revolt in the townships can be discerned.[32] The first phase, starting in the PWV area in September 1984, represented an outbreak of protest against educational issues and the imposition of higher fees for rents and services. Spurred on by violent confrontation with the police, the rebellion built in ferocity and scope as the township dwellers increasingly turned from protest to doing battle with government authorities. The second phase of the rebellion, commencing in January 1985, saw a geographic shift away from the Transvaal and down to the Eastern Cape region. So too, this second phase moved from the relatively uncoordinated and unfocused protest that characterized the first phase of the revolt to an active campaign centred on specific government targets and championed by the national anti-apartheid organizations.

Phase One: September 1984 to November 1984

As in the past few years, the grievances which drove township residents to demonstrate overwhelmingly centred around the poverty of education, social services and the cost of rental accommodations. Protests against the inadequacies of the education system, started in January 1984 by pupils in Atteridgeville, a township outside of Pretoria, soon spilled over into the Johannesburg townships of Tembisa, Alexandra and Soweto.[33] Coming on the heels of the student protests were flagrantly political demonstrations inspired by the UDF and directed against Coloured and Indian elections to the new tricameral parliament in August 1984. Racked by violence, these actions effectively disrupted the crucially important electoral mandate for the constitutional reforms that the Botha administration coveted from the Coloured and Indian communities.[34] And finally, coupled with the protests in education and politics was the emergence of opposition to a series of rent increases promulgated by 14 of the newly elected Town Councils on the Witwatersrand throughout that year.

These incidents were to come to a head with the outbreak of unrest in September 1984. A stayaway organized by the Vaal Civic Association on 3 September to protest the raising of rents by the Lekoa Town Council and call for the resignation of town councillors ended in violent confrontation with the police. By the end of a week of demonstrations and stayaways at least 31 people had been killed, victims of the SAP and so-called black-on-black violence. Following the outbreak of unrest, the Release Mandela Committee called for a strike on 17 September to protest police actions. Hampered by confusion, the protest generated an uncoordinated response from township residents.[35] Confronted throughout this period by demonstrations of up to several thousand persons, the perennially undermanned police force reacted characteristically by firing birdshot and rubber bullets at the crowds, as well as arresting and detaining hundreds of demonstrators. In the wake of these heavy-handed tactics by the authorities, which between August and October had resulted in 65 deaths, demonstrations multiplied across the townships of the Transvaal.[36]

Against this background of escalating violence into October, official government complacency gave way to alarm. The Minister of Law and Order, Louis le Grange, describing the unrest as 'war, plain and simple', announced that cooperation between the SAP and the SADF would be increased in order to combat the problem in the townships.[37] Within twenty-four hours of the Minister's speech the police and military had acted jointly in Joza township in the Eastern Cape region. Over the next few weeks the security forces launched house-to-house searches and set up roadblocks in townships in the PWV area and the Eastern Cape region looking for 'criminal and revolutionary elements'.[38]

The reaction to the stepped-up presence of security forces by the anti-apartheid movement was to organize, in conjunction with the normally politically reticent black trade unions, a nation-wide stayaway for two days in early November. The success of the strike, called to protest the introduction of the SADF into the townships among other demands, was evident as an unprecedented 500 000 persons participated in the action.[39] Notably, black consciousness organizations, which had chosen to stay aloof from the strike, were critical of the aims and timing of the stayaway.[40]

By the year's end, after nearly four months of sustained civil unrest, the death toll stood at 149 – four of the victims being town councilors killed by angry mobs – several hundred persons had been arrested and detained by police and property damage was estimated in the tens of millions of rand.[41] While the acts of civil disturbance had dropped off, some 350 000 township residents were still engaged in a boycott on rents and services in the PWV area[42], the education system remained under assault by student organizations, and consumer boycotts of town councillors' and government-sponsored businesses were continuing in the Witwatersrand and the Eastern Cape. With grievances still mounting within the townships, the stage was set for the next phase of the rebellion.

Phase Two: January 1985 to July 1985

As South Africa moved into the new year, it appeared that a period of relative tranquillity had settled over the black townships. This hiatus in the major protests and violence was, however, to be short-lived. A new cycle of unrest, starting in earnest in March, gripped the black townships of the Eastern Cape, eventually spilling over into the Western Cape and the Witwatersrand. In this case, the issues which had initially fuelled the disturbances the previous year – rental and service increases by the town councils and continuing problems associated with the conditions of 'Bantu' education – had become incorporated by the anti-apartheid movement into a wider national agenda. As the actions of the state's security forces aimed at quelling the rebellion began to be felt, the wave of protest increased in both size and intensity. This in turn gave rise to a concerted effort by some ANC-inspired activists to transform the character of the township rebellion from incidents of civil disturbance to incipient insurgency.[43]

From the beginning of the year, the focus of unrest shifted from the Witwatersrand area to the Eastern Cape region. Utilizing the familiar tools of strikes and consumer and school boycotts, the civic associations began to broaden the scope of their protests to take up national issues.[44] Pebco, the civic association 'flagship' stepped out onto the national stage to 'declare war on the community council system'.[45] In conjunction with local unions and other anti-apartheid organizations in the Eastern Cape, Pebco organized a comprehensive strike in March to protest price increases in consumer goods and petrol. As this campaign evolved, the tempo of protest and reaction in the Eastern Cape increased, climaxing with the police killing 19 protesters in Langa township outside of Uitenhage. The result was a huge upsurge of rioting which engulfed the townships of the region and, once again, brought local black trade unions into the conflict to protest the actions of the SAP/SADF. Further stoking the flames of rebellion was the assassination in late June of four leaders of the Cradock Residents Association which, along with the death and detention of numerous heads of the anti-apartheid movement, sowed confusion and anger within the ranks of these organizations.

While the Eastern Cape remained the hub of unrest in the first half of 1985, outside of Cape Town a huge squatter settlement at a sandy spot called Crossroads became the focus of national and international attention. Various government attempts to remove the squatters to nearby accommodations provoked a series of clashes between the SAP and demonstrators, the worst of which resulted in 18 deaths.[46] But perhaps the most disturbing trend from the government standpoint was the renewal of unrest in the Witwatersrand in June. There, attacks on black councillors and police multiplied, as did the sophistication of the weaponry used in such acts.[47] With the death of eight Cosas activists, killed when their hand grenades inadvertently exploded, the character of the rebellion in the Witwatersrand began increasingly to take on the appearance of an armed insurgency. Seen against the background of the public shift in January by the external mission of the ANC towards sanctioning strikes at 'soft' (i.e. civilian) targets and calling for a 'people's war' to make the townships 'ungovernable', as well as a 209 per cent increase in recorded insurgency acts during that year, the situation in South Africa appeared to be spiralling out of the government's control.[48]

Throughout the second phase of the township rebellion, tensions between the ideologically opposed UDF and the NF which always seemed to be simmering beneath the surface, continued to erupt into outright conflict. In January the first manifestations of this feud came to light with the controversy surrounding American Senator Edward Kennedy's visit to South Africa. Three months later in the Eastern Cape region fighting between the two anti-apartheid organizations resulted in the death of four activists.[49] By the early part of the following year, after months of intermittent fighting, Azapo and its affiliates had been driven out of the Eastern Cape.[50]

In addition to the UDF–NF split, this period saw the further development of friction between the UDF and Inkatha.

Inkatha, a politico-cultural organization founded by KwaZulu homeland leader Chief Mangosuthu Buthelezi, increasingly came into conflict with UDF affiliates in the Natal region as the two organizations vied for local support. In particular, the UDF's (and Azapo's) rejection of local black government set the organization on a path of direct confrontation with Inkatha, which chose to field candidates in many of the local elections in its bid to extend its influence both inside and outside of KwaZulu.[51] With a large number of Inkatha members among the community councillors of Natal, the UDF–NF attack on the structures and individuals comprising the black local government system was naturally seen as an assault on Inkatha and the KwaZulu government. Linked to this situation were the ideological divisions between the ethnically based nature of the Inkatha movement, which was fundamentally traditionalist in its outlook, and the distinctly non-racial approach of the UDF, which appeared to become a bastion of radicalism as the unrest progressed. The result was tension which eventually exploded into violent clashes in Natal's townships and the surrounding countryside.

The Rise of Black Opposition to the Reform Programme: the Politicization of the Black Trade Union Movement

While the UDF and NF might claim to act for the masses of disenfranchised blacks, it was actually the black trade union movement that came closest to deserving this mantle. As the largest, best organized and most diverse cross-section of South African society, the trade unions commanded a veritable army of support which could potentially be mobilized behind any number of concerns. Despite this position, the black trade unions had proven remarkably reluctant to put their strength in the service of issues beyond those of the shop floor. This attitude was particularly pronounced in the approach adopted by the nation's largest black trade union federation, Fosatu, which had deliberately stood aside during the student protests of the late seventies.[52]

The development of community-based organizations in the black townships and the subsequent rise in protest put new pressures on the black trade unions to engage in political activities. While the country's largest black trade union federation drew criticism from elements within the anti-apartheid movement for its refusal to cooperate with community organizations, it remained steadfastly outside of overt political activity. The leadership felt that the federal structure of an organization such as the UDF – which allocated equal voting strength to organizations irrespective of membership – would ultimately tie the unions to decisions that did not best represent their interests.[53]

This stance was in the process of changing when the townships erupted into violence in September 1984. With the onset of the rebellion, the unions were pulled irresistibly towards protest as more of their members began to feel the direct effects of the unrest. The turning-point came with the two-day stayaway organized on 5 November 1984 to protest the intervention of the SADF in the townships of the Vaal triangle. For the first time Fosatu, in conjunction with the Release Mandela Committee, participated in a UDF-sponsored action. The result was the largest strike that the country had ever seen, with 500 000 workers staying home from their jobs.

This shift in support of political activity by Fosatu was, as UDF leaders were to discover, not indiscriminate. Rather than throwing its support behind the myriad local and national causes espoused by the UDF and its affiliates, the federation chose to participate selectively in political actions. An example of this was the stayaway and boycott conducted in the Eastern Cape in March 1985 by Pebco and local UDF affiliates. Called to protest an increase in consumer prices, the unions refused to take part in the action. Worker participation was characterized by union officials as the result of UDF intimidation.[54]

The politicization of the black trade union movement was realized with the founding of the Congress of South African Trade Unions (Cosatu) in November 1985. Born in the heat of the partial state of emergency, Cosatu brought together under one umbrella organization Fosatu, the National Union of Mineworkers and various UDF-affiliated unions. Led by President Elijah Barayi (a former member of the ANC Youth League), General Secretary Jay Naidoo and Vice-President Chris Dlamini (former president of Fosatu), Cosatu injected a new militancy into the labour movement that reflected the increasingly revolutionary climate.[55] And, with over 460 000 members signed up on the day Cosatu was founded, the organization had the muscle to back up its claims of worker representation.[56] As its first major act, the federation called for a strike in 1986 to win official observance of the symbolic workers' holiday, May Day, and an estimated one and half million workers supported the stayaway.

Conclusion

Nine months after the unrest started in the Vaal triangle, the newly established black local authorities system carefully nurtured into place by the Botha administration was on the verge of collapse. Against a backdrop of carnage which had produced 381 deaths and 1497 injuries, among them several town councillors, only five of the 38 fully established black local authorities were in fact in operation.[57] Over a hundred town councillors, the backbone of the new system, had been attacked since September 1984 and a full 240 of them had chosen to resign their positions.[58] The state's attempt to introduce changes in the structure of local government affecting the urban black population was immobilized.

The importance of the rejection of the newly enhanced black local authorities by the black communities cannot be overemphasized. As the preliminary pillar in the government's political reform programme, the black local authorities represented a crucial component of the government's overall effort to manage political change in the country. Recognition of the importance of these structural changes to Botha's reform programme by the anti-apartheid movement had actually inspired it to focus resources on discrediting the black local authorities.

By the eve of the government's imposition of a partial state of emergency, the sources of discontent within the affected black communities had multiplied. Initial efforts by the government to restore order to the townships through recourse to standard police action had merely exacerbated tensions with the black population. In fact, under the tutelage of the newly formed UDF and NF, opposition to state-managed change grew in depth and scope. While the black local authorities remained a target of protest and unrest, the anti-apartheid movement's new-found strength gave it the wherewithal to effectively challenge virtually all aspects of the Botha reform programme. A coordinated response to this threat by the South African government was not long in coming.

SECURITY

Despite warning signs from a variety of sources, the sustained ferocity of the township rebellion caught the Botha administration by surprise. The initial response by the government was to turn to conventional security measures, relying heavily on police actions to bring demonstrations by township dwellers under control. When eleven months of virtually continuous unrest proved this approach to be inadequate, the government imposed a partial state of emergency in the 36 magisterial districts experiencing the preponderance of the disruptions. Armed with a battery of security legislation to back up their actions, the SAP – supported by the SADF – seemed initially to have successfully stifled unrest within the effected areas. Nevertheless, the inherent deficiencies in the scope of the emergency regulations, coupled with the severity of the methods employed by the security forces, actually served to fuel further dissent within townships. Internationally, the shortcomings of the state's response to the civil disturbances were reflected in the deterioration of gains recently won in the international environment which, despite the maintenance of a successful regional foreign policy by the Botha administration, moved ever closer to imposing additional political and economic sanctions on South Africa.

Security: the Internal Dimension

The government's response to the outbreak of unrest in the townships reflected a fundamental misperception of both the depth of discontent which underlay the actions of township dwellers and the sophistication of activists involved in the rebellion. Hence, the initial reaction of the government was to allow the security forces to employ standard policing methods to bring the rebellion under control. When this combination was unable to halt the disturbances, the Botha administration turned to the extraordinary legalistic device of imposing a partial state of emergency on unrest-affected areas. The first state of emergency was in many respects nothing more than an expansion of the means utilized before its introduction as applied to a designated portion of the country. As was to become evident following the lifting of the emergency in March 1986, while the security forces had been able to quell unrest in those districts identified under emergency regulations, both within and without those areas the conditions which spawned the unrest remained fundamentally in place.

The Security Response: September 1984 to July 1985

As described in the previous section, the government's initial response to the protests which swept the Vaal Triangle at the beginning of September was to rely on established strategies and methods employed by the SAP in similar situations. Utilizing unsophisticated methods of crowd control – which included the recourse to sjamboks (whips), rubber bullets and birdshot – the security forces battled demonstrators numbering at times in the thousands.[59] Legal tools such as the power of arrest and detention were exercised both against protesters identified in the heat of the demonstrations and activists heading up the various anti-apartheid bodies. Incidents of torture of detainees, sometimes causing the victim's death (or, as the official explanation often went, suicide) were also a common feature of the security clampdown.[60] The abduction and even murder of activists by government-sponsored assassination teams, ranging from the notorious Civil Co-operation Bureau to 'hits' organized informally through vigilante groups, decimated the ranks of the opposition.[61] All of these actions by the government contributed to the climate of fear and intimidation which beset the townships during this period.

As unrest dragged into the New Year, the State Security Council (SSC) grappled with strategies that might defuse the opposition developing in the black community. With one of the major demands of both the internal opposition and the international community centring on the release of long-standing prisoners, administration officials decided to take the unprecedented step of proposing that the state make a conditional offer to the liberation movements. Thus on 31 January 1985, the State President publicly announced that his government was willing to release Mandela and other top ANC and PAC officials contingent upon their renunciation of violence. Within a week's time, Mandela and his colleagues had rejected the offer; however, 18 members of the PAC accepted the government's terms and were freed.

But by far the most heated debate within the SSC centred on the decision to impose a state of emergency over those areas of the country severely affected by unrest. The government had been receiving intelligence since the early eighties which indicated that should popular protest to reformist measures develop within the black community, the mobilization of the civic organizations and independent black trade unions would provide activists with a concrete means of sustaining such protest.[62] As early as six months preceding its actual declaration, against a background of continuing disturbances in the Witwatersrand and Eastern Cape region, the proposal to introduce a state of emergency was put on the agenda of the SSC.[63] Consistently turned down at subsequent meetings on the grounds that police action alone was sufficient to contain the situation, the renewal of disturbances in the PWV area prompted a reassessment of the motion by senior officials within the government. According to senior military officials, the decision to invoke only a partial state of emergency – one which not only failed to utilize the SADF-inspired National Security Management System to its fullest capacity but in essence continued to employ the strategy of 'containment' which had marked SAP efforts to date – was taken on the recommendation of the Minister of Law and Order.[64] An important feature of this decision was the government's desire to placate international sensibilities, which were already heightened by the unrest in the townships. It was felt that by invoking a partial emergency – one which did not impose severe restrictions on the media – the government would obviate international criticism and avoid any action on the sanctions issue.[65] It was thus on 21 July 1985 that the State President declared 36 magisterial districts to be under emergency regulations.

The Partial State of Emergency, July 1985 to March 1986

The introduction of a partial state of emergency in the country called into play a number of institutions and legal procedures which were to be the foundation of the government's response to the crisis. In the first instance, administering the State of Emergency required the activation of an executive body, the National Coordinating Council (NCC), to oversee the day-to-day procedures of the emergency. Implicit in this move was the activation of the National Security Management System (NSMS) which, as will be shown, was not fully brought into operation at this stage. Secondly, concurrent with the recourse to a state of emergency would normally be the introduction of additional legalistic tools tailored to the requirements of this extraordinary situation. The failure to do so was another anomaly of the government's application of a state of emergency. All of these instruments were brought to bear on the unrest-affected areas by the government over the period between July 1985 and March 1986.

The strategy employed throughout the period covering the partial state of emergency was based on the application of 'counter-insurgency' (Coin). Formulated by the South African Police, counter-insurgency strategy consisted of the introduction of a 'dynamic policy of change' engineered by the state while simultaneously engaging in police work based on an extensive intelligence network.[66] With reliance upon the SAP's traditionally strong circle of informants within black activist groups as the centre-piece of the security side of counter-insurgency strategy, assaults by activists on that network were to be a key feature of the township rebellion as it moved into a more coordinated phase.

With respect to the institutions which coordinated and implemented this strategy, the NCC played the leading institutional role in directing the implementation of the partial state of emergency. It was the NCC, located in the Office of the State President, that acted as both the liaison and coordinating body between the two secretariats of the National Security Management System and the National Welfare Management System.[67] Playing an important role throughout the partial state of emergency, the NCC was to be replaced with the elevation of the Inter-departmental

Committee on Security (renamed the National Joint Management Centre) at the point in which the full State of Emergency came into existence in June 1986.[68]

Theoretically, the National Security Management System (NSMS) would under conditions of a state of emergency play a decisive role in carrying out the daily tasks that constituted the work of the state in such an extraordinary period. In fact, while at the regional level the JMCs had been conducting a variety of civic action projects in their respective areas as well as serving as an 'early warning' instrument since their inception, at the central level the administration structure of the NSMS had essentially remained dormant. By their own admission, NSMS officials in the upper echelon of government were 'just keeping the seats warm'.[69] According to one source, the organization of the NSMS during the period which preceded the imposition of a *full* state of emergency (June 1986) was:

> found to be lacking as far as proper communication and control channels were concerned, apart from the fact that it was designed for a totally different function and was not geared for the day-to-day running of the Emergency.[70]

The declaration of a state of emergency in selected magisterial districts allowed the formulation, in terms of the Public Safety Act of 1953, of a range of security-based laws designed to combat unrest situations.[71] Among the legalistic devices utilized extensively by the government during the emergency, put forth as Proclamation R121 of 1985, was the restriction on gatherings deemed to be a threat to security, the banning of individuals and organizations, the establishment of curfews in designated areas, and the selective arrest and detention of suspected anti-government activists. The employment of these legally sanctioned actions by the police represented a continuation of the methods utilized prior to the actual declaration of a state of emergency.

Contrary to expectation no emergency regulations for the media were formulated by the government in the early stage of the emergency. As a result, the international community, which had been privy to numerous television accounts of the bitter cycle of unrest in its first eleven months, was able to observe through the eyes of reporters the extent of the government crackdown.[72] All of this was to have a devastating effect on the credibility of the Botha reform programme and significantly boosted the fortunes of the international sanctions campaign. In Chester Crocker's words:

> Incredibly, these guys [the South African government] actively facilitated foreign media coverage of township unrest, imagining that the TV footage would help their cause by focusing on 'terrorists and hoodlums' causing the violence, and not on the police and defense forces conducting their heavy-handed township sweeps.[73]

This security oversight was partially reversed in November 1985, when the government banned the electronic media from recording or publishing material derived from unrest incidents.[74]

It was, however, the designation of emergency status to only selected unrest areas in the country which, in the eyes of some senior military officials, constituted a supreme strategic blunder by the government.[75] Allowing certain areas to fall outside of the scope of the emergency served to encourage the spread of the rebellion to unaffected regions. Thus by forgoing the advantages fully available to it through the extra-ordinary recourse to an emergency situation, the Botha administration effectively negated the worth of one of its major and most brutal weapons for combating the rebellion in the townships.

Implementing the Partial State of Emergency

On 21 July 1985, P.W. Botha appeared on South African television to announce the imposition of a partial state of emergency in South Africa.

> Every responsible South African has, with growing concern, taken note of conditions of violence and lawlessness which, in recent times, have increased and have become more cruel and more severe in certain parts of the country, especially in the black townships. These acts of violence and thuggery are mainly directed at the property and persons of law-abiding black people, and take the form of incitement, intimidation, arson, inhuman forms

> of assault, and even murder . . . I cannot ignore the insistence of all responsible South Africans, especially of the majority of the black communities, who ask that conditions are normalised and that they are granted the full protection of the law to continue their normal way of life . . . In view of the prevailing conditions, it is essential that the situation be normalised in such a way that the climate for continued dialogue in the interest of all people in the constitutional, economic, and social fields is ensured. Against this background, the government has . . . decided to proclaim a state of emergency.[76]

The areas affected by the decree included 36 magisterial districts located primarily in the PWV area and the Eastern Cape region.[77] In those designated areas, the government authorities moved to quell the rebellion through the application of unrest-related techniques. In the Eastern Cape, the continuing spectacle of protest and rioting, coupled with the maintenance of consumer boycotts, came under assault by the security forces. In the Port Elizabeth and Uitenhage areas, while rioters and police clashed with deadly results at protests and funerals, the security forces on patrol were subject to attack. Up north on the Witwatersrand, joint SAP/SADF operations in townships like Tembisa and KwaThema resulted in the arrest of hundreds of persons. These actions were followed by the introduction of preliminary 'supportive projects' (a feature of the civic action programme) by the SADF, in coordination with local town councils. Among the projects implemented were the construction of recreational facilities, sinking of bore-holes, and assistance in the administration of schools, hospitals and other public facilities.[78]

After a slow start, the arrest and detention of activists achieved the intended result of curbing the effectiveness of these organizations in the designated unrest areas. Following up on the banning orders issued in March, the Minister of Law and Order banned meetings of 64 organizations – including the UDF, Azapo, the Detainees' Parents Support Committee, the Release Mandela Committee, various youth and student organizations, and certain civic associations – in 30 magisterial districts.[79] Along with their followers, many of the heads of student organizations, civic associations and the national anti-apartheid organizations were brought into police custody, swelling the number of persons arrested in the first six months of the partial State of Emergency to 7996.[80] In their absence, some organizations became paralysed and ineffectual as the second tier of activists attempted to take up the reins of leadership.[81] Concurrently, a pattern of assassinations and disappearances of individuals associated with these organizations developed, sowing further confusion within the ranks of the anti-apartheid movement. The abduction and murder of the four leaders of the Cradock Residents Association at the behest of the regional JMC on the eve of the emergency, an event which threatened the tenuous unity achieved by the feuding UDF and NF, drew an angry response within the black communities.[82] Other similar events included the deaths of UDF activists Victoria Mxenge and Toto Dweba in separate incidents in August 1985.

With the government ban on mass meetings and some anti-apartheid organizations (such as Cosas),[83] the people of the townships turned to other forums for political expression. It was under these circumstances that funerals, attracting at times tens of thousands of mourners, became elevated to the status of *de facto* political gatherings. In spite of specific restrictions on the conduct of everything from the delivery of the eulogy to the demeanour of the mourners, funerals continued to serve as a highly-charged vehicle for the communication of political material and information, and sometimes themselves became the focal point of further unrest. Opposition to the government spilled over to leaders of the South African Christian community, which issued the Kairos ('moment of truth') Document in September 1985 denouncing the state theology of apartheid, asserting that the impetus for genuine change lay with the oppressed, and – while condemning violence – questioning whether resistance actions could be equated with that of state-inspired violence.[84]

Accusations of excesses and brutality, including the use of unreasonable force in quelling protests, as well as complaints of abuse during detention, continued to dog the security forces during the emergency. While the SAP continued to take the lead in curbing the unrest during the emergency, the SADF – which had deployed 35 372 soldiers in 96 African townships by the end of the year[85] – also came under growing criticism. Responding to charges against it, the Minister of Defence announced the formation of 28 complaint centres where township residents could submit claims against the SADF and, if validated, receive remuneration. The poor response by the community, attributed by the security forces to intimidation, rendered the programme inoperative.[86]

During the period of the partial state of emergency, the incidents of unrest actually increased more than twofold over the first four months from approximately 1000 on the eve of the imposition of emergency to almost 3000 during September–October with the worst of the violence occurring outside of the specific emergency districts.[87] As was becoming evident as the emergency progressed, activists who escaped (or were released from) the security net thrown over the unrest areas simply moved to those areas still unaffected by the regulations. So too, the anti-apartheid organizations made a concerted effort to step up protest in those districts, both taking advantage of the lack of security regulations and seeing an opportunity to spread the rebellion further afield. This approach was illustrated in the Western Cape when UDF leader Alan Boesak mobilized supporters for a march on Pollsmoor prison, home to incarcerated ANC leader Nelson Mandela. The banning of the march, coupled with the detention of Boesak, sparked sustained riots in Cape townships and the city itself, eventually causing the government to put these areas under martial law.

As the focus of the rebellion shifted outside the designated emergency districts, the Botha administration responded by adjusting its tactics. On 25 October it lifted the State of Emergency in six of the magisterial districts and, on the following day, extended the emergency to eight new districts in the Cape.[88] This action was followed on 3 December by the lifting of the state of emergency in eight other districts[89] and then, two months later, the removal of emergency restrictions from six more.[90] Finally, 229 days after its imposition, the government announced that it was lifting the partial state of emergency completely.

Hiatus in the Rebellion

With the removal of the state of emergency on 7 March 1986, the government hoped to undercut the negative publicity which had accompanied the recourse to special security measures both at home and abroad. The decision to lift the emergency was directly linked to the deteriorating international climate and, faced with Western threats of economic sanctions, the Botha administration seemed poised to reconsider its position on a host of issues – most particularly, the position of famed ANC prisoner Nelson Mandela. They allowed the Commonwealth to send a special mission, the Eminent Persons Group, to the country, and its subsequent discussions between Pretoria, the ANC and Mandela appeared to harbinger a breakthrough in the political impasse.

Nevertheless, despite these measures, the government remained fully cognizant of the security dilemmas facing it. Having this in mind, the Botha administration endeavoured both to strengthen the domestic covert capacity of its special forces and to replace the extraordinary regulations utilized during the state of emergency with statutory legislation that accomplished much of the same thing.

In February 1986, the Deputy Minister of Law and Order, Adriaan Vlok, convened a special committee to study counter-insurgency responses to the burgeoning crisis. In an interim report, the committee called for the creation of a covert force outside of the SADF and SAP which would be 'specifically organized, equipped and trained to plan, co-ordinate and execute counter-revolutionary actions' to thwart unrest. Two months later, the Civil Co-operation Bureau (CCB) was officially created, though it was in fact to retain links with the SADF until 1988.[91] That year, its operations were 'privatized' and all ties with the SADF were severed. Denied access to government intelligence sources and management, thereafter the CCB appeared to act as a 'renegade' unit, selecting targets and executing operations on its own initiative until it was shut down in mid-1990.

At the same time that the government's covert operations were being strengthened, the Botha administration introduced emergency-style legislation. Addressing parliament three days before the lifting of the partial state of emergency, Botha announced his intentions.

> Sporadic and isolated cases of violence are . . . still being instigated in various parts of the country. Nevertheless the situation has improved sufficiently for me to announce that a proclamation will be issued in the near future . . . which will lift the state of emergency in the remaining magisterial districts in which it still applies. To enable the authorities to deal with continuing cases of unrest without subjecting the population to the inconvenience of a state of emergency in terms of our internal security legislation, existing legislation will be revised . . . to give the authorities the statutory powers necessary to protect lives and possessions effectively. In the meantime the security forces will preserve order and safeguard communities in terms of existing legislation.[92]

While the government was attempting to steer the new security legislation through the tricameral parliament, the country was plunged into a new cycle of township violence. In this case, it was the spectre of growing conflict between rival forces within the townships themselves which marred the peaceful transition away from martial law. So-called vigilantes (or *amabuthos*), which had become a feature of the township rebellion in the latter half of 1985, launched brutal attacks against the incipient structures and individuals put into place as a result of the township rebellion. Representing a conservative response to the self-styled 'comrades' who were at the forefront of the unrest, the vigilantes were given tacit – and in some cases overt – support by the security forces as they attempted to drive their enemies out of the townships.[93] In a similar fashion, parts of Natal became a battleground between UDF supporters and the Inkatha movement.[94] Under the guidance of the local JMC in the rural settlement of Trust Feed, Inkatha militants and the SAP joined forces to wipe out UDF supporters in 1988.[95] The emergence of these counter-weights to the forces of 'radicalism' in the township rebellion fuelled a new wave of destruction in the already volatile situation.

It was in the Western Cape and Natal that this phenomenon was most vividly apparent. At the squatter settlement known as Crossroads, political violence erupted on 18 May between the *witdoeke* (fathers) and the 'comrades' as the government attempted to move the squatters to a newly established settlement at Khayelitsha. By the month's end, this ongoing generational skirmish had resulted in the death of 45 people, the destruction of 2000 shacks and the creation of 20 000 homeless.[96] In Natal, pitched battles between UDF and Inkatha broke out leaving dozens dead, while on the Witwatersrand and in the Eastern Cape clashes between vigilantes and black youth caused further destruction. In addition, the homelands – particularly KwaNdebele, whose proposed 'independence' sparked three months of extended fighting and over 100 dead – were swept into the cycle of violence which gripped the rest of the country.[97] Overall, in the 97 days between the lifting of the partial state of emergency and its reimposition, 622 persons were killed, 221 persons dying in May alone.[98]

Security: the External Dimension

The dawn of a peaceful and cooperative regional environment envisioned at the time of the signing of the Nkomati and Lusaka agreements seemed to recede with every passing day. The collapse of the understanding between South Africa and Angola was marked by a renewal of the border war. In Mozambique, covert South African support for the increasingly autonomous Renamo phenomenon stretched the limits of the Nkomati Accord to the breaking point. With the outbreak of unrest in the black townships and the dramatic growth in ANC-sponsored insurgency incidents as a backdrop, the South African state redoubled its efforts to deny the ANC any substantive regional support. But, while Botha continued to score successes on that front, it became apparent that the biggest external security threat to South African government came not from a military source but rather an increasingly effective international campaign to encourage disinvestment and economic sanctions against South Africa. It was this latter menace which the government found itself to be virtually powerless to counter.

Angola and Namibia

The shaky peace between South Africa and Angola signed at Lusaka in February 1984 held for nearly eighteen months. While both sides took steps to reduce the possibility of direct armed confrontation, the use of indirect conflict through the support of insurgency forces – Swapo and Unita – belied their commitment to a full cessation of hostilities. Three events in particular signalled the collapse of the understanding at Lusaka. First, at the same time that the American Assistant Secretary for African Affairs was conducting his 'shuttle diplomacy' between Luanda and Pretoria in May 1985, word was received that the SADF's elite 'recces' were captured on a mission of sabotage in the far-flung province of Cabinda. Secondly, a few months later, the United States forfeited its somewhat tarnished position as an 'honest broker' with the US Senate's repeal of the Clark Amendment, thus paving the way for a return to covert American support for Jonas Savimbi's Unita forces. Finally, in September that same year the Angolan government launched a massive attack against Unita's position in the south-eastern corner of the country. The battle for the strategic town of Mavinga, which pitted a combined Angolan-Cuban force of 4000 with air support against 5500 Unita troops, was one of the most fearsome of the entire civil war. Only the intervention of the South African Air Force, which wrought havoc on the exposed Angolan positions, saved Unita from what would have been certain defeat.[99]

In the aftermath of the collapse of the Lusaka Agreement, the military forces in the region prepared themselves for further confrontation. In the case of the Angolans, the narrow margin of Fapla's defeat at Mavinga acted as a spur to Luanda and its supporters to build up military forces for what it hoped would be a decisive victory over Unita. Massive resupplying efforts by the Soviet Union and its allies over the next eighteen months laid the foundation for what was expected to be a military campaign of lengthy duration. For its own part, Unita benefited from joint South African and American assistance as it readied itself for another assault against their position. At the same time, Unita's insurgency campaign spread to virtually every province in the country, tying down Angolan forces and crippling the economy.

To the south in Namibia, the improved security situation on the border region seemed to signal success for the SADF's counter-revolutionary strategy. While the border itself remained problematic, the SADF could point to the fact that Swapo forces had not penetrated the security fence established 200 km south of the Angolan frontier and into the white farming area since 1983.[100] The continuing implementation of the SADF's Civic Action programme in the most contested areas of the territory – Ovamboland, Kaokoveld, Kavango and Caprivi – held out the hope that the border region could be won over to the government perspective. The process of shifting responsibility for security over to local Namibian control continued with the turning over in May 1985 of control of the South West African Police to the local commissioner of police. All of this had the effect of enhancing the Botha administration's ability to employ a two-track strategy of negotiations with the international community on the subject of independence while extending the process of self-government within the territory, implicitly threatening to proceed with an 'internal solution' to the Namibian question.

The establishment of the Transitional Government of National Unity (TGNU) on 17 June 1985, was a major step towards realizing this 'internal solution' in Namibia. Made up of the six parties which participated in the Multi-Party Conference, the TGNU was given wide powers of governance in all spheres but that of defence and foreign policy. The newly appointed Administrator-General, though empowered to review legislation emerging from the TGNU in terms of a Bill of Fundamental Human Rights, indicated from the outset that his role would principally be that of a figurehead. Along with the Constitutional Council, a 16-member body founded in late 1985 to draw up a constitution for the territory, the TGNU represented a major step towards the realization of Pretoria's long-standing goal in Namibia: the development of a strong administrative infrastructure capable of governing the territory and, simultaneously, the creation of a credible (and if possible internationally acceptable) alternative to Swapo.[101]

Despite this development, the first two years of this new dispensation in Namibia were marked by almost continual controversy which threatened the viability of the 'internal solution'. The National Assembly's repeal in April 1986 of AG8, the legislation promulgated in 1980 which effectively instituted 'grand apartheid' in Namibia, sparked off a heated debate in the government. White parties, unwilling to abandon the principle of 'own affairs' in matters like education, used the courts to block the implementation of laws which contravened their interests. These measures were themselves countered by moves within the TGNU by other parties to scrap any vestige of apartheid legislation. Such was the level of internal debate in these institutions that the Constitutional Council was only able to come up with a draft constitution one and a half years after its establishment.[102]

Coupled with this was the reluctant recognition by officials in Pretoria that the TGNU enjoyed little support either within the territory or abroad. The strength of Swapo's Ovambo ethnic appeal and the shortcomings of Windhoek's administration, coupled with the outspoken criticism of the church community, all served to limit the popularity of the TGNU.[103] Swapo's internal wing continued to draw large crowds of supporters at its rallies, despite restricted access to publicity mechanisms and the ongoing 'hearts and minds' campaign. And on more than one occasion the South African government itself contributed to undercutting the legitimacy of the 'internal solution' by fixing an independence date and subsequently scrapping it.

Regional Policy in Southern Africa

While the Botha administration had been partially successful in winning official recognition of its regional ambitions, be it in the form of security accords or economic cooperative agreements, there remained substantial regional holdouts like Botswana and Zimbabwe. Faced with a rise in ANC guerrilla activity and the continuing spiral of rebellion and violence in South Africa's townships, Pretoria saw fit to maintain its destabilization policies towards states in the region. Mozambique in particular suffered at the hands of increasingly autonomous proxy forces while the BLS countries were subject to both direct and indirect intervention by the SADF. The result was that by the end of 1986, with the exception of a circumscribed presence in Zimbabwe and Botswana, the ANC had effectively been neutralized or driven out of the adjoining states of the region.

Regional Policy in Southern Africa: Zimbabwe

The peculiar mix of public hostility, peppered by intermittent acts of violence, and the pursuit of stable trade relations continued to characterize Zimbabwean–South African relations. The low point of relations centred around Pretoria's accusation that ANC guerrillas used Zimbabwe as a staging area. The explosion of limpet mines in the Northern Transvaal, in one instance killing six persons, led the Minister of Foreign Affairs to declare that the SADF reserved the right to engage in 'hot pursuit' missions against its neighbour.[104] Informal contacts between the security forces of both countries, resulting in tighter border restrictions, forestalled direct SADF intervention.[105] During the same period, in what some interpreted as a quid pro quo measure, dissident activity in Matabeleland abated.

However, in May 1986 the SADF finally acted upon longstanding threats and struck out at ANC offices in downtown Harare. Coupled with this blatantly hostile act was the continuing destruction in neighbouring Mozambique. With the vital Beira corridor under continued assault by Renamo, Zimbabwean found itself unable to withdraw its estimated 7000 troops without risking further damage to its aspirations for economic delinkage from South Africa. This in turn had the unwelcome effect of bringing the insurgency into eastern Zimbabwe in early 1986 as Renamo guerrillas retaliated for Harare's involvement in Mozambique.

In direct contradiction to the hostility generated by these incidents, trade with South Africa actually increased during this contentious period. In part this could be attributed to the effective closure of the Beira corridor, channelling Zimbabwean trade south. Ironically, while trade with South Africa grew, Robert Mugabe took on the mantle of premier spokesperson for the application of economic sanctions against the Republic. This stance was adopted against the advice of members of his cabinet who felt that the imposition of sanctions would be disastrous for the Zimbabwean economy.[106]

Regional Policy in Southern Africa: Mozambique

The pomp and circumstance that accompanied the signing of the Nkomati Accord in March 1984 could not hide the fact that Samora Machel's regime had come as a result of pressure exerted through the application of South African security policies. The discovery of the Vaz diaries in a Renamo camp in 1985, which revealed that elements within the SADF were continuing to provide the guerrilla movement with support, caused Maputo to suspend the Nkomati Accord's joint security commission. While the South African government attempted to placate Mozambican authorities by claiming that steps would be taken to eliminate SADF collusion with Renamo, its destructive activities continued to exact a heavy toll in Mozambique and, through the disruption of the Beira corridor, Zimbabwe as well.[107] Machel's growing reliance on a combination of Western financial aid, Eastern Bloc military assistance and the troop strength of the Zimbabwean and Tanzanian armies, still seemed no match for the South African-fostered insurgency movement. At the same time, Renamo's ability to survive and in fact prosper under conditions of reduced external support from South Africa in the post-Nkomati environment – a function of its ability to extract resources from the peasantry as well as assistance from abroad – meant that the organization was in the process of developing its own direction.[108]

The end result of the maintenance of South African destabilization policies was that the Mozambican government found itself in the invidious position of being unable to defeat Renamo and, because of the patent unwillingness of erstwhile allies in the Eastern Bloc to provide support comparable to that given Angola, it had nowhere to turn but South Africa and the West for assistance. The days in which the Mozambican government could pursue a cooperative policy with the outlawed ANC were never to return.

Regional Policy in Southern Africa: Botswana, Lesotho and Swaziland

The three 'captive states' – Botswana, Lesotho and Swaziland – were subject to a continuation of destabilization on the part of their powerful neighbour during this period. After the signing of the Nkomati Accord, all three countries acted to a greater or lesser degree as a conduit for ANC infiltration and/or assistance. The South African government, intent on denying any contiguous territorial sanctuary to the revolutionary organization, undertook to maintain pressure on the BLS states to withdraw such support. While neither Botswana nor Lesotho would join South Africa in promulgating a non-aggression pact such as the one signed by Mozambique and Swaziland, by the end of 1986 they had in effect agreed to the content of such an accord through their actions and statements.

In Botswana, the fragile balance between cooperation and conflict which guided Botswanan foreign policy towards South Africa was shaken by SADF incursions into the country.[109] On 14 June 1985, the SADF launched an attack on its neighbour, striking at alleged ANC offices in Gaborone and killing 12 persons. The SADF claimed that through this particular office, the ANC had planned and executed 36 acts of insurgency since August 1984.[110] The timing of the assault, coinciding with the visit of the Commonwealth's Eminent Persons Group (see below), provoked an international outcry.

Lesotho continued to experience pressure to formally agree to a non-aggression pact with South Africa, thereby ousting the ANC presence in the country. On 20 December 1985, an armed attack in Maseru resulted in the deaths of nine persons, including two ANC personnel. The Lesotho National Liberation Army took responsibility for the raid, though officials in Maseru claimed that the SADF was behind the action.[111] The subsequent imposition of an economic blockade by South Africa in January 1986, and Botha's warning that the lucrative Highlands Water Project (a South African–Lesotho joint venture) could be cancelled, helped bring on a military coup against Chief Jonathan on 20 January. The new government reaffirmed an agreement struck in the final days of Jonathan's regime in which both countries undertook to refrain from allowing the planning or execution of terrorist acts against its neighbour.[112] It also agreed to oust members of the ANC and the PAC as a quid pro quo for lifting the economic blockade. Six months later, the government expelled 63 South African refugees, among them members of the ANC.

Finally, building on the non-aggression pact of 1982, Swaziland and the South African government maintained their mutually beneficial security and economic relationship. The opening of an official South African trade mission in early 1985, as well as South African financial and technical support for development projects, served to highlight the advantages of cooperating with South Africa. In addition to receiving South African investment, the Swazi government was offered territory which would give the land-locked state access to the sea. The collapse of this deal, brought about by indignant homeland leaders, did not harm relations. At the same time, despite this cooperative relationship, the ANC managed to develop 'an extensive and sophisticated underground network' in Swaziland.[113] This became the target of the Swazi security forces which was, on occasion, assisted by the SADF.

The International Environment

The spectacle of sustained violence in the black townships, coupled with the meagre show of support for the new constitutional dispensation among the Coloured and Indian populations, contributed to the lukewarm reception that the international community had given to Botha's reforms. With the imposition of the partial state of emergency in June 1985, international censure of the South African state increased dramatically. Fuelled by the ever-rising death toll in the townships and the growing organizational sophistication and strength of the anti-apartheid movement, the international community moved closer to imposing a range of sanctions on South Africa. Two events in particular – Botha's disappointing performance in an internationally televised speech, the so-called 'Rubicon' speech, in August 1985 and the subsequent collapse of the Commonwealth's own mediation effort – were to tip the scales in favour of the introduction of sanctions by the international community.

The elevation in importance of the international sanctions campaign was directly related to the closure of ANC bases in states adjoining South Africa. A product of the South African government's policy to 'destabilize' countries which offered the ANC sanction and support, the severe constraints imposed by this development forced the organization to focus a growing portion of its resources on the international sanctions campaign. ANC officials hoped that the imposition of sanctions on the South African economy would bring pressure to bear on both the state and the local business community and serve as a force for change. The sanctions campaign took place on four fronts: the United Nations, the Commonwealth, the United States and the European Community.

In the case of the United Nations, the General Assembly of the UN had traditionally taken a strong position against South Africa. The Security Council, dominated by the Western powers, remained reluctant to impose sanctions beyond those already in place (the 1977 mandatory arms embargo) for reasons which had much to do with economic rationale and Cold War politics. This situation was particularly acute in the case of Great Britain which had substantial economic interests in South Africa and, under Prime Minister Margaret Thatcher, was loath to take steps which would jeopardize those interests. The result was the passage of an annual resolution condemning South Africa by the General Assembly, seconded by the Security Council and the spearheading of efforts to further isolate South Africa from international organizations and forums of all kinds.

The Commonwealth's approach to the divisive issue of South Africa alternated between caution and histrionics. The Gleneagles Agreement of 1977, which introduced a sports boycott against South African athletics, was largely adhered to by member states. By 1985, the Commonwealth Summit in Nassau put South Africa on top of the organization's agenda once again.[114] Recognizing that the Commonwealth had yet to devote significant resources to the particulars of a sanctions campaign and coupled with Britain's intransigence over the sanctions issue, Commonwealth leaders elected to put together a mediation effort to assist in negotiating a transition to majority rule in South Africa. The Eminent Persons Group (EPG), headed by distinguished members drawn from Commonwealth nations, was strongly backed by Thatcher and Reagan and it was their combined persuasion which caused Botha to consider participating in the process.[115] The EPG mission coincided with personal and secret initiatives by imprisoned ANC leader Nelson Mandela directed towards opening discussions with the government. Building upon informal contacts with Minister of Justice Kobie Coetsee, which had begun in November 1985, Mandela says:

> I had concluded that the time had come when the struggle could best be pushed forward through negotiations. If we did not start a dialogue soon, both sides would be plunged into a dark night of oppression, violence and war.[116]

There followed the lifting of the partial state of emergency and the official abandonment of influx control measures, seemingly signalling a basic shift in the Botha administration's policy towards both domestic reform and the outlawed ANC. Operating from February to May 1986, the EPG mission shuttled between the State President's office, Nelson Mandela, ANC leadership in Lusaka and other elements within the South African community. On the government side, the *sine qua non* of further progress in opening the domestic political process was the renunciation of violence by the ANC; for its own part, the ANC continued to press for a lifting of prohibitions on political activity and concrete steps towards ending apartheid.[117] Despite the obstacles, for a brief moment it appeared that the EPG mission would succeed in bringing together South Africa's warring factions.

However, in a decision still wrapped in mystery, on 19 May Botha approved a series of strikes against ANC targets in Botswana, Zambia and Zimbabwe. Well after the event, Botha and the Secretary of the State Security Council continued to evince confusion as to the depth of the international criticism over the strike.[118] As there was no formal cessation of hostile events, it is possible that Botha believed he was employing a time-honoured stratagem in negotiations to launch a military action to support positions taken at the negotiating table. At the same time, the unwillingness of Western leaders to take up the South African government's position on violence, which would have had profound implications for the issue of the conditional release of Mandela and the unbanning of the ANC, greatly angered Botha.[119] With the EPG-sponsored debate shifting in early May to an official suspension of the use of violence by both parties it was provocative at the very least, if not a deliberate effort on the part of Botha, to launch military actions against ANC headquarters. Knowledge of the attack was limited to a few select Cabinet Ministers (amongst them Foreign Minister Pik Botha) causing acute embarrassment to Chris Heunis who only learned of the attacks while in the midst of discussions with the EPG mission.[120] The ANC, which had been openly sceptical of the process to begin with, repudiated the mediation effort. Faced with mounting criticism in the West, Botha chose to defy the international opprobrium rather than bow to its demands.

The scuttling of the Commonwealth initiative marked a turning-point in the international campaign for the isolation of South Africa.[121] At the mini-summit convened to consider the EPG mission's report in August of that year, the heads of the Commonwealth adopted the mission's position that economic sanctions were imperative. However, Margaret Thatcher's patent reluctance to harm British interests resulted in only a selective imposition of restrictions on investment and the importation of a range of South African products.

In the United States, the call for sanctions increased in the wake of the township rebellion and the imposition of the partial state of emergency. Anti-apartheid activists lobbied federal and state officials on the issue of sanctions, organized protest campaigns on university campuses, and publicized boycotts of companies doing business in South Africa. Following his visit to South Africa in early 1985, Senator Edward Kennedy introduced legislation which called for the banning of all new investments, the halting of the sale of Krugerrands, a prohibition on the sale of computers and a range of other punitive measures. Seeking to steal the thunder from Congressional Democrats, the Reagan administration imposed limited restrictions on trade between the United States and South Africa in September 1985.[122] However, in the wake of the adverse publicity accompanying the 'Rubicon' speech and the new state of emergency, by next October the Congress was able to override a Presidential veto and pass the Comprehensive Anti-Apartheid Act (CAAA). The CAAA further restricted American investment in South Africa, curtailed trade in South African primary and secondary products, and withdrew South African Airways' landing rights.[123] With public pressure building, a number of American businesses and universities with interests in South Africa divested themselves of their assets.

All of this occurred despite the willingness from some officials within the conservative Reagan administration to support the Botha reform process. Most notably, CIA Director William Casey met in secret with Botha administration officials in Southern Africa in the early eighties and, in addition to expressing sympathy for the position of the South African state, promised to press for further American support for South Africa's efforts in Namibia and Angola.[124] The hardening of the Reagan administration's position towards the South African government was an outgrowth of its overall disappointment with that government's failure to make rapid and substantial progress on reform, characterized by the disappointing 'Rubicon' speech and the scuttling of the EPG mission. A contentious meeting between American Ambassador Herman Nickel and Botha in May 1986, in which the State President flatly accused the American government of interference in South Africa's internal affairs, marked a turning-point in South African–American relations. Declaring that 'sanctions are your problem, not ours', thereafter, Botha sought to pursue his security and reform programme in defiance of international considerations and threats of sanctions.[125]

The European Community also moved to impose comprehensive sanctions against the importation of South African goods in the mid-eighties. Acting the same month that the Reagan administration imposed its initial sanctions package, the European Community issued a ban on the sale of oil and restrictions on military, scientific and cultural ties with South Africa.[126] With France taking a leading role, the European Community passed further sanctions legislation in 1986 prohibiting new investment and iron and steel imports. When Japan followed suit within days of the European Community decision, the South African state found itself to be moving towards full isolation from the major industrial powers of the world.

But arguably the sanctions which had the most impact were those applied by the private international banking system. In July 1985, Chase Manhattan Bank broke with its standard policy and refused to rollover South African debt, thus forcing South African corporate borrowers to pay both the interest on loans and the principal. This action was to precipitate a drop in international lending institutions' confidence in the country and, coupled with the new investment restrictions imposed by the industrialized countries, the subsequent shrinking of capital flows to South Africa caused a crisis in the country's balance of payments and a 50 per cent drop in the value of South Africa's currency.[127] Coming in the midst of an economic slowdown, the withdrawal of needed financial support from the international banking system exacerbated the magnitude of the crisis facing the state.

Conclusion

This period was brought to a close with the declaration of a full state of emergency in June 1986. According to government calculations, between September 1984 and January 1986, 955 people had been killed during the unrest, 628 of which had died as a result of actions by the state. Among the dead were 203 blacks whom the government described as 'moderates', many of whom had died through the 'necklace' method. Security force casualties between September 1984 and August 1986 included 56 dead and 711 injured.[128]

Viewed from the government's perspective, the partial state of emergency had been an unmitigated disaster. From the initial absence of regulations curbing the media to the decision to limit the emergency to selected magisterial districts, the formulation and implementation of the emergency served to actually foment further unrest in the townships rather than reduce it. Even a government committee of inquiry convened to investigate the outbreak of violence in September 1984 came close to accepting that the actions of the black community were, in contradiction to official interpretations, the product of spontaneous protest:

> [A]gitation and intimidation did undoubtedly play an important part. It would be short-sighted and unrealistic, however, to attach too much weight to this factor. On the other hand, what is shocking is the large extent to which people have played into the very hands of the agitators, thus making the agitator's work so much easier.[129]

An unanticipated result of the imposition of the emergency was that the black community was mobilized as never before. The range of demands by the anti-apartheid activists emerging out of martial law is indicative of the degree of politicization that community had undergone. In addition to issues of a local nature (improvement of conditions within the townships) the organizations now called for the lifting of the state of emergency, the withdrawal of the SADF from the townships, and the abolition of the black local authorities structures. In effect, the introduction of the emergency, bringing with it the concentrated action of the security forces against not only a broad spectrum of anti-apartheid activists but hitherto inactive members of the townships, served as something of a catalyst for what had been a relatively uncoordinated and disparate opposition.

Finally, the failure to move beyond military-inspired methods of dealing with the insurrection had a high cost for the South African state. With the undermining of the negotiation process launched by the EPG in 1986, the Botha administration had taken a definitive step away from accepting international norms on the situation in South Africa. This effectively narrowed the opportunity for winning outside acknowledgement of Botha's domestic political and social reforms and, concurrently, placed considerable pressure on the South African government to come up with an acceptable 'internal solution' to stem the tide of unrest. While Botha desperately attempted to win black support for a recently unveiled 'internal solution' (see below) the price of turning away from the international community would be weighed not only in terms of the increasing isolation and economic hardship in South Africa but also in terms of thousands of lives over the next three years.

REFORM STRATEGY IN THE EYE OF THE STORM: ECONOMIC, SOCIAL AND CONSTITUTIONAL POLICY IN THE MID-EIGHTIES

The outbreak of sustained unrest in 1984, aimed principally at the political reforms initiated by the Botha administration, did not in fact interrupt the introduction of substantial changes in the economic, social and political spheres by the South African government. Seeking to retain the initiative in spite of the rising tide of protest, the South African government continued to put forward new proposals on the economic, social and political restructuring of the polity. At the same time, recognition of the limitations of the reform strategy adopted in the early eighties caused government policy-makers to grope towards the formulation of a new approach to reform. This debate within government circles on the nature and content of further change, sharpened by the ongoing rebellion in the townships, resulted in bold initiatives in the socio-economic sphere. At the same time the government, fearful of losing political control, moved cautiously towards a further broadening of the political spectrum.

Reassessing the Botha Reform Programme

P.W. Botha's opening address to the tricameral parliament in January 1985, calling for the establishment of a National Statutory Council of white and black leaders to discuss 'power-sharing', was a sure indication that his government was intent on setting political reform on a different course. But it was the publication in May 1985 of an NP document which marked the official shift in policy away from the reformist vision of the early eighties drawn from the Riekert, Wiehahn and the Theron commissions.[130] Entitled '. . . And What About the Black People?', the pamphlet admitted that the homelands had proved to be a failure on a number of counts, among them the government's inability to create a viable political link between urbanized Africans and the homelands, that the existence of mistrust of government intentions had impeded the government's capacity to draw credible African leaders into the reform process and that the government had been unable to secure international acceptability for the scheme.[131] With the 'group nature of South African society' and the non-negotiability of a segregated educational system and residential areas as the government's condition, the broadside reopened the public debate on the parameters of the reform process as they had been defined in the early eighties. The evolution of a comprehensive post-Riekert urbanization policy, one which dispensed with influx control and the rigid attempt to implement the homeland scheme in favour of 'orderly urbanization', was to be an outgrowth of this new debate on the Botha reform programme. Another product was the decision to extend political participation to the African population through the establishment of a national forum for negotiation of a future political dispensation between all population groups.

While the debate over the scope and direction of reform began anew, the actual implementation of promised changes in the socio-economic sphere quickened from the mid-eighties onwards. Critical to this process was the consolidation of the position of the DCDP over virtually all aspects of the government's reform programme. The dismantling of the DCD in 1985 signalled the collapse of the last internal bureaucratic bastion against Botha's reform programme. Thereafter, though the process of political restructuring remained under fire – stalling the introduction of aspects of the government's proposed political reforms – tangible movement continued in the area of socio-economic reform.

Socio-economic Reform Policy

Throughout the mid-eighties, under the shadow of the township rebellion, socio-economic reform continued to proceed methodically towards eliminating much of the onerous aspects of socio-economic legislation promulgated in the name of apartheid. At the same time, the government's acknowledgement of its inability to give substance to the Riekert 'insider/outsider' approach to African urbanization paved the way for the introduction of a new strategy of urbanization. Produced by the President's Council and reviewed by a Cabinet committee, this new approach to the question of African urbanization reflected both an official acceptance of unworkability of Riekart's proposals and an effort to bring urbanization policy in line with the proposed regional development strategy.

Government Initiatives

At the opening of the tricameral parliament in January 1985, the new State President signalled his administration's intention to promote further alterations to the structure of socio-economic relations in the South Africa. Botha announced that full property rights for Africans in urban areas (in accordance with the exigencies of the Group Areas Act) would be established, that influx control would be altered to eliminate its discriminatory aspects, and that the policy of removing population groups in fulfilment of apartheid criteria would be reviewed.[132] In a series of addresses at NP provincial congresses later that year, Botha expanded upon the content of these statements, indicating that the government was still attached to the notion of further reform in the socio-economic sphere. Legislative action in this area was not, however, to take place until the tabling of the President's Council's report on urbanization and the government's review of that report several months later.

At the request of the State President, the President's Council set about reviewing South African policy on urbanization in early 1985. Put together by the Committee for Constitutional Affairs, the issuance of *An Urbanisation Strategy for the Republic of South Africa* in August marked a radical departure from past government policies which had guided urbanization. Specifically, the committee's report declared that the underlying principle which directed the Riekert Commission's work on the subject, that – with the exception of an African 'insider elite' – the African population was neither economically (nor politically) a part of 'white' South Africa, was deemed to be obsolete.[133] Flowing from this acceptance of the inevitability of African urbanization was the committee's call for the elimination of influx control and the passbook system and its replacement by a strategy of urbanization whose focus lay in managing rural-to-urban migration. Application of this policy would put urbanization strategy in line with the government's broader regional development strategy.

The Botha administration's reaction to the President's Council's report on urbanization was slow in coming. The *White Paper on Urbanisation* finally issued in April 1986, concurred with the bulk of the content of the President's Council's report.[134] The long-standing policy of management of rural to urban migration through the implementation of influx control and the passbook system was singled out in the White Paper as being marginally effective in fulfilment of its original intent but had caused tremendous harm to the country in a variety of respects. Thus the White Paper recommended the scrapping of this onerous legislation, calling for its replacement by a system that centred around the acquisition of provisions for housing as a controlling mechanism as well as the establishment of a universal identity card for all South Africans.[135] While the policy of forced removals of population groups in racially designated areas other than their own was upheld by the White Paper, it emphasized that such actions should take place in the context of negotiations with the affected groups. Overall, the new urbanization policy recommended by the White Paper was to encourage 'orderly urbanization' along the lines employed by the regional development strategy.

Further reviews of socio-economic policy were to follow on the heels of these government initiatives. In January 1984, the Strydom Committee recommended that the Group Areas Act, along with a host of other laws effecting residential segregation, be scrapped for whites, Coloureds and Indians.[136] In April 1985, following up on this report, the President's Council began to review the Group Areas Act. With residential segregation as one of the most explosive issues for the white community, the coming election in May 1987 caused the release of its report to be delayed.

Socio-Economic Reform Legislated

The scrapping of apartheid legislation and the introduction of laws that were in keeping with the government's new urbanization strategy were taken up in the first full session of the Tricameral parliament. Principal among these was the repeal of the Prohibition of Mixed Marriages Act of 1949 and Section 16 of the Immorality Act of 1957, initially broached by the State President in 1980. The passage of this reformist legislation by the Tricameral parliament was, according to senior government officials, deliberately delayed by Botha until the establishment of the new parliament so that Coloured and Indian politicians who participated in the controversial political dispensation would have something concrete to take back to their constituencies.[137] Other legislative matters acted upon during this period included the replacement of the hated passbooks – vital to the enforcement of the influx control system – in April 1985 by a universal identity book for all South Africans. In December, Heunis announced that the ninety-nine-year property leasing system for qualified Africans in urban areas would be supplanted by freeholder rights.

Political Reform Policy

More so than socio-economic initiatives, the crisis between 1984 through 1986 ruptured the implementation of Botha's reform policies in the political sphere. As one of the main objects of protest, the newly established Black Local Authorities as well as other proposals at the third-tier level such as the Regional Services Councils were effectively rendered inoperative or still-born. Concurrently, reform at the second tier of government, focusing on the provincial councils, continued to go forward as the government gave shape to its wider regional restructuring plans. And at the national level, with the newly created Tricameral parliament in place, the Botha administration moved to establish mechanisms for the further restructuring of government to accommodate African political aspirations.

Local and Regional Reform: Crisis at the Third Tier

One of the primary targets of violence since the onset of the township rebellion was the black local authorities. The councils had became the focus of anti-apartheid activisms because it was felt that acceptance of these refurbished black political structures would both constitute an acknowledgement of the legitimacy of the new constitutional dispensation – one which excluded blacks from direct participation at the national level – and serve as a support for the continuation of white domination of the political process. Throughout the upheavals, the government – increasingly in the form of the security-dominated NSMS – attempted to bolster these structures, providing in some instances comprehensive protection for the property and lives of black councillors. By mid-1985, months of sustained unrest had caused the suspension of all but five of the 38 black local authorities, rendering the newly established system inoperative.

At the same time that the township rebellion was crippling the black local authorities system, the DCDP continued to prepare the administrative foundation for the implementation of the RSCs and the future restructuring of the provincial governmental system along regional lines. The phasing-out of the four provincial councils paved the way for the introduction of a newly created multiracial decision-making structure. In place of the all white elected provincial administrative bodies, the new system consisted of a multiracial executive committee appointed by the State President and answerable to the parliament. Charged with the management of 'general affairs' at the second tier, the new provincial administrations were empowered to work jointly with homeland officials.[138] Not only did this encourage the development of consultation and cooperation between the two political entities, but, as the legislation initiating the changes in provincial administration allowed for the actual subdivision of the provinces themselves, the legislative foundation was laid for comprehensive regional restructuring. In the meantime, the provincial administrations were to act as caretakers of the provinces which in future looked to be increasingly obsolete as the state moved towards restructuring polity within a wider confederal system.

Reform at the National and Supra-national Levels

It was evident from the statements of senior government officials that the process of constitutional reform would not end with the passage of the legislation establishing the Tricameral parliament in 1983. Rumours that the government planned to bring Africans into the new parliament through the introduction of a fourth chamber were strengthened with the convening in February 1983 of a cabinet committee to investigate the constitutional status of Africans.[139] The Cabinet Committee on the Constitution was to play a key role in the Botha administration's reformulation of its political reform strategy. It was here that everything from the possibility of introducing a fourth pillar to the tricameral system to the contours of a future confederal system were debated. Here too, in later years, the reform process itself stalled as decision-makers failed to agree upon the direction or extent of reform, as well as the critical issue of negotiations with the ANC.[140]

Under the chairmanship of the Minister for Constitutional Development and Planning, the Cabinet Committee on the Constitution established six principles, representing the essence of the government's position on the next stage of reform, to guide its deliberations. They were:

> Everyone, individually and in a group context, should have an effective say in decision-making processes that affect his interests;
> Domination of one group by another should be eliminated and the rights and rightful aspirations of each group should be defended and satisfied;
> The rights of each group to self-determination should be respected, protected and furthered;
> Provision should be made for opportunities for cooperation with regard to common interests;
> Order and stability must be maintained and promoted throughout;
> And, any further action should be accompanied by constant consultation and negotiation.[141]

In reworking African constitutional rights, the committee first sought to shift the relationship between the government and the homelands from that of a series of bilateral contacts to that of a multilateral relationship.[142] As in the case of the National Liaison Committees – whose informal multiracial structures for local government were to serve as the model from the RSCs – a working committee was established which would lay the foundation for the multilateral forum envisioned in the government's confederalist ambitions. Starting with the introduction of homelands leaders into the process on an ad hoc basis, the informal status of the working committee allowed NP leaders and their African counterparts to accustomize themselves to working together on what were perceived to be highly volatile issues. Government reformists hoped to gradually widen the net to include those African leaders still outside of the negotiation process.[143]

In keeping with its brief, the working committee of the Cabinet Committee on the Constitution began to lay the groundwork for negotiation over a range of issues with leaders of the 'independent' homelands during the early part of 1984.[144] The immediate fruit of these discussions, announced in November 1984 by Heunis, was the committee's recommendation that South African citizenship be restored to all citizens of the homelands. Other subjects broached at the meetings at the request of African leaders were the abolition of influx control measures including the creation of a single identity document for all South Africans, and property rights in urban areas for Africans.[145] All of these issues were in fact taken up by the committee on urbanization and, over the next eighteen months, introduced before parliament.

A final recommendation by the working committee, that an informal negotiating forum comprising the government and African leaders be established so as to broaden the range of South African participation in the political reform process, was to be the genesis of a statutory body, the National Council. This institution, a forum for debate amongst political elites within South Africa, was to form the basis for what the Botha administration hoped would be the next step in the reform process: broad-based negotiations on a future political dispensation with all parties which renounced violence as a tool for change.

The Provincial Congresses of the National Party

In keeping with his previous policy of seeking the consensus of the white electorate before embarking on significant socio-economic and political change, Botha outlined the key elements of the Cabinet Committee on the Constitution's recommendations at the NP's four provincial congresses held in mid-1985. Taken together, the State President's addresses to the provincial congresses on his administration's new strategy on urbanization and the proposed establishment of the National Council represented an important preview of his revised reform programme. One of the speeches in particular – the so-called 'Rubicon' speech – was to play an unexpectedly pivotal role in redefining the international community's relationship with South Africa.

At the NP congress in Durban, Botha's speech focused on the need for the abandonment of the 'outdated' system of influx control, one of the cornerstones of apartheid.[146] This was followed by the provincial congress at Bloemfontein where Botha declared that South African citizenship would be restored to Africans living inside and outside the homeland structure. In the Transvaal, administration officials addressed the party delegates about the need for a negotiated process for change, one which would include black leaders 'who do not basically agree with the Government' as long as they renounced violence as a tool for change.[147] Finally, at the NP congress in Port Elizabeth, Botha stated definitively that his administration was committed to a geographically united South Africa, one common citizenship, and a universal franchise.[148] This was accompanied by a promise to restructure the state's official 'think tank' – the President's Council – to include African members and a reiteration of the call for negotiations with a range of leaders, African and otherwise, outside of the established system.

The significance of these speeches lay in the fact that it represented the Botha administration's revised blueprint for political and socio-economic reform in the wake of the creation of the Tricameral parliament and the violent upheavals of the last two years. Tying together what appeared to be disparate threads and degrees of the reformist activity as conducted by his administration up to the mid-eighties, Botha signalled that he was ready to embark on further changes of the structures and substance of the state. At the same time, the limits of apartheid reform were clearly delineated: any proposed change in the status quo would not significantly alter the nature of group or racial basis of political representation in South Africa nor threaten the integrity of group identity.

It was, however, Botha's 'Rubicon' speech which received the greatest scrutiny. Addressing an international audience, encouraged by the DFA to expect the announcement of a momentous shift in government policy, Botha's focus on limited reforms of aspects of apartheid all the while emphasizing the government's determination to resist revolutionary violence and foreign interference was greeted with general dismay.[149]

The disappointment which accompanied Botha's performance spelt an end to the alliance between the government and business as well as strengthened the international campaign for sanctions (see above).[150] One month after the Rubicon speech the Chairman of the Anglo-American corporation, Gavin Relly, led a delegation of major business representatives to Lusaka to conduct face-to-face talks with the ANC. This action was followed by the publication of a full-page advertisement in the local press calling on the government to end the state of emergency. Finally, the issuance in January 1986 of what amounted to a counter-strategy of reform – the 'Business Charter of Social, Economic and Political Rights' – by the South African Federated Chamber of Industries sealed the break in the cooperative alliance between the government and business.

The National Council

Following up on the recommendations of the working committee of the Cabinet Committee on the Constitution, Botha announced in his opening address to parliament in January 1985 that the government planned to establish a negotiating forum comprising the government and African leaders to debate the future direction of political reform. Seeking to draw prominent figures from the homelands and black local authorities into the process, Botha declared that the National Council would be empowered to discuss a range of constitutional matters in the hope of creating 'a more favourable basis for negotiations aimed at arriving at mutually acceptable development steps in the constitutional field'.[151] In a parliamentary debate later that month, Botha went further, offering to release Nelson Mandela if he 'unconditionally rejected violence'.

Addressing the opening session of the Tricameral parliament a year later, having now won the support of the NP's provincial congresses, Botha clarified the terms of the next step in political reform:

> I intend to negotiate the establishment of a national statutory council, which will meet under my chairmanship. I propose that this council consist of representatives of the

> South African Government, representatives of the governments of the self-governing National States, as well as leaders of other Black communities and interest groups. Pending the creation of constitutional structures jointly to be agreed upon for our multi-cultural society, this council should consider and advise on matters of common concern, including proposed legislation on such matters.[152]

Statements by the Minister of Constitutional Development and Planning, whose position as chairman of the Cabinet Committee on the Constitution tied him closely to the proposals, outlined the substance of the State President's planned negotiating forum.

> It is crucial that the council not be regarded as another advisory body. The truth is that the council, by reason of the executive State President's involvement, will be a very influential and powerful body . . . In fact, as the State President will chair both the council and the Cabinet, there is no closer link possible between the council and the executive authority of South Africa.[153]

Its initial focus would be community issues and matters of general concern, but Heunis held out the promise that the National Council would tackle the thorny issue of developing a new political dispensation. The National Council was to be, in Heunis's words, 'a starting point for power-sharing'.[154]

The persistent unwillingness of any African leaders to participate openly in the proposed forum, despite the credentials of some as beneficiaries of approved governmental structures, was to render the National Council stillborn. In particular, Chief Mangosuthu Buthelezi's equivocal stance towards the project was especially discouraging for Pretoria as the inclusion of the KwaZulu leader was imperative to the success of any such institution. Botha's desire to have Buthelezi participate was such that he appealed directly to Buthelezi to discuss any aspect of the proposed negotiation forum. For his own part, Buthelezi recognized the importance of his personal participation to the success of the project and maintained a tough stance towards Botha.

> I would start negotiation with the State President tomorrow if he was serious about addressing the fundamental

> issues of black constitutional rights in our country. But if he wants to go it alone in the national council then he is welcome to try with whomever is prepared to sit with him on it . . .[155]

As for Nelson Mandela, speaking through his daughter at a UDF rally in 1985, he issued the first of many public dismissals of government attempts to link his release with a renunciation of violence.

> I am surprised at the conditions that the government wants to impose on me. I am not a violent man . . . It was only then, when all other forms of resistance were no longer open to us, that we turned to armed struggle. Let Botha show that he is different to Malan, Strijdom and Verwoerd. Let him renounce violence. Let him say that he will dismantle apartheid. Let him unban the people's organization, the African National Congress. Let him free all who have been imprisoned, banished or exiled for their opposition to apartheid. Let him guarantee free political activity so that people may decide who will govern them.[156]

Seemingly undeterred by the lack of support for the proposed reforms from African leaders of any political stripe, the Botha administration went ahead and prepared the foundation for the introduction of this next step in the process of political reform by calling for an electoral mandate from the white community in 1987.

Political Reform Legislated

Legislation emerging out of the government initiatives in the political sphere during this period centred on fulfilling promised reforms by the Botha administration. Among the more important were the Restoration of South African Citizenship Act, the Abolition of Influx Control Act and the Black Communities Development Amendment, which granted free holder rights to qualified Africans in urban areas. The repeal of the Prohibition of Political Interference Act of 1968, which allowed political parties to accept membership from all the statutory population groups, set the stage for a return to multiracial politics in the country. The Provincial

Government Act eliminated the four white provincial governments at the end of June 1986 and put in their stead a multiracial executive committee appointed by the State President. The provincially controlled Development Boards were scrapped and their functions and staff temporarily placed under the supervision of the provincial executive committees.[157] Finally, the Regional Services Councils Amendment Act, which detailed the financing mechanisms for the RSCs, gave further content to the still stymied introduction of these new structures.

But, viewed from the perspective of the Botha reform programme, the most significant legislation to emerge during this time was the government's introduction of the National Council Bill. Put before parliament in May 1986, the Bill called for the establishment of a National Council consisting of the chief ministers of the ten 'homelands', representatives of the urbanized African community nominated by that community and appointed by the State President, the chairmen of the three ministers' councils, any cabinet ministers deemed appropriate by the State President, and up to ten individuals nominated by the State President. Chaired by the State President, the National Council was empowered to consider legislation and make recommendations to the government.[158] Botha underscored the importance of the Bill to parliament:

> [The National Council] should be an interim body to give all population groups participation in decision-making until negotiation leads to an agreement on an extensive new constitutional dispensation for all South Africans . . . I must emphasize that the council is not an end in itself, but a means to an end.[159]

Conclusion

Confronted by spiralling unrest in the townships, the Botha administration nonetheless sought to maintain the momentum of socio-economic and political reform as inaugurated in the early eighties. This was despite the government's acknowledgement of substantial shortcomings in the reform programme as previously conceived, a situation which had led to a reconceptualization of reform in the socio-economic and political spheres. With the new urbanization strategy and the proposed National Council serving as cornerstones of the government's new approach to change, administration officials were confident that black South Africans would be drawn back into the process of state-managed reform.

This effort to rework aspects of the reform programme notwithstanding, the divide between the government's incremental approach to reform and black aspirations – fuelled by the tragic events in the townships over the previous eighteen months – became increasingly evident. Reform in socio-political sphere which, a few years back, would have been heralded as a significant breakthrough, was ridiculed by activists. Reacting to the abolition of the Mixed Marriages Act and Section 16 of the Immorality Act, the UDF spokesperson declared: 'What must be repealed are those laws which deny the majority of people in South Africa their political, residential, labour and citizenship rights.'[160] This sentiment was echoed by even 'moderate' Africans, such as Buthelezi, when it came to the realm of political reform.[161] The same could have been said for the government's proposed multiracial National Council which, if it had been established a few years before, would in all probability have won the support of a significant sector of the black community. The patent rejection of these reformist steps by political moderates was a measure of how the initial support for reform apartheid had all but dissipated.[162]

CONCLUSION

On the eve of the imposition of the full state of emergency, the Botha administration acknowledged yet again that the changes implemented to date would not be sufficient to carry the country through the rest of the decade. While underlining the fact that the Tricameral parliament had always been a transitional arrangement, the South African government nonetheless grappled to develop an alternative constitutional dispensation which would meet their political requirements and those articulated by the various leaders of the black majority. Determined to retain control over the process of reform, yet faced with a narrowing constituency of support amongst the white population and manifest intransigence amongst the black population, the Botha administration found itself in a quandary. A consequence of this dilemma was the deliberate shift by the government away from its leading role in formulating institutional solutions to perceived problems to one in which it sought to engage black leaders in the actual development of those solutions. This abandonment of the prescriptive approach which had characterized reform to date, in favour of an emphasis – in lieu of a set of specific proposals in the socio-economic and, most especially, the political sphere – on the process itself, distinguished the next phase of reform by the Botha administration.

The government's recognition of the shortcomings of existing constitutional reforms was coupled with the sober realization that the township rebellion had reached revolutionary proportions, threatening its very ability to manage the affairs of state. In order to regain control over the unwieldy security situation, the Botha administration determined that it would have to introduce stringent security measures on a nation-wide basis. As the previous partial state of emergency had proved to be ineffectual in quelling the township rebellion, a reassessment of security strategy was undertaken, resulting in the introduction of a new counter-revolutionary strategy based on a combination of security, socio-economic upliftment programmes and political reform. Turning away from the international community, epitomized by the scuttling of the EPG mission, the Botha administration chose to rely on its own resources to solve the pressing dilemmas facing South Africa rather than have them compromised by the international considerations. By doing so, the South African government had effectively placed all of its political eggs into one basket: the securing of black support for an internal political solution. Balanced between enticing a wary Nelson Mandela and pressuring reluctant homeland leaders to participate, this approach was to form the basis of the Botha administration's new response to the spectacle of sustained unrest in the remaining years of the decade.

Against this background, the State President took stock of the changes to the South African polity brought on by his government's reform programme. Far from disheartened by the protracted nature of the process gripping the country, Botha evinced a confidence that the progress of incremental reform would continue to move forward. At the NP's provincial congress in the Transvaal, held in September 1986, Botha reflected:

> Our reform is a process of modernization. In announcing the Twelve Point Plan for orderly change and reform seven years ago, I then stated this truth. Through the adoption of the Twelve Point Plan, we undertook to continue with meaningful reform on a wide and balanced basis. On the one hand the plan was the affirmation of a framework and a point of departure through which the realities of our multi-cultural society would serve as the guidelines for reform and modernisation. On the other hand it was also the basis on which concrete reform steps in the fields of constitutional, economic and social affairs could be implemented. It was enunciated with due cognisance of our national security, prosperity, foreign relations and our national interests. Any objective observer who has kept a close watch on developments during the past seven years since the Twelve Point Plan was announced, would have to agree that we are indeed succeeding in the realisation of those goals we have set for ourselves.[163]

A terse acknowledgement of the setbacks to the reform programme experienced by the government in the wake of the two-year rebellion was a painful reminder that the government's plans had not met with universal approval:

> Of course, as can be expected, we are also meeting with increased opposition as part of an attempt to sabotage our progress.[164]

Its brevity notwithstanding, Botha's admission reflected his government's assessment of the dire security situation facing the state in the mid-eighties. This appraisal of the security environment had only a few short months before led to the imposition of an unprecedented full state of emergency, the ramifications of which were to reverberate to the end of the decade.

6 The Security State and the Forces of Revolution, 1986–88

> *The National Statutory Council not only must succeed but will succeed.* Minister of Constitutional Development and Planning, Chris Heunis, in June 1986.[1]

> *[I]f the State President turns his national council into a castration chamber then only those who aspire to be political eunuchs will want to go there.* Chief Mangosuthu Buthelezi.[2]

The declaration of a full state of emergency in mid-1986 marked not only a shift away from early attempts to quell the township rebellion but a further reassessment of the government's established strategy of reform. With the growing entrenchment of the security establishment at the helm of government, the incrementalist approach to reform which had characterized the Botha administration's outlook in the early eighties came to be eclipsed by a new military-inspired counter-revolutionary strategy aimed at defusing the internal crisis. Employing strategies derived from the Namibian experience, the government strove to stem the tide of revolution through a tryptich of repression, socio-economic upliftment and political reform. At the same time, events in the external environment threatened the South African position on the Namibia–Angola border, ultimately spurring on the process of a negotiated settlement in Namibia. Concurrent with these events were the protracted efforts by Botha administration officials to secure black participation in the next phase of its political reform programme, that of negotiating a new constitutional dispensation. The stalemate that ensued between the government, established black leaders and the forces of protest was mirrored by the controversy within the government itself, as hard liners and reformists battled over the policy direction that South Africa should pursue. The result was an increasing paralysis in the implementation of government's reform programme, an imbroglio that was to characterize the last of the Botha years in office and ultimately contribute to the State President's downfall.

This chapter will first examine the Botha administration's effort to gain an electoral mandate from the white community for direct negotiations with black leaders, the next step in the reform process. Secondly, it will look at the shifting fortunes of the rebellion against the state and the introduction of a new security-based strategy aimed at defusing the revolutionary climate in the townships. Coupled with this will bc an investigation into the changing external security environment. Next, the status of the Botha administration's programme of socio-economic reform will receive attention. And, finally, the protracted process of reforming the political sphere will be examined.

SEEKING A MANDATE FOR NEGOTIATION AND CHANGE: THE 1987 ELECTION

The State President's announcement in January 1987 that he was to dissolve the House of Assembly and conduct elections came as a surprise. However, as in the past, Botha felt compelled to seek a mandate from the white community before embarking on a substantive change of the existing dispensation. Hence, just as Botha had fought an election around the issue of the inauguration of his reform programme (the Twelve Point Plan) in 1981, so too, when faced with the need to introduce further and more substantial change in his government's programme, he turned to the electorate to secure a mandate for that change.

The campaign itself was hard fought. Under the banner of 'Reform yes – Surrender No', the NP claimed that its incremental approach to reform was the only alternative to the chimera of old apartheid offered by the Conservatives and the 'soft left' sloganeering of the Progressive Federalist Party (PFP). The government sought to present the white community with its proposed framework within which the next stage of reform would take place. Botha indicated that two of the main pillars of apartheid – the Separate Amenities Act and the Group Areas Act – were not themselves to be treated as holy cows.[3] At the same time, NP politicians declared that certain principles underlying this legislation, such as the right to foster the identity of a statutory population group through the maintenance of some forms of segregation, was considered to be inviolable. Several key defections of known NP liberals, among them Dennis Worrall and Wynand Malan, were an uncomfortable signal that the pace of the Botha reform programme was losing support within its own ranks.[4]

In the end, the NP won 123 of the 178 seats in the House of Assembly against the Conservative party's 22 seats and the PFP's 19 seats. In the process, the white community dealt the PFP a stunning defeat, throwing their support behind the Conservative party and raising it to the position of main opposition party. For its own part, the elections demonstrated that the NP had lost a significant sector of its traditional Afrikaner support base to its Conservative party opponents while, as it adopted traditional English-speaking liberal stances like federalism, it was able to pick up votes from PFP supporters.

The election of 1987 was an important bellwether of the attitude towards the Botha reform programme within the white community. The predominance of security concerns in the campaign, eclipsing the rhetoric of reform, reflected both white South Africans' genuine fears and the NP's skilful manipulation of these concerns. Ensconced within this framework of security, the next phase of the NP's reform programme involving negotiation and further changes to the status quo would move forward with the approval of a majority of the white electorate. As Botha himself declared:

> [T]he support given the Government by the voters endorses the evolutionary approach followed by the Government in respect of economic, social and constitutional development and advancement . . . [I]t confirms the Government's point of departure that security, order and stability in all of our communities are preconditions for reform and that the proponents of radicalism and violence will have to renounce that course before they may participate in constitutional processes.[5]

Secure in this endorsement from the white community, the Botha administration forged ahead with the implementation of the twin imperatives of security and reform. Aligned against it were the anti-apartheid movement and the forces of revolution which had re-emerged in strength in the mid-eighties.

REVOLUTION

Since the outbreak of violence in September 1984, the course of unrest had moved from open rebellion to incipient revolution. In the process, the revolt in the townships began to develop a momentum of its own, sweeping black South Africa into a conflagration which both set it against the armed might of the state and increasingly set the community against itself. Imbued with the belief that the Botha administration was teetering on the brink of collapse, the township youth took command of the anti-apartheid struggle, lending an untutored militancy to the conflict. However, by the end of the following year, the euphoria which characterized the first years of the rebellion had – under the full weight of the state security apparatus – given way to the recognition that the armed struggle would not topple the regime in the near future. It was this sober realization which ultimately opened the way for a debate within the UDF and the ANC as to the pursuit of alternative approaches to power, namely participation and negotiation.

Revolution versus Anarchy

Internally, the UDF – which had served as the backbone of the challenge to state authority since its formation – had weathered the partial state of emergency intact if not fully operational. With the lifting of emergency regulations in early March 1986 and the subsequent release of many of its leading activists, the UDF was poised to rejuvenate its campaign against the state. The youth, having heeded the ANC's call for the creation of alternative governing structures to those of the state, established street committees and 'people's courts' in the townships, linking these to the local civic organizations. Based on the plan devised by slain civic leader Matthew Goniwe, the street committees took over the administrative functions of the township and, in addition to soliciting and attempting to act on community concerns, presided over an array of politically motivated directives to the local residents covering everything from consumer boycotts to the taxation of black businesses.[6]

Disciplined action in the name of the street committees by township activists won the respect of black communities; however, in some instances, the revolutionary fervour of the youth resulted in the perpetration of questionable deeds. The instigation of trials in the self-styled people's courts, which meted out harsh sentences against those offenders who contravened street committee directives, as often brought additional fears to township life as justice. Suspected informers, the lifeblood of the SAP's intelligence network, were subject to the gruesome method of execution known as 'necklacing'. Sensing victory in the air, township youth by the thousands abandoned their studies to participate in the final overthrowing of the state. The slogan 'liberation before education' took its place beside the ANC's call to make the country 'ungovernable' and these became the watchwords of the numerous youth groups which manned the barricades of the revolution. As the reactionary vigilante forces came into play in the latter half of 1985, contributing to a cycle of fratricide which reached particularly horrific proportions in the Natal midlands, the 'comrades' became engaged in running street battles with their opponents which seemed to take on a life of their own. A criminal element, the so-called *com-tsotis*, took command in some of the townships in the name of the revolution and used the mantle of anti-regime politics to terrorize township residents.[7] An activist in Alexandra township, speaking at the height of the rebellion of April 1986, captured the dilemma facing the anti-apartheid movements in the wake of the unravelling of discipline in the township rebellion.

> There had been calls for ungovernability, particularly from the ANC. Well, the township got ungovernable in the post-Six Day War era.[8] Police weren't in the township. The township was ungovernable to the enemy. Now people got ungovernable to their own organizations. Elements went around demanding money from shopkeepers, who in turn complained about this intimidation campaign.[9]

For many of the older township residents as well as much of the leadership of the anti-apartheid movement, these developments represented not a step on the road to revolution but rather a slide towards anarchy. However, given that youth and student groups represented half of the UDF structures[10] and considering the heightened atmosphere of the rebellion itself, it was difficult for more conservative voices within the movement to take steps to curb the situation without risking severe censure. The establishment of the National Education Crisis Committee (NECC) in late 1985 by concerned parents and elders signalled the determination of this segment of the anti-apartheid movement to regain their authority over the unruly revolutionaries.

The turning-point came with the convening of a national meeting of the newly formed NECC in Durban in late March 1986. At this forum, Zwelakhe Sisulu – editor of the *New Nation* and son of jailed ANC stalwart Walter Sisulu – criticized the approach of some of the 'comrades':

> We are not poised for the immediate transfer of power to the people. The belief that this is so could lead to serious errors and defeats. We are however poised to enter a phase which can lead to the transfer of power. What we are seeking to do is to decisively shift the balance of forces in our favour. To do this we have to adopt the appropriate strategies and tactics, we have to understand our strengths and weaknesses, as well as that of the enemy, that is, the forces of apartheid.[11]

Thereafter, despite losing some militants to black nationalism, the UDF began the process of reasserting control over the struggle. With the NECC taking the lead, students were urged to return to school and engage in 'people's education' as a feature of the revolutionary struggle.[12] The South African Youth Congress, a national student organization, was launched in 1987 in part to provide a disciplined outlet for township youth. These assertive measures proved to be an important dimension in the conflict with the government in the waning years of the decade as the anti-apartheid movement started to grapple with alternative strategies of gaining power.

At the same time, the grassroots democracy and openness

which had distinguished the first years of the UDF, reeling under the dual assault of faltering control over the township rebellion and counter-revolutionary measures (see below), was replaced by an increasingly secretive approach to politics.[13] The adoption of the Freedom Charter in August 1987, signalling an end to the strategy of seeking to build a broad front against the state, coincided with a rise in official UDF hostility towards other anti-apartheid organizations such as Azapo and its affiliates.

> At this stage we cannot tolerate competing ideologies ... We cannot waste our time confusing people ... We must learn from Algeria in the 1950s, where everyone was smashed into one movement.[14]

International financial support for the UDF, which had bolstered the movement in the early eighties, was curtailed in late 1986 by the government causing annual revenues to tumble from R2 million to R200 000.[15] Coupled with these developments was a growing disillusionment with the movement, born of the inordinately high expectations in the mid-eighties. As a member of the executive committee of squatters in Thokoza township remarked in 1988:

> [W]e will never see change in our lifetime. The UDF tried and failed. The Front is still trying but nothing is coming right.[16]

The People's War

The practical implications of the shift to a 'people's war' meant that the ANC had abandoned the high-profile sabotage missions of the late seventies and early eighties in favour of massive infiltration of guerrillas into the country. In order to realize this strategy, the ANC leadership had banked on the establishment of a mobile guerrilla army based within South Africa itself.[17] This would be effected through the expanded infiltration and recruitment of insurgents trained in small arms and mine-laying, the establishment of rudimentary alternative governing structures linked with the civic organizations and backed by the founding of political-military structures within a regional framework. Integrated into the Goniwe plan in the townships, the politico-military structures called Regional Political-Military Councils (RPMCs) were established in Botswana, Swaziland, Lesotho and Zimbabwe. They were composed of representatives from local committees for Security and Intelligence, SACTU (the South African Congress of Trade Unions) and the Political department and made answerable to the newly created Political-Military Council in Lusaka. The task of the RPMCs was to establish Area Political-Military Councils (APMCs) in the South African territory contiguous with the RPMC and, using infiltrated Umkhonto we Sizwe guerrillas as a nucleus, build up the components of a 'people's army' in preparation for the next phase of revolutionary warfare.[18]

In light of the extraordinary developments in South Africa since late 1984, the ANC convened a conference in Zambia in June 1985 to assess the status of the uprising and its role in this process. At the close of the Kabwe conference, the newly elected National Executive Committee issued a confident appraisal of events:

> Our conference will be remembered by our people as a council-of-war that planned the seizure of power by the masses, the penultimate convention that gave the order for us to take our country through the terrible but cleansing fires of revolutionary war to a condition of peace, democracy and the fulfillment of our people.[19]

Following on the heels of the Kabwe Conference the pace of military activity picked up. There was an increase in landmine explosions from 50 in 1984 to over 200 by 1986.[20] APMCs were created in a preliminary fashion by the RPMCs in some regions – three in the Cape and one in the Northern Transvaal – and, in the case of the APMC founded in the Western Cape, were able to go so far as to put together autonomous military units.[21] The seeds of the guerrilla warfare phase of the revolution appeared to be near fruition.

Conclusion

The utilization of the expedient of calling for a 'people's war', which presented the insurrection within the townships as directly attributable to ANC actions, was a double-edged sword for the organization. Only partially in control of events, the status of the revolutionary struggle became tied to the conduct of the township rebellion in all its manifestations. Attempts by the ANC and the UDF to reel-in the township youth met with only partial success; as the battle against the vigilantes and the security forces raged within the townships, the impetus for violence continued to foster militancy within the ranks of the 'comrades'. With the imposition of the full state of emergency in June 1986, the anti-apartheid movement suffered a severe blow to its ability to carry out both illegal and legal operations. Reeling under the twin assaults of security force action and phenomenon of vigilantism, the anti-apartheid movement's optimistic forecasts of toppling the Botha regime in the mid-eighties gave way to sober realism. By October 1986, in a directive issued by the ANC's Political-Military Council, the organization admitted:

> Despite all our efforts, we have not come anywhere near the achievement of the objectives we set for ourselves.[22]

This gloomy assessment of the situation within South Africa, echoed by UDF activists, resulted in yet another review of ANC strategy. A statement issued in October 1987 by the ANC's National Executive Committee reaffirming the organization's commitment to 'genuine negotiations provided they are aimed at the transformation of our country into a united and non-racial democracy' reflected its reduced expectations of a military-inspired victory over the South African government.[23] Coupled with this was the growing pressure from the Soviet Union, prevalent since 1987, to seek out a negotiated solution to South Africa's political divide rather than a revolutionary one.[24] The subsequent publication of constitutional proposals, formed in the liberal democratic mould, in the middle of 1988 gave content to the ANC's shift away from a militant strategy of overthrowing the government to one in which power was attained through negotiation.[25] This step was ultimately to have far-reaching consequences for the reform process in South Africa.

SECURITY

The expanding nature of unrest in South Africa, coupled with the re-emergence of a military threat to the South African position on the Namibian border, caused the Botha administration to engineer two seemingly contradictory shifts in its approach to security. Internally, the two-year rebellion in the townships had developed into a revolutionary insurrection, threatening not only the government's reform programme but the very legitimacy of the state itself. Shedding the uncoordinated response which characterized the first state of emergency, the Botha administration simultaneously imposed country-wide emergency regulations while introducing a new counter-revolutionary strategy aimed at quelling the incipient revolution. In the case of the external environment, the launching of a massive conventional campaign against Unita and the stepping up of Swapo infiltrations strained the capacity of the SADF to respond effectively. Fierce fighting on the Angola–Namibia border brought the enervated combatants once again to the negotiating table and, after decades of conflict, resulted in the signing of a peace accord paving the way for Namibian independence and the withdrawal of Cuban troops. Finally, the ever-present danger of further international sanctions began to bite into South Africa's economic well-being and brought with it the first signs of change in its covert nuclear programme.

Security: the Internal Dimension

The failure of the partial state of emergency to even dampen the revolutionary fervour that gripped the townships was manifest by the middle of 1986. With the number of unrest incidents climbing by the week, coupled by the escalation of revolutionary activity on the part of the ANC or those who claimed to act in its name, the government faced a crisis of enormous proportions. Its response was to return to the mechanism of imposing a state of emergency in South Africa. However, drawing on the lessons of the immediate past, in this instance the Botha administration extended both the scope of the emergency regulations themselves and the territorial purview of the emergency to include the entire country. Concomitant with this action was the introduction of a new military-inspired counter-revolutionary strategy tailored specifically at combating the unrest. Principally a derivation of American strategist J. J. McCuen's work and the SADF's experience in Namibia, counter-revolutionary strategy as employed in South Africa proper dominated the state's security response to the end of the decade.

Counter-revolutionary Strategy

Just as Beaufre exerted determining influence over the development of the SADF's radical military doctrine Total National Strategy, so too other foreigners were to play a critical role in the development of the South African government's specific approach to counter-insurgency. Chief among these were Lt.-Colonel J. J. McCuen, an American military strategist with experience in Vietnam, whose penned a detailed account of the intricacies of combating revolutionary warfare through the application of a counter-revolutionary strategy. McCuen's *The Art of Counter-revolutionary War: The Strategy of Counter-insurgency* served as a textbook for the South African military in its campaigns in Namibia and, as the SADF became more involved in combating domestic upheavals, its lessons was increasingly applied to South Africa itself.[26]

McCuen's study of counter-revolutionary warfare centres on the notion that the development of a theory of counter-revolutionary warfare necessitates an investigation of revolutionary warfare itself. Drawing on the principal proponents of revolutionary warfare, Mao Tse-tung and V. N. Giap, McCuen outlines the four stages of revolution: the organization phase, the terrorism phase, the guerrilla war phase and the mobile warfare phase.[27] To combat each phase, he recommends counter-measures which in many respects mimic the approach adopted by the revolutionaries. Specifically, he calls for the use of civic action programmes in the organization phase; the use of police actions in the terrorism phase; the use of low-level military actions in the guerilla war phase; and the use of conventional military actions in the mobile warfare phase.[28]

To counter a massive insurrection, McCuen calls for the employment of what he terms the 'oil spot strategy'.

> The problem of the governing power is not merely the defensive one of stopping the rebel attacks, but the offensive one of winning back control of the country . . . [T]he governing authorities must evolve a step-by-step plan which is based on the realities of the situation and which accomplishes the critical objectives in a logical order. It is of greatest importance that this plan be predicated on the fact that winning is going to take a long time – years rather than months. It is essential that the plan be based on the oil spot strategy: that is the establishment and expansion of strategic bases until the entire country has been rewon.[29]

Through this selective establishment of these strategic bases in the heart of the insurrection, the governing power can operate against revolutionary forces and, utilizing the five critical elements outlined above, gradually recover the population and territory.

According to the SADF's principal proponent of counter-revolutionary warfare, Lt.-General C. Lloyd, while many different texts on combating insurgent movements were studied in the early seventies, it was McCuen's account which 'fit our case best'.[30] Notwithstanding, there was a realization within military circles that conditions in South Africa – that of a highly industrialized sector coupled with extremes of rural poverty, a large concentration of the population in urban areas, the unique cast of its ethnic problems, and a vast territorial expanse – militated against a direct translation of the tenets of counter-revolutionary warfare into action. In particular, as the preponderance of counter-revolutionary strategists focused on *rurally based insurgencies,* South African strategists found themselves obliged to engage in improvization. They drew on a variety of cases – Algeria, Northern Ireland, the Philippines, South America and Israel – to supplement McCuen's work and, most importantly, Lloyd and others built upon their own 'hands on' experience in Namibia.[31]

The result of the SADF's ruminations on the subject was the development of a threefold approach to countering revolutionary insurrection. The first phase involved establishing stability in the affected territory. As Lloyd explained:

> It is part of the security forces' strategy to remove the enemy leaders, to take them away from the masses so that you can inform them [the masses] and convey to them the real situation.[32]

The second phase focused on the introduction of socio-economic upliftment projects in the affected territory. As Lloyd explained:

> [T]he SADF involved itself in these social upliftment programmes because of the vitally important role the local population has to play in counterinsurgency in the RSA and SWA. The loyalty, goodwill and cooperation of the local population have to be secured and the insurgents have to be denied every opportunity of exploiting friction points, grievances or dissatisfaction. At the same time the SADF utilizes the opportunity to demonstrate to the local population that they are there to help and to protect them and not to harm them.[33]

The third phase involved the introduction of political change which, if done with the cardinal principle of establishing 'good government' in mind, would sustain the community against the revolutionary threat in future.[34]

Lloyd, the commanding officer of the SADF in Namibia during the crucial years between 1979 and 1983, employed the doctrine of counter-revolutionary warfare to the military's activities in the northern part of the territory. While serving as the commanding officer for the Far North Command in the mid-eighties, Lloyd conducted seminars on counter-revolutionary warfare to senior civil servants operating within his jurisdiction. In 1986, he was brought in by Pretoria to brief the Cabinet on this new strategy.[35] Impressed with his presentation, the State President began to consider shifting primary responsibility for security policy out of the hands of the SAP – which had played the dominant role in the first state of emergency – and into that of the SADF. In the words of contemporary observers:

> "Counter-insurgency" [SAP's policy] was seen to have no answer to the unprecedented scale of the 1984 to 1986

> uprising, or to the powerful local and international pressures for fundamental change.[36]

With the declaration of the full state of emergency, the SADF's counter-revolutionary warfare had moved to the centre of the state's strategy for combating unrest.

The Imposition of the Full State of Emergency

With the rescinding of the partial state of emergency in March 1986, the pace of the rebellion quickened once again, with unrest incidents escalating into the thousands and the death rate averaging over six persons per day.[37] Concurrently, the Botha administration's efforts to replace the extraordinary measures invoked through the declaration of a state of emergency with statutory legislation incorporating much of the content of emergency regulations had bogged down in the intervening period. These bills, the Internal Security Amendment Bill, which extended the period of lawful detention from 48 hours to 180 days, and the Public Safety Amendment Bill, which empowered the state to declare any area an unrest area and thereby invoke a host of security steps, would in effect give the government the requisite powers recently cast aside with the lifting of the partial state of emergency. Fearing the onus of being seen as accomplices to the introduction of security measures by their respective communities, both the House of Representatives and the House of Delegates had asked that these bills be referred to a standing committee on law and order.[38] At the same time, armed with intelligence reports of massive protest actions planned for the anniversary of the 16 June uprisings by the anti-apartheid movement, on 4 June the government served banning orders on all gatherings commemorating the Soweto uprisings or the Freedom Charter.[39] As the appointed date for the nation-wide protests drew closer and with its proposed security legislation still outstanding, Botha took the decision to impose a full state of emergency. On 12 June 1986 he announced before parliament the declaration of a country-wide state of emergency:

> [S]poradic cases of violence have begun to increase again and they have begun to assume such proportions that I

> am of the opinion that the ordinary laws of the country which are now on the statute book are insufficient to enable the government to ensure the safety of the public and to maintain public order. In fact, the government has information at its disposal concerning what is being planned for the coming days by radicals and revolutionary elements. This constitutes a real danger to all population groups in this country . . . I have decided to introduce a state of emergency throughout the entire country, including the self-governing states.[40]

Unlike the previous partial state of emergency, the new decree represented a cohesive package aimed at defusing the internal crisis. Reflecting the experiences of the previous two years, the array of regulations promulgated under the emergency were designed in such a way that they covered virtually all aspects of the existing and potential revolutionary threat.[41] According to former Secretary of the State Security Council, Lt.-General Pieter van der Westhuizen, the spectacle of resurgent violence in the townships caused the government to abandon the 'half measures' employed previously.[42] In particular, the government replaced the haphazard restrictions on the media with a body of regulations that effectively limited its ability to report on the unrest.[43] The scope of the state of emergency, covering all parts of the country, obviated the situation of activists moving to non-emergency regulated areas which characterized the previous partial state of emergency.

Structures

The imposition of a full state of emergency coincided with the restructuring of the National Coordinating Committee (NCC) which, as the committee charged with coordination and liaison activities between the National Security Management System (NSMS) and the National Welfare Management System (NWMS), had served as a focal point for decision-making during the partial state of emergency. Problems encountered by the NCC resulted in its restructuring and transformation into a new institution, the National Joint Management Centre (NJMC).[44] Placed at the centre of the state structures, the NJMC not only developed policy recommendations but it coordinated policy implementation between the NSMS and the NWMS, and by answering directly to the Office of the State President, it ensured that the day-to-day running of the emergency was accessible to the highest office in the land.[45] Within the NJMC two committees, one a Joint Security Committee and the other a National Constitutional, Economic and Social Committee, were charged with the specific task of coordinating policy between the 'security community' and the 'welfare community'.[46] Critical to understanding the importance of the establishment of the NJMC was the fact that it represented the elevation of the security establishment to the centre of power.

> The most decisive institutional expression of [the proponents of counter-revolutionary strategy] new ascendancy in the state was the dissolution of the National Coordinating Committee and the transfer of its functions to the NJMC. For the first time, the security establishment was entrusted with the coordination of both security and welfare decision-making functions.[47]

The institutional lifeblood of the full state of emergency was the now fully activated NSMS (or, as it came to be called, the National Management System). With the imposition of the full state of emergency, the entire NSMS was geared to the implementation of the demands of counter-revolutionary strategy. Through seminars conducted on counter-revolutionary strategy at the regional and local level by NJMC and Bureau of Information officials, the JMCs and their subunits turned their attention to the administration of the three main components of the new strategy as constructed by the NJMC: stability, socio-economic upliftment and political reform.[48]

The first task which the newly established NJMC set for itself was an analysis of the crisis facing the country. It concluded that the township rebellion was rooted in five fundamental factors: 'unsound local authorities, unemployment, poor housing, insufficient education and inadequate medical services.'[49] These conditions were deemed to be particularly prevalent in 36 of the black townships where, as NJMC research demonstrated, 90 per cent of all of the unrest incidents occurred. It was these same adverse socio-economic conditions which, in the view of the study, were exploited by the revolutionary activists to serve their particular cause. Linking the study with the principal objectives of the full state of emergency as outlined by Botha – the restoration of law and order (stability), the return to normality (normality)[50] and the creation of circumstances which would be conducive socio-economic and political development (development) – the NJMC devised a counter-revolutionary plan to thwart the course of the revolution. It consisted of:

> Establishing short-term stability by neutralising those actions taken by the revolutionaries which could not be classified as actions of a democratic nature. These steps were:
> (a) To limit intimidation by isolating those members of the 'People's Army' who were responsible for deeds of intimidation. This meant that quite often people had to be locked up without trial.
> (b) Limiting armed propaganda by restricting the publication of visual images of violence and destruction. This was done by means of media regulation.
> (c) Restricting the political activities of organisations furthering the aims of the ANC and the SACP. Thirty-three organisations had various restrictions placed upon them. It should be stressed that these are short-term actions and are only reactive measures.
> Developing a long-term plan to eliminate the causes of unrest. Socio-economic development was introduced in three phases:
> Phase 1 was directed at 36 critical towns; Phase 2 involved an additional 16 towns; Phase 3, which commenced in January 1989, involved every one of the more than 700 black towns in South Africa.
> Once stability had been created and the socio-economic needs of the people were being satisfied, the political aspirations had to receive high priority.[51]

Through the employment of this newly devised strategy, the NJMC hoped, in the words of the Secretary of the State Security Council, General van der Westhuizen, to 'lower the revolutionary climate' in the townships and lay the groundwork for socio-economic and political reform.[52]

Establishing Stability and Normality

The first requirement of the new counter-revolutionary strategy was the establishment of order in the flash points of the rebellion. With unrest incidents running at 12 255 in the first half of 1986,[53] the security forces were faced with the daunting prospect of reining-in an insurrection of revolutionary proportions. Their response was to increase security personnel in the townships (upwards of 8000 SADF troops served in the townships),[54] to rely upon the extended powers given to the security forces under the state of emergency – allowing for the massive detention of suspected activists and the imposition of martial law restrictions – coupled with the introduction of outright military-style action and support for local vigilante forces. The institution which served as the primary vehicle for directing and coordinating this response at the local level was the mini-Joint Management Centre.

The initial step taken by the mini-JMCs in unrest areas was to establish a Joint Operations Centre (JOC) within the affected location. This was invariably set up at the local police station within the township itself. Ensconced within the JOC, the Security committee (VEIKOM) consisted of local SADF and SAP commanders, intelligence officers from NIS as well as members of other relevant government departments. The chairman of this committee, usually drawn from either the SADF or the SAP, supervised an array of forces including SADF troops from the local command, SAP forces, auxiliary police (*kitskonstabels*)[55] and municipal police. Coordination with security personnel from the homelands as well as private security firms was emphasized in certain cases. These forces were charged with the task of patrolling the township, conducting house-to-house searches, and setting up roadblocks. Supporting the work of the JOCs, was the Joint Intelligence Centre (GIS/JIC) which monitored the activities of townships organizations such as the civic associations, youth groups, trade unions and political organizations. Staffed principally by employees from the military and national intelligence services, the GIS/JICs also served as a link between local events and the JMC's own Joint Intelligence Committee as well as the Intelligence committee at the submanagement level.[56] Finally, a Communications committee (KOMKOM) assisted the process through its propaganda campaign aimed both at the local community and the national (and international) media at large.

To take one example, the township of Alexandra, situated on the edge of one of the wealthier suburbs of Johannesburg, had been a centre of acute unrest in the period between 1985 and 1986. The murder of a student activist in February 1986 set off a cycle of ever-escalating violence in the township, with councillors and policemen accused of collaboration and coming under assault.[57] As the death toll mounted, massive funerals and illegal gatherings attended by thousands of township residents multiplied under the watchful eye of the security forces. Reacting to the emergence of vigilantism, activists established self-defence units in early May 1986, putting Alexandra at the forefront of the insurrection.[58] With the 'comrades' gaining the upper hand in the daily street battles, the situation was such that the township was declared to be 'a liberated zone' by street committee youths.[59]

With the imposition of the full state of emergency in June and the reintroduction of the security forces in strength into Alexandra, the township underwent a transformation. Under the auspices of the Security committee of the mini-JMC established to administer the township in September, the security forces launched house-to-house searches, arrested known or suspected activists, and engaged in the careful monitoring of anti-apartheid organizations, thereby successfully stifling the incipient rebellion. In addition, vigilante attacks on activists – which had been an ongoing feature of the conflict since the beginning of the year – multiplied, driving activists further underground.[60] A 24-hour roadblock was established at the entrances to the township. The result of these strident actions by the mini-JMC was that during the whole of 1987, no incidents of unrest were reported by the security forces in Alexandra.[61]

Within one hundred days of the imposition of the full state of emergency, UDF officials had conceded that their movement had been thrown onto the defensive.[62] By January

1987, with the full state of emergency only six months old, administration officials judged that stability had essentially been achieved and normality was within reach.[63] The following September, security forces felt sufficiently in control of the situation in Alexandra to withdraw roadblocks which had been in place since March 1986; however, SADF troops continued to be stationed in the township.[64]

Socio-economic Upliftment

The next step in the counter-revolutionary framework was the introduction of substantive socio-economic upliftment programmes. Targeting some of the most egregious examples of deprivation, the government's upliftment projects sought to meet the fundamental socio-economic causes that fed unrest in the townships. This approach, which deliberately echoed McCuen's 'oil spot' thesis, saw the infusion of significant financial and other resources into townships such as Alexandra (Johannesburg), Mamelodi (Pretoria), New Brighton (Port Elizabeth), and Bonteheuwel (Western Cape). All in all, 36 townships were targeted for special attention by the state.

As in the case of securing stability and normality within the townships, the mini-JMCs took the lead in introducing the socio-economic phase of counter-revolutionary strategy. While in the first instance the Security committee of the mini-JMCs played a leading role in the process, at this point the Constitutional-Economic-Social committee – known as the Welfare committee – occupied the central position. Composed of representatives from government departments and local political structures, the Welfare committee set the priorities and administered the introduction of socio-economic upliftment programmes in the affected areas. As in the previous phase, the Communications committee provided support for the efforts of the Welfare committee. Another component was the establishment of the smallest units in the whole NSMS structure, local management centres and joint liaison forums, to provide linkages between the private sector and the NSMS institutions on issues of common concern.

The approach taken by the Welfare committee was to utilize

consultation with the community and intelligence sources as a means of identifying key socio-economic problems plaguing the community. A strategy for tackling these problems would then be devised by the Welfare committee, incorporating the expertise and resources made available by the range of government departmental representation on the committee. In those instances in which outside knowledge and/or resources were required, the Welfare committee would seek to establish joint liaison forums with the private sector. Among the most common rationales behind the creation of a joint liaison forum was the mini-JMC's need to secure financial assistance for a particular project such as housing developments or direct involvement in the construction or maintenance of such projects. An imperative of this entire socio-economic upliftment programme was the effort to bolster the battered position of the black local authorities in the townships. Therefore, whenever possible, the Welfare committee sought to utilize existing officially recognized local government structures as the vehicles for the introduction and implementation of projects in an effort to confer greater authority and legitimacy upon these structures in the eyes of township residents. In fact, one of the primary tasks of the Communications committee was to portray the introduction of various socio-economic programmes as directly attributable to the actions of black local authorities.

Finally, one of the crucial issues facing virtually all the Welfare committees in unrest areas was that of the rent and service boycotts. Crippling the financial status of the black local authorities from the outset, the Welfare committees identified the termination of the boycotts as central to the re-establishment of these structures in the townships on a permanent and viable basis. For this reason, the Welfare committee devoted significant resources to the development of strategies to break the boycotts.

Again, in the case of Alexandra, the re-establishment of stability – albeit done through the imposition of strict security measures – allowed for the introduction of a significant array of socio-economic programmes. Entitled the 'Alexandra Urban Renewal Proposal', the new development plan castigated the previous approach to the township as failing to:

> improve the standard of living of some ninety per cent of the residents of Alexandra . . . [and contributing] towards the worrying security situation and the resignation of the former councillors.[65]

Following consultation with members of the community and outfitted with a budget of R116 million, the mini-JMC in charge of the area set about building 6000 new houses and 700 apartments equipped with basic services. Infrastructural improvements featured high on the Welfare committee's priorities, and subsequently paved roads, sewerage and drainage systems, installation of electricity and indoor plumbing, and street lighting were introduced to the township. Longer-term projects included the establishment of new schools, a health clinic, a technical training centre and a sports stadium.[66] Critical to the success of this venture was an emphasis on black home ownership which would help recoup the cost of infrastructural improvements, foster conservative values among home owners and provide employment within the community.[67] White businesses located on the outskirts of the township were encouraged by the mini-JMC to participate through its joint liaison forum in these socio-economic upliftment projects. The 'Progress Through Employment' campaign launched in November 1987 – which featured a host of business, employment and training opportunities – was an outgrowth of this cooperative effort between the mini-JMC, the Sandton business community and the Alexandra Civic Association.[68]

Linked with the implementation of socio-economic upliftment programmes in Alexandra was an ongoing propaganda campaign administered by the Bureau of Information through the Communications committee of the mini-JMC. Operating with the principle that 'good government . . . must see and be seen', newspapers such as the *Newsletter to the People of Alexandra* and the *Metropolitan Digest*, as well as a comic strip called *Alex and Friends*, explaining the government's position on issues ranging from the rent boycott to the Freedom Charter were distributed.[69]

Turning to the mini-JMCs' efforts to break the rent and service boycott, the case of Lekoa township is illustrative of the strategy typically employed. In late 1985, several months before the institution of the full state of emergency, a document outlining a strategy for overcoming Lekoa's costly rent and service boycott was circulated at the Lekoa Town Council. The document proposed that 'local collection action groups' composed of councillors, police and other officials be established and mandated to secure back payment of rents by any means available.[70] Among the suggested strategies to be utilized by the mini-JMCs were: to identify those township residents with sufficient income and bring legal action against them; convince employers to deduct rental costs from employees' salaries; establish recreational weekend camps for township youths where they would be lectured on the process of constitutional change and the need to pay rent, and would in turn convince their parents to do so; overturn alternative structures such as street committees and replace them with government-sanctioned 'law and order committees'.[71]

The document singled out the mini-JMCs as the main mechanism for implementing the breaking of the rent and service boycott, but it noted that all decisions regarding the introduction of further increases in rent were to be taken at the Cabinet level, stating that, 'All actions are to be taken in mini-Gesamentlike Bestuursentrums [mini-JMCs] and [in that] context . . . within [the] ambit of the National Security Management System.'[72] Furthermore, it urged officials to avoid dealing with organizations not sanctioned by the government in resolving the boycotts declaring that, 'No acknowledgement through negotiations must be given to revolutionary groups or organisations.'[73]

Finally, the potential for 'winning the hearts and minds' of the local population through the application of this counter-revolutionary strategy, and the danger that this posed to anti-apartheid activists, was ably demonstrated during this period. To cite one example, the local MP in the Bonteheuwel and Bishop Lavis areas who sat on both local management committees, had a seat in the mini-JMC committee structure and headed up a local civic association.[74] His ability to retain these posts (though he eventually left the civic association), despite their fundamentally antithetical perspectives, underlined the potential for cooptation of the even those non-governmental structures specifically aligned against the state. The cooperative relationship established between the mini-JMC, the white business community and the Alexandra Civic Association (a UDF affiliate) – which nearly resulted in officials from the civic association participating in the 1988 municipal elections – was further confirmation of the strength of the counter insurgency propaganda campaign. Local activists in the Bonteheuwel region, while extremely critical of the ultimate ends of the projects introduced by the mini-JMCs, recognized both the benefits to the community and the dangers to their own aims.

> We don't reject these things [the socio-economic projects]. These are demands that the community has been campaigning about for several years. But we know we are getting these things though [*sic*] our struggle, and the committee should not be getting the credit.[75]

Political Reform

The decision to call for nation-wide municipal elections in January 1988 was both a demonstration of the Botha administration's confidence in the success of the full state of emergency and a recognition that the political structures put into place in the early eighties were in dire need of the legitimizing influence of electoral politics if they were to play a role in the proposed next stage of political reform. With ten months until the actual polling took place, the government and anti-apartheid forces began squaring up for the contest that promised to be a barometer of their respective abilities to exercise influence and power over the black population.

As a direct result of the success of the security forces in curtailing the anti-apartheid movement, for the first time since the inception of the UDF there commenced a debate within that organization over participation in government-sponsored structures. UDF leader Archie Gumede signalled on more than one occasion that the anti-apartheid organization was considering whether, in utilizing the elections in order to gain control of the black local authorities, it would be bestowing legitimacy on an institution against which it had defined itself so ardently.[76] The Alexandra Civic Association also tentatively broached the subject of participation and while this position was shelved, civic leaders did in fact subsequently join the town council.[77] In the end, the UDF chose to embark on its existing strategy of boycotts and, despite government prohibitions against these measures, calls were issued by its national executive for non-participation in the elections.

In order to combat the threat of a boycott, the government decided to spread the actual polling dates over a ten-day period. This step was coupled with the passage of legislation in June allowing for postal voting by township residents. As the polling date(s) neared, the Bureau of Information launched an all-out propaganda campaign at a cost of R4.8 million to encourage Africans to vote.[78] For its part, acting under the shadow of emergency regulations prohibiting such action, the anti-apartheid movement launched a counter-propaganda campaign involving the issuance of pamphlets, paid advertisements and graffiti, as well as informal meetings urging township residents not to vote.[79]

A large show of force by the SADF and the SAP, stationed at key polling stations as well as patrolling the townships, contributed to the relative calm surrounding the election. In spite of this, incidents of intimidation did apparently occur, including 40 armed attacks on local authority structures.[80] Concurrently, the anti-apartheid movement accused the government of coercion through implied threats to Africans under its employment and that of para-statals. Nevertheless, according to some observers, 'Mobilisation against the election, though present in the 1988 elections paled into insignificance compared to the vigorous campaign mounted during the 1983 elections.'[81]

In the end, the results of the elections were disappointing for the government, with it claiming an overall poll of 25.1 per cent, while the UDF declared that a more accurate figure was 5 per cent.[82] Amongst the African population, the low overall turnout represented a strong rebuke for the government's programme of winning support for the local authorities. Nonetheless, however precarious their mandate (and the implications therefore of their ability to sustain themselves), with 247 of the 260 town councils participating in the elections, the African local authorities structures were back in place and running.[83]

In the Coloured and Indian communities, the polling indicated a growing level of support and legitimacy for the local authority structures. In this case, 44.5 per cent of Coloured voters went out to vote for local authorities[84] while within the Indian community, overall participation was lower, averaging 34.8 per cent.[85] Any analysis of levels of voter participation in these communities must take into account the strength of the government propaganda campaign and the security force presence during the election; nevertheless, when compared to polling rates in the municipal elections of the early eighties, there was a marked increase in participation. This fact seems to point to a growing degree of acceptability and legitimacy within these communities for the structures of the new political dispensation.

While the results of the municipal elections could be said to have issued a partial verdict on the efficacy of counter-revolutionary strategy, they did not represent the fullest expression of that strategy for two reasons. In the first instance, the necessity of having a significant security force presence in place during the electoral campaign was an indication that the strategy was still in process and not ready to challenge revolutionary forces without recourse to some form of implicit or explicit coercion. Secondly, it would be inaccurate to label the elections as the last phase of counter-revolutionary strategy. McCuen's call for the introduction of significant reforms to the political structure in the wake of restoring stability and implementing socio-economic reforms was yet to be heeded by the government. Rather, the 1988 municipal elections were a feature of the previous wave of institutionalized political change and as such did not represent any new alterations to the political structure. This point is underscored by the former Deputy Minister of Law and Order, Roelf Meyer, whose position placed him at the centre of the day-to-day administering of the state of emergency. Meyer characterized the period between 1987 and 1989 as one in which progress was made on the socio-economic side (of the counter-revolutionary equation) but no significant 'progress was made on the political side.'[86]

Natal

While the imposition of a full state of emergency brought sharp reductions in the levels of violence across the country, there remained one outstanding exception to this rule: Natal. In the townships which surrounded the city of Pietermaritzburg, the cycle of killing between UDF and Inkatha supporters rose in a new, sharper crescendo. There, the death toll reached 399 in 1987, a staggering 60 per cent of all killings in South Africa.[87] Underlying the escalation in violence were a combination of political rivalries, deep-set ethno-cultural animosities and, ultimately, a cult of violence which, once ignited, seemed inextinguishable.[88]

The formation of UDF affiliates in the Pietermaritzburg region was seen as threatening the traditional power base of KwaZulu's Inkatha Freedom Party. Given the ideological differences between the two groups, with the UDF hostile to participation in government-sanctioned political structures and Inkatha's willingness to engage in qualified participation, there was certain to be friction between the two organizations. Recruitment and counter-recruitment drives by the UDF and Inkatha in mid-1985 and the calling of various boycotts by civic associations and trade unions which were opposed by Inkatha, all became fodder for a conflict which rapidly escalated into violence. The South African security forces' open hostility to the UDF and its allies contributed to a willingness to either stand by passively or actively cooperate with Inkatha and the KwaZulu police in curbing the endeavours of these organizations.

Layered into this conflict were generational and ethno-cultural issues which were a feature of the confrontation in other parts of South Africa. With the UDF aligned organizations in the townships dominated by self-styled radical youth and those participating in local government structures overwhelmingly composed of the older generation, the issues of breakdown of the traditional rural authority structure came into play. Concurrently, the perception amongst the Zulu-dominated Inkatha movement that the UDF was controlled by Indians and Xhosa-speaking Africans, groups with whom the Zulu people have had a history of friction, fed into the hostility between the organizations.

Finally, while difficult to quantify, by the late eighties the conflict in Natal could be said to have developed into the kind of intractable situation which characterizes problems in the Middle East. The raids and counter-raids engineered by forces supporting the UDF or Inkatha, often led by youths with little understanding of the issues which motivated the rivalry in the first place, continued to occur against a backdrop of verbal recriminations by the leadership of these organizations.[89] The situation was such that, following the unbanning of the ANC and the establishment of a climate for peace at the highest level in these rival organizations, the fighting continued unabated.

Security: the External Dimension

The external environment posed an acute and contradictory dilemma for the South African government. On the one hand, the direct military threats to the Republic continued to be limited in nature, focused exclusively on the Angolan/Namibian issue. Outside of this area, the Southern African region remained not only quiescent but, in the case of Mozambique, actually moved closer diplomatically to South Africa. However, on the international front, the proliferation of the sanctions movement brought another dimension to the struggle, one in which the South African government was hard-pressed to find solutions.

Angola/Namibia

With the collapse of the Lusaka Agreement in mid-1985, the Angolan and South African governments returned once again to open hostilities. With Cuban troop strength increased to 40 000 and new Cuban and Soviet commanders in place, a second attack against Unita strongholds began to take shape in June 1986. Fapla and its allies – including three ANC battalions consisting of 300 men each – started its drive to the south-east but an alert Unita force checked the assault before it was able to gather momentum at the town of Cuito Carnavale.[90] Undeterred, yet another massive offensive was launched in September 1987 with Fapla troops – supported by tens of thousands of Cuban troops, sophisticated Soviet weaponry, and led by Soviet General Konstantin Shaganovitch – pressed once again towards the key provincial town of Mavinga. As the tide of battle began to shift away from Unita, the South African military was called in and, as in the last campaign, it brought in the 32 Battalion and threw its air power against Angolan troops. This time, the Angolans' improved performance and utilization of sophisticated Mig-23s against an increasingly aged South African Air Force dealt South African forces some significant losses.[91] The impact of the UN's mandatory arms embargo, effectively cutting South Africa off from much of the most contemporary and sophisticated military hardware, seemed to have played a part in this development.[92] Fapla and Cuban forces held their own for six months, under the personal command of Fidel Castro, against a combined Unita–SADF counter-offensive. While the withdrawal of SADF troops was touted as a victory in Luanda and Havana, the fact remained that the Angolan government was frustrated once again in their objective to dislodge Unita.[93]

The twin setbacks suffered by the SADF and the combined Angolan–Cuban forces in the 1987 Angolan campaign proved to be a watershed event. No longer able to guarantee the relatively cost-free (in terms of losses of white lives and irreplaceable military equipment) victories of the past and faced with the prospect of another defence of Unita the coming year, Pretoria looked to a diplomatic resolution of the conflict more keenly than ever. With the internal security situation in Namibia stabilized and the apparent success of the Civic Action programme in spreading socio-economic benefits to the Namibian community, circumstances appeared to favour an election which could usher in a friendly government in Windhoek. Coupled with this was the dissolution of any faith in the viability of maintaining the internal solution in the territory which, after three years of the Transitional Government of National Unity (T.GNU) had produced little more than a state of constant squabbling in Namibia.[94]

On the Angolan side, in spite of a tremendous expenditure of resources the hoped-for military victory over Unita still evaded the best efforts of the government and its communist allies. Linked with this was the dual burden of a stagnant economy and the grinding civil war. Dependent upon the Eastern Bloc for weaponry, training and troops, Luanda was particularly vulnerable to the policy changes emerging under Gorbachev. The reluctance of Soviet Union to fund the Angolan conflict, which had put it in the position of that country's major creditor,[95] began to have an impact on the fortitude of the Angolan government.

Faced with these adverse circumstances, both the South Africans and the Angolans moved away from the military option and began embracing a diplomatic solution to the conflict. Linkage between a Cuban withdrawal and the implementation of UN Resolution 435 was accepted in July after a series of meetings involving top South African, Angolan and Cuban officials. In early December 1988, the negotiating parties sat down in Brazzaville to discuss a formal settlement to the 13-year-old war. This was followed by a meeting in New York on 22 December at which the final version of a peace accord was signed.[96] The New York Accords called for the phased withdrawal of Cuban and South African troops from Angola and Namibia respectively, followed by the implementation of Resolution 435 and the independence of the former League of Nations mandate. An unwritten but vital part of the agreement was the simultaneous withdrawal of South African support for Unita and the rescinding of training bases for the ANC in Angola itself. The latter step, the fulfilment of a long-standing goal of Botha's regional policy, effectively put the South African state beyond the reach of the ANC's military wing, as thousands of Umkhonto we Sizwe guerrillas were shifted north to camps in Tanzania, Zambia and Uganda.[97] In the words of ANC and SACP biographers:

> The New York Accords were a bitter pill indeed . . . For the Soweto generation, teenagers who had left South Africa in 1976 determined to come home with guns to fight for their freedom, it was a heavy blow. They were now further from South Africa than they had been ten years earlier.[98]

Regional Policy in Southern Africa

Outside of Namibia and Angola, the regional environment diminished in relative importance during this period as the principle goal of destabilization – the collapse of the ANC support network in neighbouring countries – had in essence already been achieved. Having won this direct confrontation in Southern Africa, the theatre of conflict shifted to the wider international stage as the countries of the region played a leading role in formulating and promoting the case for sanctions against South Africa.

Regional Policy in Southern Africa: Zimbabwe

As in the past, relations between Zimbabwe and South Africa were marked by contradiction and conflict. Zimbabwe's hosting of the non-aligned movement conference in 1986 set the tone for Zimbabwean–South African relations for the rest of the decade. Concurrently, Mugabe's efforts to reroute Zimbabwean trade away from South Africa continued to be frustrated by his country's dependency upon the Republic and the debilitating civil war in Mozambique.

The convening of the Non-Aligned Movement Conference in Harare, held from 28 August to 7 September 1986, put the international spotlight on Southern Africa as never before. At the conference, delegates endorsed a nine-page policy statement on South Africa calling for wide-ranging sanctions as well as the establishment of a fund to assist those states bordering South Africa and provide financial support to the liberation movements. Despite this show of unity on the issue of South Africa, disagreements amongst key heads of states marred the proceedings. Worried that the implementation of sanctions by frontline states – especially if the West itself would not endorse them – would only serve to cripple their economies, Zambia's Kenneth Kaunda declared that taking such a step would be 'suicide'.[99] Kaunda was equally disparaging of Mugabe's call for an international military force to be levied against South Africa.[100] Subsequent efforts by the Zimbabwean government in July 1987 to eliminate all but the most essential imports from South Africa met with failure as the extent of Zimbabwean economic dependency on its neighbour became obvious.[101] Linked to this assessment was the inability of Harare to transform the rail link through Mozambique into a viable alternative to South African transport networks for reasons as varied as the guerrilla war in that country and the shortcomings of the Mozambican facilities.

With the outstanding exception of a bombing near an ANC office in 1988, direct South African intervention into Zimbabwean territory was nil during this period. Nevertheless, the ongoing indirect conflict in Mozambique crippled Zimbabwean efforts to reduce trading links with the Republic and drained government coffers in Harare, exacting a high toll on Zimbabwe. With an estimated 10 000 troops in place guarding the Beira corridor at a cost of $1 million (Zimbabwean) a day, Mugabe's government found itself in the position of playing a supportive role in a war which increasingly seemed unwinnable.

Regional Policy in Southern Africa: Mozambique

The failure of South African diplomacy to bring the government and Renamo together in October 1985, coupled with the revelations surrounding continued SADF covert support for the rebels, effectively scuttled the Nkomati Accord. South African–Mozambican relations reached a nadir with Samora Machel's untimely death in a mysterious plane disaster over South African territory twelve months later.[102] Once Machel's successor Joaquim Chissano had consolidated his position, the process of reconciliation between Mozambique and South Africa began anew through its revival of the Nkomati process. With the encouragement of Western sources, talks were reopened with South Africa over the reactivation of the Nkomati Accord's joint security commission in August 1987. This was followed by a meeting between Botha and Chissano in Tete province on 12 September 1988 in which the two leaders called for the 'reactivation and reinforcement' of the Nkomati Accord.[103] These discussions paved the way for the shipment of US $4.5 million of South African military equipment to protect Cahora Bassa and an opening of economic relations the like of which had not been seen for over a decade.[104] An array of joint committees were convened to discuss areas of mutual cooperation, including transportation, agriculture, economics and cooperation and development. Finally, Mozambique concluded a preferential trade agreement with the Republic that waived or reduced import surcharges on a number of Mozambican goods.[105]

Regional Policy in Southern Africa: Botswana, Lesotho and Swaziland

During this period, South African involvement in the BLS countries continued to focus on maintaining cooperation in dismantling remaining ANC structures such as the RPMCs and ousting ANC officials. In the case of Botswana, which had attempted to find a middle ground between Pretoria and the ANC, the South African government maintained pressure on the government in Gaborone to join other states in the region and adhere to a non-aggression pact. The Botswanan government, backed diplomatically by Britain and the United States, continued to resist any such official recognition of what amounted to its de facto compliance to South African demands. An SADF raid into Botswana in April 1988 resulting in the death of four persons accused by Pretoria of being members of the ANC received international condemnation. Clashes between the SADF and the ANC on the border in August were followed by the imposition of stricter movement control between the two countries and the construction of a security fence by South Africa.[106]

In the aftermath of the coup which toppled Chief Leabua Jonathan in January 1986, Lesotho moved away from confrontational politics to cooperative relations with South Africa. This was reflected in the development of a close relationship between the two countries' militaries and the establishment of an unprecedented level of economic cooperation. Specifically, the South African government gave R2 million for the construction of a military hospital in Maseru, seconded SADF troops for the project and provided military equipment to the Lesotho army.[107] On the economic side, the Highlands Water Treaty signed ten months after the coup paved the way for the development of a longstanding hydro-electric project between the two countries which promised to provide Lesotho with power and significant revenue.[108]

Finally, relations between Swaziland and South Africa continued to reflect the condition of inter-state harmony which emerged following the signature of the non-aggression pact of 1982. As was the case in post-coup Lesotho, cooperation between South African and Swazi security forces and South African economic assistance directed to Swaziland combined to make for a stable relationship between the two neighbours. In particular, the imposition of sanctions against South Africa by the international community afforded Swaziland an unprecedented opportunity to boost its trade, as the tiny kingdom became a conduit for many illegal South African goods.

The International Environment

Events in 1986, which saw the imposition of economic and financial sanctions by the United States, the Commonwealth and other Western states, marked the high point of the international campaign to isolate South Africa. Thereafter, despite some domestic pressures to introduce new sanctions or strengthen existing legislation, the governments of key Western states desisted from taking further steps against South Africa. In the case of the United States, the Comprehensive Anti-Apartheid Act required an annual Presidential report on the situation in South Africa which was to serve as the basis for further action, if deemed necessary. Given President Reagan's disinclination to impose sanctions to begin with, there was little likelihood that, barring egregious changes in the country, he would recommend additional sanctions. In the case of both the Commonwealth and the European Community, with British Prime Minister Margaret Thatcher playing an active role against sanctions in both organizations, the limitations of action had for the time being apparently been reached.

While by the late eighties the international sanctions campaign had come to a virtual standstill, its impact in South Africa was only beginning to be felt. Capital shortages, critically important to everything from socio-economic development projects to the introduction of new technology, threatened the future viability of the South African economy, as did the $22.1 billion losses due to the oil embargo.[109] A 1988 report on the impact of sanctions by one of the main mining houses declared:

> [S]anctions are beginning to have an adverse effect on the economy ... The expansion of the South African economy is being restricted by the continued absence of substantial capital inflows. There is a consensus that the confidence of overseas investors must be restored, before adequate funds from that source will again be available.[110]

The confidence of the foreign investor and the South African business community were shaken by events in the mid-eighties; the sanctions campaign, which proposed to turn white South Africans into a pariah nation, contributed to the beleaguered and embattled mentality amongst whites. The number of white immigrants exceeded that of emigrants in 1986, the first time in the modern era.[111] In psychological terms, the cultural, scientific and academic boycotts also acted to transform elite opinion from one of support for the government to hostility. The steady stream of white business, academic and political figures visiting ANC headquarters in Lusaka following Botha's disappointing Rubicon speech in August 1985 testified to this erosion of elite support.

The end result of the combination of world-wide economic slow-down, the fall in the price of South Africa's primary commodity, gold, and the costs attendant to the overcoming of the sanctions campaign was that the South African economy experienced a decline in its annual growth rate from a high of 5.9 per cent in the sixties to 1.7 per cent in the eighties.[112] With capital outflows increasing, and foreign investment since the mid-eighties nil, the prospects for a resurgence in prosperity for the country looked relatively bleak.

The impact of sanctions seemed to have the effect of thawing South African secrecy on its nuclear programme. On 21 September 1987, with pressure mounting to suspend South Africa from the International Atomic Energy Agency, the Botha government broke with its past policies on nuclear issues and announced that it was willing to 'commence negotiations with each of the nuclear weapon states on the possibility of signing the non-proliferation treaty.'[113] While clearly continuing to serve its original purpose as a bargaining chip with the international community on important issues such as Angola, the South African government was moving closer to dismantling its nuclear deterrent.

But the most momentous change in the international environment came with the ascension to power of Mikhail Gorbachev in the Soviet Union in 1985. Burdened by the exorbitant financial costs of simultaneously maintaining a modern military deterrent to the United States and supporting client regimes in the Third World, all underpinned by a stagnant economy and sterile political system, by the onset of the eighties the Soviet Union had reached a state of profound crisis. The depth of the crisis had been publicly acknowledged by the country's leadership since 1986, the year that Gorbachev's reformist regime initiated a significant reworking of the Soviet Union's approach towards the Third World. This dramatic policy reorientation was officially announced by Gorbachev:

> We are in favour of stepping up collective searches for ways of defusing conflict situations in the Middle East, in Central America, in Southern Africa, in all the planet's hot spots.[114]

It was against this background that the Soviet Union, previously a supporter of revolutionary means in Southern Africa, began to urge compromise with the South African government as the best avenue to power in light of the military setbacks experienced by the ANC.[115] With this came the gradual withdrawal of financial support for the liberation movements in the late eighties by both the Soviet Union itself and its client states in Eastern Europe; these developments were to play a significant part in fostering a climate conducive to a negotiated settlement in South Africa.

Conclusion

On the eve of Botha's resignation in August 1989, the security situation in Southern Africa had – from Pretoria's perspective – achieved a level of overall stability such as the government had not experienced since the advent of the township rebellion five years earlier. Domestically, the introduction of the full state of emergency had effectively crippled the anti-apartheid movement within a few short months of its imposition. The prosecution of counter-revolutionary strategy in the townships, while not free from mis-steps and controversy, had begun the long process of simultaneously ameliorating the worst features of township life and rebuilding the government's local government system. Despite efforts to disrupt the elections of 1987 and 1988, the successful conclusion of these events underlined the relative balance of power between the government and those organizations aligned against it. The determination of the government to retain the security measures introduced under the State of Emergency was reflected in Deputy-Minister Roelf Meyer's assertion that the State of Emergency could last for three years or more if that was deemed necessary to restore political balance.[116]

Externally, the Gordian knot of Namibian independence and massive Cuban involvement in Angola was cut with the signing of the New York Accords. Thereafter, Soviet and Cuban influence in the region – already in eclipse globally – rapidly declined. With respect to Namibia, even the prospect of a hostile Swapo government in place in Windhoek, long a source of concern for the South African government worried about the establishment of another sanctuary for insurgency, was muted through the terms of settlement itself and the development of a favourable international environment. In the rest of the region, the destabilization campaign of the first part of the eighties had neutralized those states pursuing policies which had been actively hostile towards South Africa. Furthermore, through a combination of the conscious targeting of alternative structures such as SADCC and the overall ineffectiveness of those institutions to realize their potential, economic ties with South Africa were actually reinforced during this period. As for the liberation movements themselves, relentless South African military and diplomatic measures had forced their withdrawal to bases far removed even from Southern Africa. Only the failure to stave off the introduction of sanctions by the international community, partially a product of diplomacy on the part of states of the region, marred the otherwise auspicious security environment fostered by the South African government in support of its ambitions.

SOCIO-ECONOMIC REFORM POLICY

The introduction of socio-economic reforms by the Botha administration, after gaining momentum in the middle of the decade, had reached an impasse by the end of the eighties. With the bulk of the most onerous apartheid legislation publicly discredited by its own officials if not actually repealed, the government was confronted with the problem of tackling the remaining so-called pillars of the apartheid system: the Separate Amenities Act and the Group Areas Act. As Botha had maintained throughout the reform process that the retention of separate educational facilities and separate residential areas was a *sine qua non* of any socio-economic change in the country, and indeed had recently campaigned on the sanctity of these very issues, it was difficult to broach the subject without alienating his white constituents. At the same time, the exigencies of the reform process increasingly demanded that these issues be confronted. Caught between the two imperatives, the government vacillated, effectively casting further doubt upon the credibility of its commitment to the stalled reform programme.

Government Initiatives

The President's Council's report on the Separate Amenities Act and the Group Areas Act was not released until September 1987, well after the white elections. The content of the document, entitled the *Report of the Committee for Constitutional Affairs of the President's Council on the Report of the Technical Committee, 1983 and Related Matters*, was both critical of the implementation of these Acts over the years and, simultaneously, served as an endorsement of certain features of that legislation. Specifically, the report called for the repeal of the Separate Amenities Act, declaring not only that in implementation it had failed to live up to the 'separate but equal' provisos of the law but that it no longer reflected the actual norms of the South African community itself.[117]

With respect to the Group Areas Act, the President's Council recommended that the principle of separate residential areas be retained by the government.[118] At the same time, the report recommended that municipalities be given the option to designate their residential areas as open to settlement by all population groups, pending the review of the provincial administrator. Under this scenario, real estate developers should be allowed to apply to have their developments denoted on a non-racial basis. Further suggestions by the President's Council included that business districts in all areas be opened to commercial activity by all population groups and that restrictions on the ownership of agricultural land be modified. Significantly, however, the President's Council declined to rule on the status of separate educational facilities.

The government's response to the President's Council's report offered equivocal supportive of its recommendations. Addressing parliament in October 1987, the State President suggested that elements of the Separate Amenities Act and the Group Areas Act should still be retained as they were central to each population group's right to maintain its own institutions and identity. Concomitant with this approach was, however, a willingness to allow for the establishment of jointly utilized amenities in certain instances and racially mixed residential areas if the process was 'implemented on a planned and orderly basis.'[119] On the issue of education, while upholding segregated schools in the public realm, Botha acknowledged the right of private schools to admit other population groups.

Socio-economic Reform Legislated

The implementation of the new urbanization strategy and, following the release of the President's Council's report, the introduction of changes to legalized social segregation occupied the bulk of legislative activity in the late eighties. Three bills amending the Group Areas Act were tabled by the Ministry of Constitutional Development and Planning. The most controversial of these, the Group Areas Amendment Bill, tightened restrictions on individuals who contravened residential segregation by empowering authorities to levy fines and conduct evictions of illegal tenants. The Bill also provided for financial compensation by the government to those individuals who found that the declaration of their residential area as a 'free settlement area' had, when put up for sale, caused their property to command a lower price than its 'basic value'.[120] With the advent of widespread opposition to the measures contained within the legislation, the Bill was withdrawn from consideration. The Free Settlement Areas Act of 1988 introduced provisions for municipalities to be declared 'free settlement areas', that is to say, areas in which the Group Areas Act and Black Communities Development Act would not apply. Under the Act, free settlement boards were to be established to hear evidence in particular cases in which residential areas sought this non-racial status. After reviewing the case, the board would make recommendations to the State President, who would then take the final decision, pending the approval of the Council of Ministers.[121] And finally, the Local Government Affairs in Free Settlement Areas Act, establishing political mechanisms for non-racial municipalities, was passed in 1988.

Criticism lodged against the pace of socio-economic reform in the House of Representatives and the House of Delegates grew louder towards the end of the decade. Under pressure from their limited constituencies and the anti-apartheid movement, the Coloured and Indian members of parliament needed to produce substantive changes in the conditions of their electorate in order to justify participation in government structures. The fact that onerous legislation like the Separate Amenities Act and the Group Areas Act continued to exist damaged the reputation of Coloured and Indian parliamentarians. It was this situation which motivated the actions of the leaders in the House of Representatives and the House of Delegates, effectively holding the political process hostage to that of socio-economic reform, and provoked a constitutional crisis in the tricameral parliament (see below).

Socio-economic Reform Implemented

Preliminary changes to social segregation which had been possible through the application of exemptions or deliberate oversight on the part of government officials (see Chapter 4) were accelerated in the wake of the government's public review of these policies. Assisting the process was the fact that the Ministry of Constitutional Development and Planning had relinquished responsibility over such matters to the provincial and local authorities concerned.[122] In particular, prohibitions against multiracial use of municipal facilities such as parks, swimming pools and beaches were cast aside either unilaterally or under pressure from black South Africans. Labour party leader Alan Henrickse's contravention of segregation law at the beaches of Port Elizabeth, an act which earned him a public reprimand by the State President, was but one example of the challenges made towards desegregating facilities. During this same period, hotels, restaurants and cinemas also moved towards desegregation of their institutions, though there remained outstanding exceptions to this rule as newly captured Conservative party municipalities attempted to turn back the clock on desegregation.[123]

Labour Policy

The uneasy relationship between the government and the black trade union movement, specifically the umbrella federation Cosatu, deteriorated measurably in the late eighties. This was linked to two phenomena, the growing politicization of the black labour movement and the introduction of emergency regulations aimed at curbing such activities. In particular, the detention of 614 union leaders affiliated with Cosatu in the first days of the emergency was greeted with harsh condemnation by the trade union movement.[124] The zenith of antagonism occurred during the South African Transport Service (SATS) strike of 1987 when six workers were killed and the trade union's headquarters were occupied by the police. The extensive damage done to the building and the arrest of over 400 Cosatu members did not quell the strikers' fervour.[125] Within a few days four 'scabs' were murdered in Cosatu House, raising tensions between the trade unionists and government officials to unprecedented levels. After another police occupation of the building, Cosatu House was destroyed in a bomb attack by right-wing terrorists. Against the background of these incidents, in February 1988 the government extended emergency regulations so as to put additional restrictions on Cosatu's ability to engage in or advocate political activity.

During this same period, the Department of Manpower attempted to swing 'the balance of power back towards management'.[126] The result was the passage of the Labour Relations Amendment Act of 1988 which sought to reverse the direction of labour relations as interpreted by the Industrial Courts. While court rulings had effectively disallowed the dismissal of workers on political grounds and supported the right to strike, the new law gave the employers greater latitude in terms of laying off workers, introduced criteria which reduced the scope of what were considered to be permissible grounds for a strike, weakened the position of trade unions in collective bargaining process by disavowing the majoritarian principle, and made labour liable for losses incurred during an industrial action.

At the same time, Cosatu experienced the limitations of its strength when a series of stayaways organized to protest issues ranging from the state of emergency itself to the police shooting of a union member only met with a modest response from the rank and file.[127] Acknowledging the success of the state of emergency in disrupting political campaigns, thereafter the Cosatu leadership broached involvement in political issues with greater care.[128] Despite this sobering reassessment of the potential for trade union action in the service of politics, Cosatu continued to play an active, if somewhat circumscribed, role in the wider anti-apartheid struggle. At its second national conference, in July 1987, the organization adopted the ANC's Freedom Charter as 'a guiding document which reflects the views and aspirations of the majority of the oppressed and exploited in our struggle against national oppression and economic exploitation'.[129] By the next year, 'disciplined alliances' between trade union affiliates of Cosatu and some of the UDF civic associations, representing a break from the tradition of distance and non-cooperation which had sometimes separated the two movements in the past (see Chapter 4), were beginning to be established.[130] The formation of the Mass Democratic Movement in 1989, bringing together the UDF and Cosatu into a loose anti-government alliance, was an important step in the fulfillment of this ambition.

Conclusion

The Botha administration's progress in the socio-economic sphere towards the end of the eighties, while often significant in terms of content, still retreated before the complete eradication of crucial aspects of apartheid legislation. Thus, while the government made clear its intention to engineer modifications to legislation enforcing social segregation, at the same time the Separate Amenities Act and Group Areas Act still remained on the statute books. Complicating its task was the fact that as other issues fell away, the contentious issue of the maintenance of separate educational systems for each population group, one of the NP's 'non-negotiables' of this stage of the reform process, came to the fore. This overall process of incremental reduction or elimination of discriminatory legislation had the unintended effect of highlighting those outstanding acts which enforced statutory discrimination and, at the same time, were considered by the Botha administration to be the most politically sensitive. The government's continuing hesitation over the status of these measures cast further doubt upon its commitment to reform.

POLITICAL REFORM POLICY

As in the past, the prospect of engineering significant change in the political structures of the country was the most contentious and difficult to achieve within the parameters of maintenance of state control of the process set by the Botha reform programme. This situation was to become particularly acute in the late eighties as the Botha administration attempted to woo black leaders into participating in its next phase of political reform. With virtually all black leaders calling for the release of Nelson Mandela as a prerequisite to participation in the National Council, and the government insisting on Mandela's renunciation of violence before any release, the process of political reform at the national level ground to a halt. Coupled with this situation was the eruption of a series of constitutional crises in the tricameral parliament instigated by Coloured and Indian leaders. As a result of all of these adverse developments, the DCDP – formerly the locus of the Botha reform programme – suffered a significant diminution of its power. Despite this situation, the process of change at the local and regional levels continued to evolve, with the Botha administration introducing the multiracial Regional Services Councils into municipal government and implementing the multiracial joint executive authorities structure between the provincial administrations and the 'homeland' authorities.

Political Reform at the Local and Regional Levels

Political reform at the local and regional levels focused on the long-awaited implementation of the Regional Services Councils. These structures, which brought together representatives from all statutory population groups on an executive board within a given municipality, marked a significant shift from the racially-exclusive structures of the past. At the same time, the RSCs kept intact the 'own/general' affairs dichotomy which formed the basis of the new dispensation at the national level.

Nearly two years after the legislation motivating their creation had been passed, the government finally introduced the RSCs. By 1989, sixteen RSCs were in operation in all parts of the country except Natal. Preliminary adjustments to the RSCs' controversial voting arrangement (see Chapter 4) began to take place with the RSC in Johannesburg initiating changes.[131] While the adjustments made did not alter the balance of power between white local authorities and black local authorities, an important precedent had been established for the evolution of the RSCs.[132] Another legislative step was taken with the passage of the Regional Services Councils Amendment Act in May 1988. The new law provided for cooperation between South African municipalities and adjoining non-independent homelands on the dispersement of municipal services, including the establishment of representation on the RSCs executive boards by homeland representatives, breaking down still further the administrative barriers between South Africa and the non-independent homelands.

The restructuring of provincial government, creating multi-racial executive authorities in the place of the former all-white Provincial Councils, was put into operation in 1986. Shorn of the legislative structure of the past, the provincial administrators and the new multiracial executive committees – minus African participation – went about the business of administering the provinces. In a major step towards realizing the government's stated goal of decentralization, the DCDP delegated authority over the Development of Black Community Act, the Black Local Authorities Act, the Group Areas Act and the Prevention of Squatting Act to the provinces. At the same time, given that the provincial administrator and the members of the executive committee were all appointed by the DCDP, the central government retained a strong say in the process. Heunis indicated in his address to the first meeting of the new provincial bodies that both law-making powers could be conferred upon them and they could be established on an electoral basis in the future 'should this fit into the unfolding pattern of constitutional development'.[133]

In the Natal region, where the Joint Executive Authorities Act created to give statutory standing to the KwaZulu/Natal Indaba project was already in place, the process of joint decision-making between different racially based authorities continued to develop. In November 1987, the KwaZulu/Natal Joint Executive Authority officially came into existence, bringing the two political entities together through the mechanism of a joint executive committee. Operating under the principle of consensus decision-making by a ten member committee selected equally from KwaZulu and Natal, the central authority undertook to administer to two territories without recourse to legislative powers.[134]

Finally, the Local Government Affairs in Free Settlement Areas Act of 1988 established a political structure for those persons residing in a 'free settlement area'. Accordingly, individuals in designated non-racial residential areas would vote for a non-racial management committee which would have the power to advise the white local authorities unless the provincial administrator chose to confer decision-making status upon the management committee.[135]

Reform at the National and Supra-national Level

The Botha administration's self-stated next phase of political reform, the establishment of a forum that would negotiate a new constitution, ran into trouble from the outset. Much to the dismay of government officials, neither government-sanctioned African leaders nor those outside of the state structure would participate in such a project. Concurrently, having turned his back on winning international acceptance for his reform programme, epitomized by the failed EPG mission of 1986, Botha desperately needed black domestic support and participation to give credibility to his evolving 'internal solution'. While the Botha administration sought to both modify and extend the projected forum, reiterating their sincerity and commitment to the process as well as introducing legislation which would allow African participation at the cabinet level, black resistance to that process solidified.

Government Initiatives: Negotiating Future Reforms

With the NP's electoral victory in May 1987, which had been cast as a referendum on the next stage of the reform process, the State President went public with his proposals of the future. An advertisement placed in all the major South African newspapers called on black South Africans to support the government's process of reform through participation in the next phase of the programme.

> In this election [May 1987] the White electorate gave me an overwhelming mandate to negotiate with representative leaders of our Black communities and groups about our common future . . . I am now extending my hand of friendship to all South Africans of goodwill. Join me in talks and negotiations. We will find the answers to our questions together.[136]

In a speech given that same month before a joint sitting of the tricameral parliament, the State President promised to become personally involved in the negotiation process with black leaders. In the wake of this accelerated approach to reform, Botha embarked on an unprecedented tour of black townships, utilizing this forum to reiterate his call for black participation in the National Council, as well as addressing black South Africans on African language television.

> I promise to assist those Black communities and interest groups who are ready and prepared to bring forward their leaders and representatives to serve on the National Council. The time for excuses is over. There is no justification for models, blueprints, and declarations of intent as excuses for not negotiating.[137]

By 14 July 1987, the first meeting on the shape of the proposed negotiating forum took place between government officials and black leaders. Limited to senior representatives of the United Municipalities of South Africa, an organization composed of members of the black local authorities, Heunis's disappointment in not securing broader representation amongst the African majority was manifest.

> We have pleaded in the past, and do so again today, that people should not paint themselves into a corner by saying they are not going to negotiate unless certain conditions are met.[138]

Concurrently, in response to commentary on its proposals and meetings with black leaders,[139] the government introduced a new facet into the process, expanding the representative range of the African community by calling for the election of regional representatives of the African population outside of the homeland structure to sit on the National Council. These elected representatives would be drawn from districts corresponding roughly to the nine development regions of the country – entitled the National Statutory Council Areas – and, along with the six homeland leaders, would constitute half of the statutory members of the National Council.[140] The other members would be the three chairmen of the tricameral parliament's Council of Ministers, the Minister of Constitutional Development and Planning, and any other cabinet ministers whom the State President wished in include, as well as up to ten individuals selected by the State President. The specific enabling legislation authorized the National Council to draw up plans for a new constitution and to serve as an interim body at the executive level where Africans, sharing power with the other population groups, would have the power of review of all legislation prior to its consideration by the Cabinet.[141] The Bill was tabled in parliament on 11 September 1987 and almost immediately withdrawn for reconsideration under protest from all quarters (see below).

Though the positive response to the proposed negotiating forum on the part of opposition groups was limited to the Black Urban Councils Association and a newly created political entity, the Federal Independent Democratic Alliance,[142] the Botha administration pressed ahead with its initiatives. In early November, the government released ANC and PAC prisoners, including one of Nelson Mandela's protegés, Govan Mbeki. Speculation was rampant that Mbeki's release was a trial run for the freeing of Mandela but that event was in fact not to occur under the Botha administration. The contentious debate over Mandela's release, one which pitted security force officials and conservatives against the reformist wing of the NP, hinged on his public renunciation of violence as a means for political change. Mandela's wish to negotiate, even in the aftermath of the imposition of the state of emergency, coupled with his continuing insistence on an unconditional release, presented the government with a tantalizing, if unpredictable, path out of the political conundrum. But still it hesitated. For his own part, the newly freed Mbeki was unrepentant in his support of the ANC and SACP and, after a brief period of public scrutiny, he was served with a banning order.

Faced with continued resistance to the National Council, Botha sought to revive the flagging fortunes of his constitutional initiative on a number of occasions by re-emphasizing both his government's flexibility on the actual structure of the institution and the immutables for negotiation (maintenance of group basis of polity, no domination and protection of minority rights). In a speech before parliament in April 1988, delivered on the eve of the introduction of the Extension of Political Participation Bill, Botha committed the government to restructuring the President's Council to include Africans, as well as reduce its status to that resembling other statutory bodies attached to the Office of the State President so as to make way for the enhanced role of the negotiating forum. Rechristening the National Council the 'Great Indaba', Botha pleaded once again for black participation:

> The Government is not bound by any specific name, form, composition or functions for such a body. The Government is bound to the concept of a forum for consultation. I hope Parliament will proceed to give attention to the legislation which makes provisions for a formal forum for such consultation. I want to emphasis that the proposed legislation is not a prescriptive map. The council will be a formal forum within the framework of which the Government wishes to pursue its politics of consultation.[143]

Despite these measures, the black South African community remained unmoved by the proposals.

Reform Apartheid Collapses: Black South Africans and the National Council

From the outset, the Botha administration's proposals for the next phase in political reform had come under fire from the black South African community. For virtually the entire political spectrum of the African leaders (and many Coloured and Indian leaders as well), the government's format for political change proved to be unacceptable. At the heart of these leaders' objections were: the composition of the forum, which was not only biased in favour of government representatives but allowed the State President to exercise significant authority over the negotiation process; and the fact that discriminatory legislation remained on the statute books and that political parties and individuals remained banned or imprisoned. This latter point was most dramatically symbolized by the continued incarceration of the ANC's *de facto* leader, Nelson Mandela, by the state. It was this issue in particular which served as a stumbling block to black participation, rendering this phase of the government's political reform programme stillborn.

For those black leaders who had opted to participate in the government-sanctioned structures such as the tricameral parliament, the black local authorities and the 'homeland' system the price of cooptation had been high. Isolated to varying degrees within their communities, these individuals were particularly anxious to win legitimacy for themselves and their offices. Recognizing that at this point participation in a further mutation of the South African polity would render them, in the eyes of both their own constituencies and the global community at large, as pariahs, these black leaders balked at joining the government's forum outright. Thus Tom Boya, president of the United Municipalities of South Africa and mayor of Daveyton, indicated that he and his colleagues were unwilling to join in the next stage of reform until all political parties were unbanned, all political prisoners were released, a general amnesty was granted to exiled South Africans, and all discriminatory legislation was scrapped.[144] Buthelezi, whose claim to substantive domestic support and commensurate international standing made his participation absolutely crucial, continued to press for the release of political prisoners and the unbanning of political organizations as a prerequisite to participation in the National Council.

> They [the political prisoners] simply must be released, and once they are free then we can start talking about the unbanning of Black political organizations. Unless they are released, the State President's National Council will remain fatally flawed . . . If a free Dr. Mandela and I worked shoulder to shoulder . . . this country would make significant strides forward.[145]

Along with the Chief Minister of KwaZulu, four other homeland leaders voiced their determination to oppose the National Council.[146] Convinced that ANC participation in the negotiations was imperative to the success of any such project, the release of Nelson Mandela became the precondition of participation for most of these representatives.

In contrast to officially recognized leadership, the issue of participation in any government-inspired negotiation forum was less divisive or controversial. The UDF condemned the government's attempts to establish a negotiating forum, saying that:

> [The] proposals for a national statutory council including the planned regional services councils will fail because

> not only were they undemocratically conceived but they will represent the coming together of rejected apartheid bodies with no legitimacy.[147]

Azapo also ridiculed the suggestion that it join in such an exercise.[148] So too did the exiled ANC, which characterized the forum as 'cosmetic'.[149] In all these cases, participation in any negotiation structure was linked to fundamental changes in both the state's stance on security, including the lifting of the state of emergency, and the elimination of apartheid legislation, as well as an implicit rejection of the state's whole approach to controlling reform itself.

Standing at the centre of this entire controversy was the enigmatic person of Nelson Mandela. With virtually all black political organizations calling for his release as a prerequisite to any participation in negotiations, Mandela's position became crucial to the maintenance of the momentum of the process of change. Bolstered by a growing international campaign calling for his release, Mandela defied government attempts throughout their intermittent dialogue to draw him into the reform programme on its terms. His desire to engage government officials in a continuing dialogue notwithstanding, Mandela's steadfast refusal to categorically abandon the ANC's military option and the government's unwillingness to negotiate with individuals or organizations that espoused violence as a tool for change, put the two at loggerheads. This stalemate effectively put a brake on black participation in negotiations and consequently the Botha political reform initiatives ground to a halt.

The Decline of Heunis and the DCDP

Throughout the Botha era, the DCDP, steered by Chris Heunis, was the 'undisputed flagship of reform'. Starting out as a amalgamation of planning divisions drawn from the Office of the Prime Minister in 1982, by early 1986 the DCDP had mushroomed into a large bureaucratic institution with control over virtually all significant aspects of the reform process. This included the black local authorities, the new multiracial RSCs and the new multiracial provincial councils. But in the end, it was the personal relationship between Heunis and Botha that sustained the government's commitment to the reform programme as developed in the DCDP. As two long-time observers noted:

> As long as the State President was committed to reform and conditions in civil society were such that security concerns were not dominant, this fragile relationship acted as the conduit for reformist policy-making. When these conditions changed, so too did the functionality of Heunis' relationship with Botha.[150]

By 1986, confronted by ever-deepening rebellion in the townships and the concomitant inability to introduce proposed reformist measures there, Botha had shifted the emphasis of his incrementalist reform programme to the security side of the equation. Behind this action was a marked deterioration in the relationship between Heunis and Botha, with the State President blaming Heunis for the government's failure to anticipate black rejection of the constitutional changes implemented and the conflicts within the tricameral parliament with Coloured leader Alan Hendrickse.[151] In addition, the State President's interest in promulgating independent city states was viewed with dismay in the DCDP where it was seen as an apostasy to the long-term reformist vision held by Heunis and members of his department.[152]

Under the exigencies of the newly adopted counter-revolutionary strategy, the security establishment took on a greater role in the decision-making process through its position at the helm of the state of emergency, the NJMC. It was during this period that Heunis lost his privileged access to Botha, highlighted by his lack of knowledge about the military strike against the frontline states during the EPG mission. Subsequently, the DCDP was divided into two institutions, a Department of Information and Constitutional Planning, dealing with political change, and a Department for Development Planning, focusing on socio-economic issues. This bifurcation of the DCDP, mirroring the institutional divisions informed by counter-revolutionary strategy between security and welfare spheres, further crippled the ability of Heunis to direct events. On the eve of the imposition of the full state of emergency, Heunis reacted to events in a speech before parliament.

> I want to emphasis that it is the government's standpoint that it is not and cannot be the aim of the security forces to take over state activities but that it is the responsibility of the security forces to create conditions within which other state activities can function properly in the social and political spheres.[153]

With the NP's electoral victory in May 1987 and the subsequent launching in earnest of the campaign to secure black participation in the negotiating forum, the DCDP slipped further from the centre of decision-making. In June 1987, a trusted colleague of the State President, Stoffel van der Merwe, was appointed to the position of liaison with black leaders on the negotiation process and asked to report directly to Botha himself. The deterioration in the Heunis–Botha relationship was to continue through the rest of Botha's term in office, culminating in the withdrawal of security clearance for two senior DCDP officials in October 1988.

Political Reform at National and Supra-national Level Legislated

During this period, the legislation introduced relating to political reform at the national and supra-national level centred on the Botha administration's proposed negotiating forum. The patent unwillingness of black South African leaders to publicly associate themselves with this phase in the political process was to have an impact at the legislative level as well as outside it. Specifically, the Coloured and Indian politicians in the tricameral parliament, anxious to elevate their standing among their constituencies, deliberately fomented a constitutional crisis in an effort to win substantive concessions on apartheid legislation from the government.

The Promotion of Constitutional Development Act, the legislation establishing the National Council, was initially introduced in September 1987 but soon withdrawn under a storm of criticism. Finally, after being reviewed by a government committee, a somewhat modified version of the Bill was placed before a joint sitting of the tricameral parliament the following June. This one called for the establishment of a negotiating forum which would include Africans and would consider developing a new constitution for the country as well as empower it to make recommendations to the State President on legislation before the tricameral parliament or any other matters of national importance.[154] In addition to previous measures, the State President was empowered to select up to 13 representatives to the negotiating forum, of which only five could be government officials. The Promotion of Constitutional Development Act was voted upon separately by each house and passed in June 1988.

The Constitutional Second Amendment Act, allowing for the appointment of persons outside of the tricameral parliament to the position of minister or deputy minister, was also debated at the joint sitting of all three houses of parliament in June. With this law in place, the State President would be in a position to bring Africans in at the highest levels of government. In the wake of protest from the House of Representatives and House of Delegates, the Bill was withdrawn from consideration and put to parliament for a second reading in May 1989. It was never passed.

Another feature of the next phase of the Botha reform programme was the introduction in July 1988 of the Extension of Political Participation Bill. The result of discussions with an unspecified group of African leaders, the Bill established a series of regional councils with executive and legislative powers for Africans outside of the homeland system. Modelled on the 'own' affairs administrative structures developed for the other statutory population groups, the councils were to be empowered to rule on social welfare, education, community development, local government and other related issues. At the same time, issues like health, agriculture, water supply and various procedural matters were considered to be outside the purview of these structures. Using the nine development regions as the basis upon which the territorial boundaries of the councils were to be drawn, the State President would then call for elections in these regions. The number of representatives to sit on such a structure, their remuneration, the length of term and a host of other matters were left to the determination of the State President. The State President had the power to dissolve councils and, should any council fail to function, the Minister of Constitutional Development and Planning would take over its administration.[155]

During this period, a constitutional crisis developed over the consideration and passage of legislation which was to threaten the viability of the tricameral parliament. The first sign of the crisis appeared in November 1987 when Botha's expressed wish to postpone the upcoming elections in the House of Assembly from 1989 to 1992 was blocked by the House of Representatives. Requiring the approval of all three houses of parliament in order to implement this proposal, the resulting controversy saw the State President force Labour party leader Alan Henrickse out of his cabinet. At the next sitting of parliament in June 1988, Henrickse led what amounted to a revolt against the still-developing conventions of the tricameral parliament when he announced that the House of Representatives would not consider any aspects of the NP's reformist legislation until the government committed itself to the abolition of the Separate Amenities Act and the Group Areas Act. Consequently, the Group Areas Amendment Bill, the Free Settlement Areas Bill and the Local Government Affairs in Free Settlement Areas Bill were blocked by the actions of the House of Representatives and, later, the House of Delegates. After six months of inaction, the State President was forced to utilize once again the extraordinary constitutional mechanism of putting the legislation before the President's Council where the NP's dominance ensured the Bills would be both considered and passed.[156] Nevertheless, this recourse to the awkward process of circumventing the recalcitrant chambers in parliament had the effect of diminishing the overall legitimacy of an institution which already suffered from its absence to begin with, as well as harbingering future problems within the tricameral system.

With black resistance to the government's reform programme for the political sphere taking shape in all quarters, the implementation of measures such as the negotiating forum were rendered ineffectual. Thus, while they remained a feature of the legislative process and were a testament to the direction that the Botha administration was prepared to consider, these institutions never became an actual part of the political landscape during Botha's tenure in office.

CONCLUSION

The failure to realize the next phase of the reform process in the political sphere had profound implications for the entire reform programme engineered by the Botha administration. The dynamic of state-led reform as implemented under Botha required that the government both define the parameters of reform and maintain control of the process itself. Increasingly, however, as the process unfolded, the very nature of change allowed for the formal and informal empowerment of previously disenfranchised or marginalized sectors of society and, in so doing, created the conditions in which they could exercise power over the political system and process of political change itself. This creeping empowerment, though circumscribed by legislation, was given voice through the institutions established by the reform programme, such as the tricameral parliament, or through non-participation in the process of state-managed change by the recognized leaders of the disenfranchised majority. It was this latter action, aimed against the state's efforts to woo individuals like Nelson Mandela and Chief Buthelezi into participating in the government's negotiating forum, which more than anything brought the Botha administration's carefully calibrated reform programme to a halt.

Contributing to the political stalemate was the Botha administration's unwillingness to acknowledge the importance of winning international support for its reform programme. Intent on setting the pace and parameters of domestic change at all costs, Botha refused to acknowledge the crucial role which the international community could play in conferring legitimacy upon the elaborate programme evolving in South Africa. Concurrently, he failed to see that the South African government's hostility towards international concerns would translate into growing Western support for its enemy, the ANC.

In the wake of this situation, there developed a growing consensus within the Afrikaner elite that extraordinary steps would be necessary to bridge the emerging political impasse. A range of prominent white South Africans, from representatives of the business community to erstwhile political figures such as van Zyl Slabbert, undertook to meet with ANC officials in Lusaka. While these visits were strongly condemned in public by the government, certain officials within the Botha administration were secretly engaged in establishing tentative contacts with the ANC. By May 1988, even the State President had begun to seriously contemplate drawing the ANC into the reform process – beyond the declarations of intent on Mandela's release which had been a feature of his administration since 1985 – as a way of resuscitating his moribund negotiation forum. For its own part, a beleaguered ANC welcomed this opportunity as a means of reviving its sagging fortunes in the wake of a series of significant setbacks abroad (the Namibian settlement) and at home (the relative success of the state of emergency).

Out of these twin streams – the growing recognition by government officials that further progress in the realm of political reform would require direct ANC involvement and the strategic shift within the ANC towards embracing mediation – there developed the basis for a negotiated settlement of the conflict in South Africa. The settlement in Namibia in particular raised the spectre of continuing superpower cooperation on resolving outstanding regional conflicts and with that came the recognition that those parties reluctant to enter into negotiations would be penalized, much as the South African government's intransigence to Western approaches in 1986 had resulted in the imposition of sanctions. Steps towards laying down the conditions for genuine negotiations occupied the remaining months of Botha's tenure as State President.

7 From the Security State to a New South Africa

What we are doing is the logical consequence of what Mr Botha began. F.W. de Klerk, in an interview 8 March 1992.[1]

Since 1972 I have stated publicly at various times – even after I became prime minister – that I believe in reform that brings about change and allows all people to share in the good of the future. But I also believe in reform that takes into account the good of the past. I believe in orderly reform, and I am at a loss to understand the haste of the present consultations and negotiations. I cannot support a spirit of gradual abdication. P.W. Botha, in an interview 8 March 1992.[2]

P.W. Botha's final fifteen months in office marked the launching of a reassessment of the government's approach towards its long-standing opponent, the African National Congress. While the security situation had been brought under control through the implementation of the full state of emergency, the reform process remained deadlocked over the government's inability to woo black South Africans to participate in its negotiation forum. Faced with steadfast opposition, there developed a realization amongst government officials that the proposed next stage of reform would only succeed if the ANC itself was directly brought into the process. At the heart of this change was a determination that the transformation of the international environment, reflected in the amicable settlement of the Angola–Namibia issue, and the stable internal situation, provided the government with an unparalleled opportunity to seize and maintain the initiative in a negotiated settlement with their erstwhile enemy. In light of this analysis, tentative steps were taken towards bridging the gap between government hard-liners, Botha among them, and the ANC, which resulted in the thawing of the climate of mutual hostility. As Botha himself moved closer to considering Mandela's unconditional release, his unexpected physical collapse precipitated a constitutional crisis and, in spite of efforts to regain his pre-eminent position, paved the way for the emergence of F.W. de Klerk as NP leader. Botha's resignation and the government's subsequent dismantling of much of the administrative structure established under Botha marked the end of his contribution to the era of state-led reform in South Africa.

This chapter will first examine the Botha administration's tactical shift from overt hostility towards the ANC to that of embracing direct negotiations with the outlawed organization as a means of realizing the next phase of the reform process. Secondly, it will outline the circumstances which brought about the resignation of the State President. And, finally, an analysis and assessment of the National Security State as instituted in South Africa will be conducted.

PAVING THE WAY FOR NEGOTIATIONS

The protracted road to direct negotiations between the South African government and the ANC, the logical outgrowth of the near-universal rejection of black South African participation in Botha's proposed next phase of political reform, remained hindered by a number of factors. Principal among these was the release of imprisoned ANC leader Nelson Mandela on the condition that he renounce violence as a tool for political change and the unbanning of the ANC itself. Faced with the continued intransigence of Mandela on the question of disowning violence and the State President's equally implacable stance on the same issue, elements within the government began grappling for a way out of the political impasse. Increasingly convinced that the viability of any future political dispensation was dependent upon securing direct ANC participation in the reform process, the National Intelligence Service (NIS) and the Department of Foreign Affairs actively sought to create a climate conducive to face-to-face negotiations with the ANC. Informing this shift in perspective was the growing belief among these top departmental officials that, with the diminishing role of the Soviet Union in the region (as witnessed by the favourable negotiations which culminated in the New York Accords of December 1988), there was an unprecedented opportunity for coming to an accommodation with the ANC which would allow the government to retain the initiative. In the words of the former Director of NIS, Niel Barnard, his organization became convinced that the South African government had to strike a deal with the ANC 'before our backs were against the wall.'[3]

The launching of this initiative, which met with the approval of Botha, involved establishing secret contacts with ANC officials in exile.[4] Tentative contacts had been made in Geneva as early as 1984 when, in the wake of the signing of the Nkomati Accord, South African government officials and the ANC secretly met and had continued intermittantly through the onset of the township rebellion.[5] These links were extended and reinforced by the Institute for a Democratic Alternative in South Africa (IDASA), a private organization founded in November 1986 and headed by former PFP leader van Zyl Slabbert. Along with the support of NIS, IDASA assisted in the facilitating of an unprecedented meeting between 62 prominent Afrikaners and 18 members of the ANC and SACP in July 1987.[6] The former Director of NIS characteristically understated his organization's involvement in this ground breaking event: '[NIS] was not opposed to meeting in Dakar and we believed that there could be no political solution without the ANC.'[7]

The *tête-à-tête* in Dakar proved to be a watershed event in the shaping of the political destiny of the country. With an agenda which included discussions of future political and economic structures in a 'liberated' South Africa as well as problems of the transition to democracy and the building of national unity, the participants established a rapport that was to carry over and inform the domestic debate on breaking the political impasse. The joint communiqué issued at the end of the meeting calling for a negotiated settlement, the unbanning of the ANC and the release of all political prisoners testified to the emerging consensus between the two parties.[8] By November, the first of twelve clandestine meetings between the government and the ANC discussing a range of issues had taken place in Europe.[9]

Despite having his covert blessing, Botha's public reaction to the Dakar meeting, delivered before parliament the following month, was unequivocally harsh:

> The ANC is laughing up their sleeves at the naivety of 'useful idiots' who, as Lenin puts it, can be used to further the aims of the revolution. These people did not go to Dakar to hold penetrating discussions with the ANC. On the contrary, they went to co-ordinate strategies and to find out what the ANC expects of 'democratic patriots'. For the ANC/SACP alliance talks are only a means to an end, namely, the revolutionary takeover of power.[10]

Thereafter, the Botha administration experienced an erosion in support amongst Afrikaner and NP elites for the State President's public insistence that Mandela and the ANC renounce violence as a prerequisite to participation in direct negotiations. Reflective of this divergence was the proliferation of a number of 'treks' to visit the ANC by white South Africans ranging from Afrikaner student organizations to Afrikaner businessmen.[11] With a second split in the formerly solid 'granite wall' (to use Verwoerd's phrase) of Afrikanerdom looming, coupled with ever-increasing international pressure, Botha and his followers found themselves in the invidious position of presiding over a narrowing constituency of support on the divisive issue of the future direction of the reform programme.

In belated recognition of the need to infuse the stalled political reform process with new life, as well as respond to pressures from constituencies as divergent as the Afrikaner business community and the Dutch Reformed Church, Botha began steps towards addressing the release of Mandela and the opening of the political process to ANC participation. The government's release of ageing ANC official Govan Mbeki in November 1987 was the first concrete expression of Botha's willingness to consider a review of his policy towards Mandela and the ANC itself (see Chapter 6). Further steps were broached by Botha through his authorization of the formation of a secret contact group of NP officials, including NIS leader Niel Barnard and Mike Louw, with Mandela in May 1988.[12] According to Barnard, the contact group held discussions with Mandela on three themes: to establish whether he was truly interested in a peaceful solution to South Africa's political problems; to establish if Mandela himself was a communist or not; and to establish whether he would support the protection of minority group rights in a future constitutional dispensation.[13] In spite of the favourable reports on all of these issues emanating from the contact group, the State President remained uncommitted to the prospect of meeting with the ANC leader, temporizing on the first step in 'normalizing' the political situation and preparing for negotiations.

A partner to this process, by 1988 the ANC had reluctantly started to engineer yet another shift in strategy in response to the development of adverse circumstances both internally and abroad. Domestically weakened by the security measures and soon to be shorn of its major international support due to perestroika's thawing effect on the Cold War, the liberation movement began to look to the diplomatic option over that of the military as a means of attaining power. As ANC insiders noted:

> In 1985 it was still possible to believe rationally that the strategy of armed struggle, as the ANC and Communist Party conceived of it, would achieve its goal. By 1988, that was hard to believe.[14]

Concurrent with the revaluation of policies within the ANC, the signing of the New York Accords became the occasion which signalled a definitive break with the South African government's aggressive foreign policy towards the region. Brokered by Director-General of the DFA, Niel van Heerden, the top military commander in Namibia, General Jannie Geldenhuys, and Niel Barnard, the settlement effectively diffused the central premises of the total onslaught thesis, predicated as it was on the threat posed by international communism. Van Heerden, conscious of the momentuous change which this represented, declared that the South African destabilization policies of the past were over; a new approach towards the region, which he characterized as the 'New Diplomacy', would govern regional relations.[15] With the empirical foundation for total onslaught and total strategy fast dissipating, and with it, the justification for the elaboration of the security/limited reform matrix, it remained for van Heerden and others to push Botha towards a negotiated settlement with the ANC.

Within the ANC, the elevation of moderate Thabo Mbeki

to head up the International Department and the concomitant demise of outspoken radical MK chief Chris Hani reflected the organization's movement away from a military-based resolution to the conflict. Most importantly, the results of these changes were manifested in the public enumeration of detailed constitutional proposals in late 1988 which acceded to the liberal model of a future South African state. This was eventually followed by the issuance of the Harare Declaration in August 1989, a statement of principles which were designed to serve as guidelines for any future negotiations between the ANC and the South African government.[16] The Harare Declaration called for the unconditional release of all political prisoners, the removal of restrictions on all individuals and political parties, the removal of the SADF from the townships, the end of the state of emergency and the repeal of related security legislation, and a cessation of all political trials and executions.[17] With the public acceptance of the document by the OAU on 24 August, the stage was set for the implementation of the next momentous phase in the reform process.

BOTHA'S FALL FROM POWER

While the South African state and the ANC moved closer to opening direct negotiations, the position of the architect of the state's reform process experienced an unexpected deterioration. On 18 January 1989, hours before he was to open the new parliamentary session, a debilitating stroke forced Botha into hospital. Chris Heunis was designated as acting State President in his stead. During a month-long convalescence, Botha announced that he wished to relinquish his role as leader of the NP but retain his position as State President. Acting on the State President's instructions, the caucus of the NP elected F.W. de Klerk by a narrow margin to succeed Botha as leader of the party. With his return to office in March, the controversy over the exact role of the State President and the relationship between his duties and those of the leader of the NP came to the fore. Botha's desire to effectively separate the position of head of state from that of head of government, a move which could ultimately clear the way for a black leader as governing head of the country, had apparently been on the State President's agenda for the forthcoming legislative session.[18] Despite this situation, the ground had not been well prepared for this development and at the extraordinary meeting of the NP's federal council in March, party officials reaffirmed their commitment to the link between party leadership and head of state.[19] Much to the shock of Botha, the bulk of the cabinet threw its support behind de Klerk, isolating the State President from the party regulars in the House of Assembly.

In the wake of this development de Klerk, with the backing of the cabinet and NP stalwarts, moved to consolidate his hold on the leadership of the country. In April, Botha announced before parliament that he would not seek another term of office as the State President. Following on the heels of this announcement, de Klerk's government began preparing for an election to take place the following September. Within a few days, Chris Heunis, Botha's partner and fellow architect of the government's reform programme, had resigned.

In spite of this deterioration in power, influence and personal health, Botha still attempted to conduct policy from the Office of the State President. In addition to introducing legislation on his much-vaunted statutory negotiating forum, Botha held a highly publicized meeting with Nelson Mandela in August 1989 at his official residence in Cape Town. This action, while certainly the fulfilment of a process begun over a year before, seemed also to be a political gambit by the State President to regain the initiative as a national leader. According to Barnard, who sat in on the meeting, the convivial atmosphere between Botha and Mandela was such that it was clearly 'just a matter of time' before the government authorized the ANC leader's release.[20] The only hitch was a desire on the part of administration officials to involve external figures in the ANC in the process, a step which – according to Barnard – Mandela opposed.[21]

The *coup de grâce* for the State President came over a proposed visit by de Klerk and Foreign Minister Pik Botha to Zambia in late August about which Botha claimed to have no foreknowledge. The verbal accusations which ensued climaxed with a live television broadcast in which P.W. Botha, enraged and ailing, denounced the duplicity of de Klerk and his ministers and tendered his resignation from public office. After half a century in South African politics and a decade as leader of the South African state, P.W. Botha retired to a small Cape village appropriately named Wilderness.

THE NATIONAL SECURITY STATE IN SOUTH AFRICA: AN ASSESSMENT

As outlined at the beginning of this book, the National Security State developed as a response to the threat posed by revolutionary warfare against those Third World governments aligned with the West. Its aim was to counter communist-inspired rebellion by marshalling all the resources available to it – military, political, economic and diplomatic – into a cohesive strategic programme based on the application of security measures and the introduction of substantial reforms by the state. With security concerns and reform imperatives at the centre of policy-making in the National Security State, it is appropriate that any evaluation of the National Security State in South Africa must first examine the relative successes and failures of the state to achieve its goals in these two areas.

The role which the security side of the Botha programme occupied in the National Security State was essentially one which was subordinated to that of the reform programme. It sought to create and maintain a 'breathing space' in which the complex task of state-led reform could take place unhindered by revolution. In the service of this task, proactive steps were taken by the South African security forces which were deemed to fulfil or realize this objective. Externally, destabilization against those states harbouring the ANC or forces aligned with the ANC (as in Angola) was successful in establishing buffer zones outside of South African controlled territory. The combination of direct military intervention on the part of the SADF and support for surrogate forces, seconded by the introduction of South African economic pressure, secured a raft of formal and informal non-aggression pacts with hostile neighbours. Internally, following the outbreak of significant unrest in 1984, the South African security forces launched an aggressive counter-revolutionary campaign of repression and socio-economic upliftment which stifled the rebellion and began to make inroads into the daunting socio-economic conditions in the townships. Certainly neither military incursions abroad nor acts of repression at home did much to 'win the hearts and minds' of those audiences targeted by the security forces. In both of these cases, the seeds of further violence against the South African state were sown and it was only the absence of means – and here, Angola's determination to pursue the military option even in the face of growing Cuban and Soviet reluctance comes to mind – which curbed or curtailed altogether recourse to more violence.

Nevertheless, on balance the security forces did achieve their primary aim of eliminating many sources of external support for the ANC, a process which was capped at New York in December 1988 and resulted in the shutting down of the ANC's military option. This success was offset to some extent by the state's inability to develop an adequate response to the politico-diplomatic challenge of the international sanctions campaign. Internally, the outbreak and continuation of politically-inspired violence represented a significant setback to the security of the state. While the institution of a full state of emergency in mid-1986 did demonstrably contain unrest, as witnessed by the relative calm which accompanied the municipal elections of 1988, it nonetheless was recognized amongst the 'securocrats' themselves that such measures were only a partial solution to deep-rooted problems which would ultimately require a political solution. The fact remained, however, that security-force action limited the viability of revolutionary options available to the ANC and its allies within the country, thus paving the way for the initiation of negotiations and a political settlement with the state.

Turning to the reform side of the National Security State, the verdict on this process is as fraught with contradiction as that of the security side. Certainly the South African socio-political landscape in 1979, when Botha launched his much-touted reform programme, had been radically transformed in many important respects by 1989, the close of the Botha years. Economic reform, the most thoroughgoing of the changes instituted under Botha, had transformed the workplace from a bastion of white privilege and power to one in which black workers and trade unions were dominant. A decade of social reform had eroded statutory segregation to such an extent that its total demise was foreseeable in the near future. This was especially true in the latter part of the eighties, which saw the government introduce local option clauses in remaining areas of social segregation such as housing and municipal facilities. And in the political sphere the structure of local, provincial and national government had been, if not revolutionized, something not for short of it. Through the convoluted mechanism of the 'own' affairs/ 'group' affairs dichotomy, the foundation of multiracial government had been laid, albeit still formally constituted along racial lines. As in the case of social segregation, while the form of racial division was retained, most *verligte* government reformers expected – and pointed to examples such as the new Provincial executive committees and Regional Services Councils – these new institutions to evolve away from their initial racial foundation to ones which were more truly multiracial in character. Legislation tabled in 1988 allowing for a multiracial voters' roll in selected districts was indicative of the direction of government planning in this area. At the same time, this entire evolutionary reform process was characterized by a determination on the part of the Botha administration to retain white control of the process itself and, at the end of the day, substantial white influence and power in any final political resolution.

All this took place against the background of rising conflict amongst government decision-makers over the direction and shape of state policy. The consensus which marked the period between 1979 and 1984, the high water mark of the National Security State, deteriorated in the wake of the onset of the sustained township uprising and international opprobrium. This was particularly evident in the controversy which surrounded the 'Rubicon' speech, the security strikes abroad which scuttled the Eminent Persons Group endeavour in 1986, the continued covert support by the SADF for Renamo rebels in Mozambique and the diminishing importance of Chris Heunis and his reformist DCDP in the late eighties. The friction between security and reform interests was made manifest as it became clear that further reform would require relinquishing additional state power, something which had produced a loss of state control over the process of reform as witnessed in the 'rebellion' engineered by the Coloured and Indian representatives of the tricameral parliament. This conflict was to be a major contributing factor in the stalemate which characterized the final years of the National Security State.

In light of this analysis, the verdict on the National Security State in South Africa must necessarily be that of failure. First and foremost, it was a failure in its own terms, that is to say in developing a form of government which was acceptable to all South Africans and nonetheless retained white pre-eminence in decision-making. Rejected by the majority of black South Africans and castigated by the international community, the Botha administration's concerted efforts to restructure the South African political system without fundamentally jeopardizing white power and interests atrophied in the face of overwhelming denunciation. This situation struck at the heart of Botha's programmatic approach to transforming the South African polity, overshadowing any achievements or partial successes in a range of other spheres. Secondly, the National Security State was a failure in convincing the majority of South Africans that evolutionary reform was preferable to revolutionary change. The sustained nature of unrest in the country, triggered by the imposition of the black local authorities system and the establishment of the tricameral parliament, was not abated by government appeals that 'orderly reform' was the only basis for change. This was particularly evident towards the end of the decade when the Botha administration began to make significant concessions to black interests, moves that were greeted with derision and hostility by a jaded black community. Thirdly, the National Security State was a failure because of its inability to recognize the importance of the international community to the success of the programme upon which it had embarked. Unwilling to acknowledge the crucial role that the international community played in legitimizing states and their policies, the South African government was unable – and even outright defiant of international interests – to convince this critical audience of the merits of its case. The outcome of this situation was the development of policies which took little cognizance of international norms, such as destabilization, and which gave rise to a vigorous sanctions campaign against South Africa. And finally, the National Security State was a failure in that it was unable to build upon the successes which did accrue to it over the course of the decade. Most notably, the actions of the security forces in curtailing external support for the ANC and in curbing domestic unrest (albeit temporarily) – which had effectively stripped the ANC and its internal allies of the military option – were not followed by dramatic political manoeuvres or changes in the agenda or pace of the reform programme. Instead of using these situations to, for example, bring the enervated ANC to the negotiating table, the Botha administration doggedly attempted to breathe life into established institutions or formulas which clearly had lost all credibility. The lack of imagination with respect to Botha's vaunted National Council, which was revamped and revived under F.W. de Klerk as the Convention for a Democratic South Africa (Codesa), and the simultaneous mishandling of Nelson Mandela's release, was a particularly dramatic case in point.

The explanation for this failure lies at both the ideological and methodological levels. Clinging to the increasingly hollow shell of apartheid legislation, ostensibly in the name of retaining support from its white constituency, the Botha administration managed to launch a programmatic assault on many of the manifestations of apartheid policy while simultaneously conveying to the world a singular reluctance to tackle the root racialist assumptions which underlaid these policies. If, as his successor de Klerk was to do in 1991, Botha had summarily abandoned the remaining legislative 'pillars' of apartheid – the Population Registration Act, Separate Amenities Act and Group Areas Act – his programme would in all probability have won international accolades and encountered less resistance from black South Africans.[22] But, fundamentally tied to the racist outlook which informed apartheid, Botha was unwilling to break completely with the structures of South Africa's past. The result in the political sphere was the institution of a byzantine parliamentary structure established on a racial basis, despite the fact that it was a significant break from the fundamentalist apartheid policies of the previous thirty years, which retained the form of the apartheid state and consequently engendered suspicion amongst black South Africans; and, in the area of social segregation, an over attentiveness to what were fundamentally racist sensibilities on the part of the white community at the expense of black sensibilities and dignity. Both of these circumstances were influential in the rejection of the Botha programme by black South Africans and the international community.

In methodological terms, the state's decision to pursue reform through the application of incrementalism was, in retrospect, a fatal blunder. While Botha and Heunis proclaimed the virtues of 'evolution versus revolution', the strategic value of incrementalism over that of 'blitzkrieg tactics and fabian strategy' was, in the end, negative. By introducing reforms in piecemeal fashion, done so in keeping with the dictates of incrementalism, the state failed to accrue the political kudos both internationally and domestically which would have accompanied a much more rapid introduction of reforms. Concurrently, while the selection of a gradualist approach to reform certainly eased the process of change for the white community, preparing it for the more substantial changes to come, it had the adverse effect of alienating much of the black community through its constant promise of substantive reform and subsequent unwillingness to implement such measures in full. Finally, as was aptly demonstrated by de Klerk, the rapid introduction of meaningful concessions which met many of the key points of contention central to the anti-apartheid movement actually dimmed the aura of moral sanctity which informed the international community's view of the ANC and served to throw the organization off balance politically. Notably, it took more than two years of talks with the government, coupled with the failure of the radicals' 'Leipzig option', for the ANC to fully adopt an approach to governance which was not predicated on revolutionary or opposition politics.

However, in spite of this negative assessment of the National Security State in South Africa, it is important to acknowledge that it did play a critical role in the transformative process in that country. When viewed as a transitional instrument, that is to say one which presided over the dismantling of the apartheid state and the establishment of the foundation for a 'New South Africa', the influence of the National Security State is undeniable. As noted above, in the economic and social spheres – and to a lesser extent in the political sphere – far-reaching reforms had substantially and irrevocably altered the South African landscape. Linked to this was the fact that the exclusion of revolutionary-oriented organizations such as the ANC from the process of domestic reform until after the collapse of Eastern Europe and the Soviet Union effectively undercut the ideological and material backing that was vital to these organizations. Shorn of these familiar pillars of support and operating without a credible alternative developmental model, the ANC entered the negotiations with the South African government at a distinct disadvantage.

As for Botha and the National Security State, both are castigated in all quarters as the source of a variety of contemporary problems. Violence, now endemic across all sectors of South African society, has moved from threatening the viability of the political transition to endangering development and stability in the new state. The lingering fallout of South Africa's regional policies continues to reap a bitter harvest of shattered economies mingled with internecine conflict in the neighbouring states, most notably in the recent destruction of Angola. And the great reconciliation between black and white, the crucible of nation-building for the New South Africa, is still in its infancy. It was once observed that South Africans from all walks of life had yet to experience the 'loss of innocence' which came in the wake of the accumulated horrors of twentieth century warfare, tearing the very fabric of European society apart.[23] With Utopianism of the Right and the Left discredited, an economy shackled by the twin legacies of apartheid and sanctions, and a society riven by the brutal heritage of militarization, South Africa today is no longer a stranger to these defining contours of modernity.

Against this background, it is ironic that despite a tradition of unremitting antagonism it is apologists for the South African Communist Party and the ANC who have seen fit to resurrect the architect of the National Security State and put his tenure in office in a historical context.

> [W]hile it is clear that President de Klerk has shown rare qualities of political skill and courage, it would be wrong to over-estimate his personal contribution. The fact is that even his irascible predecessor, the Great Crocodile P.W. Botha, regularly encouraged some of his ministers to visit Mandela in jail, and even to invite him to their homes. Botha himself publicly received Mandela for tea at his official Cape Town residence. Botha, generally regarded as a man little endowed with patience, tolerance or tact, went further than he has generally received credit for in opening the way for the unbanning of the ANC and the Communist Party.[24]

Botha's resignation from the government paved the way for a major shift in strategy by the NP government. The National Security State, once the chosen instrument for combating the 'total onslaught' facing South Africa, was dismantled by his successor, F.W. de Klerk. In November 1989, just two months after his election as State President on a negotiation platform, de Klerk shut down the nerve centre of the counter-revolutionaries, the National Security Management System. Following a review of South Africa's nuclear programme, de Klerk ordered the six nuclear bombs destroyed and the decommissioning of the nuclear enrichment plant.[25] Signalling the seriousness of his intention to release Nelson Mandela, de Klerk freed seven top ANC prisoners in October and held private discussions with Mandela himself in December. The securocrats, poised to serve de Klerk as they once had Botha, found that de Klerk was not a proponent of the total onslaught thesis and, as such, was ill-disposed to the formula of maintaining the established system of control while implementing limited reformist measures. Some of these individuals were to quit the government in frustration and take up positions with the emerging right wing opposition; others continued at their posts, all the while using their position in the SAP or SADF to covertly foment chaos and division in the townships. Another group, true to the bureaucratic impulse, retained their jobs within the government and adjusted to the new circumstances. As for programmatic reform as constituted under Botha, it had already been dealt a fatal blow with the closure of the DCDP and Heunis's resignation in May 1989.

But all of this was merely prelude to the dramatic unveiling of a new chapter in South African politics. On 2 February 1990, de Klerk went before the opening session of the tricameral parliament and announced his intention to unconditionally release Nelson Mandela and lift the ban on the ANC, SACP and PAC. The die which had moulded twentieth-century South African politics was irrevocably shattered.

Notes

INTRODUCTION

1. The principal exponents of modernization were G. Almond and J. Coleman, eds, *The Politics of the Developing Areas* (Princeton, NJ: Princeton UP 1960) and (if somewhat revisionist) S. Huntington, *Political Order in Changing Societies* (New Haven, CT: Yale UP 1968). L. Pye, R. Ward, and D. Rustow also contributed significantly to the debate.
2. K. Marx and F. Engels, 'Manifesto of the Communist Party', in *The Marx-Engels Reader* (2nd edition), ed. R. Tucker (New York: Norton 1978), 469–500; V. Lenin, 'Imperialism, the Highest Stage of Capitalism: A Popular Outline', in *Lenin on Politics and Revolution: Selected Writings,* ed. J. Connor (New York: Pegasus, 1968), 111–48.
3. As one scholar of political development suggested, 'We think a political-development strategy for American foreign policy may be necessary not for its own sake, but because it can advance the interests of the United States.' R. Packenham, 'Political Development Doctrines in the American Foreign Aid Program', *World Politics* 3 (April 1966): 195.
4. A debate emerged around the contentious term 'political development'. See S. Huntington, 'The Change to Change: Modernization, Development, and Politics', *Comparative Politics* 3 (April 1971), 283–322.
5. W. Shinn, 'The National Democratic State: A Communist Program for Less-Developed Areas', *World Politics* 3 (April 1963), 377–89; A. Klinghoffer, *Soviet Perspectives on African Socialism,* (Madison, WI: Fairleigh Dickinson UP 1969), 209–15.
6. See K. Marx, 'Theses on Feuerbach', in Tucker, op. cit., 143–5; V. Lenin, 'What is to be Done?', in Connor, op. cit., 31–78.
7. See Mao Tse-tung *On Guerrilla Warfare,* trans. S. Griffith (New York: Praeger 1961); C. Guevara, *Guerrilla Warfare,* (Lincoln, NB: UP of Nebraska 1985).
8. See R. Thompson, *Defeating Communist Insurgency: The Lessons of Malaya and Vietnam,* (New York: Praeger 1966); A. Beaufre, *A Strategy of Action,* (London: Faber & Faber 1967); J. J. McCuen, *The Art of Counter-revolutionary Warfare: The Strategy of Counter-insurgency,* (London: Faber & Faber 1966).
9. The term 'National Security State' is Daniel Yergin's but he does not provide a substantive definition of it nor does he locate the construct in the Third World context. See Daniel Yergin, *Shattered Peace: The Origins of the Cold War and the National Security State* (Harmondsworth: Penguin, 1977).
10. See S. Huntington, 'Reform and Stability in a Modernizing, Multi-Ethnic Society', *Politikon* 8:2 (December 1981). Huntington's paper was delivered at the annual meeting of the Political Science Association

of South Africa on 17 September 1981. Top officials from South Africa's newly formed Department of Constitutional Development and Planning, including Minister Chris Heunis, participated in the conference.

CHAPTER 1

1. *Debates of the House of Assembly.* (Hansard) 18 May 1959, Cape Town: Government Printer, col. 6023.
2. For historical accounts of the first two hundred years of white settlement in South Africa, a period which saw the development and entrenchment of many of the trends that dominate twentieth-century events in the country, see: C.W. De Kiewiet, *A History of South Africa: Social and Economic,* (Oxford: Oxford UP 1941); M. Wilson and L. Thompson, eds, *The Oxford History of South Africa.*, vols I & II (Oxford: Clarendon 1969–71); R. Elphick and H. Giliomee, eds, *The Shaping of South African Society, 1652–1820.* (London: Longman 1979).
3. An investigation into poverty in the white community conducted by the Carnegie Commission in 1930 estimated that almost 40 per cent of white families were unable to provide food or clothing for their children. Of these families, nine out of ten were Afrikaners. M. Meredith, *In the Name of Apartheid: South Africa in the Post War Period,* (London: Hamish Hamilton 1988), 18–19.
4. See T.D. Moodie, *The Rise of Afrikanerdom: Power, Apartheid, and the Afrikaner Civil Religion,* (London: University of California Press, 1975); L. Thompson, *The Political Mythology of Apartheid,* (New Haven, CT: Yale UP 1985).
5. M. Lipton, *Capitalism and Apartheid: South Africa, 1910–1986,* (Cape Town: David Philip 1985), 21–2.
6. It would be wrong, however, to link policies of racial segregation as exclusively the province of Afrikanerdom. Virtually all of the laws which were systematized under the National party were on the statute books in some form before the Nationalists took power. See S. Dubow, *Racial Segregation and the Origins of Apartheid in South Africa, 1919–36,* (Hong Kong: Macmillan 1989).
7. South African Institute for Race Relations (SAIRR) 1978, *Laws Affecting Race Relations in South Africa,* (Pietermaritzburg: Natal Witness 1978), 19–20. The South African Institute for Race Relations will henceforth be abbreviated as SAIRR.
8. Ibid., 16.
9. Ibid., 71–2.
10. Ibid., 113–14.
11. Ibid., 295–9.
12. *Union House of Assembly Debates* (Hansard) 3 March 1950, 21 April 1950, cols 4141–2.
13. Moodie, op. cit., 263–8.
14. H. Giliomee and L. Schlemmer, *From Apartheid to Nation-Building* (Cape Town: Oxford UP 1989), 71.

15. See T. Lodge, *Black Politics in South African since 1945*, (London: Longman 1983).
16. The SACP had been outlawed since 1950 and had used a variety of front organizations, of which the Congress of Democrats was one, to sustain its existence. S. Ellis and T. Sechaba, *Comrades Against Apartheid: The ANC and the South African Communist Party in Exile*, (London: James Currey 1992), 26–8.
17. J. Barber and J. Barratt, *South Africa's Foreign Policy: The Search for Status and Security, 1945–1988*, (Johannesburg: Cambridge 1990), 90.
18. Ellis and Sechaba, op. cit., 34; 37–8.
19. Barber and Barratt, op. cit., 79–80.
20. Ibid., 66–9.
21. Upon taking office, Vorster stated: 'My role is to walk further along the road set by Hendrik Verwoerd.' Cited in Meredith, op. cit., 122.
22. The National party retained an hostility towards the Asian community's presence in South Africa, despite the abandonment of its official policy of repatriation in 1961.
23. *Financial Times* (Johannesburg) 30 May 1974, 14.
24. Ellis and Sechaba, op. cit., 83.
25. Ibid., 241.
26. Between 1960 and 1970, despite government removals of 'surplus people' without the proper documentation, the proportion of Africans residing legally in the urban areas ('white' South Africa) rose from 31.8 per cent to 33.1 per cent. Meredith, op. cit., 132.
27. Cited in Giliomee and Schlemmer, op. cit., 123.

CHAPTER 2

1. Cited in *Fighter and Reformer: Extracts from the Speeches of P.W. Botha.*, compiled by J. J. Scholtz, (Pretoria: Promedia 1989), 33.
2. Ibid., 35.
3. B. Porter, *The USSR in Third World Conflicts: Soviet Arms Diplomacy in Local Wars, 1945–1980*, (Cambridge: Cambridge UP 1984), 18–19.
4. J. Spence, *Republic under Pressure: A Study in South African Foreign Policy*, Royal Institute of International Affairs, Chatham House Essays, No. 9. (London: Oxford UP 1965), 9.
5. J. Barber and J. Barratt, *South Africa's Foreign Policy: The Search for Status and Security, 1945–1988*, (Johannesburg: Southern 1990), 56.
6. J. Barber, *South Africa's Foreign Policy, 1945–1970* (London: Oxford UP 1973), 58.
7. Barber and Barratt, op. cit., 55.
8. D. Austin, *Britain and South Africa*, (London: Oxford UP 1966), 130–1; 134–6. Since its seizure at the beginning of the nineteenth century, Imperial strategists had made control of the Cape route a cardinal principle of British foreign policy. See C.W. de Kiewet, *The Imperial Factor in South Africa*, (London: Cambridge UP 1937).
9. R. Bissell and C. Crocker, eds, *South Africa in the 1980s*, (Boulder, CO.: Westview 1979), 76–7. The commitment of South African forces

in these earliest of Cold War actions did result in an agreement with the United States in 1952 authorizing the sale of American military hardware to the Republic under the terms of the 1949 US Mutual Defense Assistance Act.

10. See *The United Nations and Apartheid, 1948–1994* (New York: United Nations 1994).
11. R. Bissell, *South Africa and the United States: The Erosion of an Influence Relationship*, (New York: Praeger 1982), 8–11; 52–5.
12. J. Barber, *South Africa's Foreign Policy, 1945–1970*, (London: Oxford UP 1973), 62; S. Nolutshungu, *South Africa in Africa: A Study in Ideology and Foreign Policy*, (Manchester: Manchester UP 1975), 51–2.
13. Ibid., 83–4.
14. Barber and Barratt, op. cit., 58.
15. J. Spence, *The Political and Military Framework*, Study Project on External Investment in South Africa and Namibia (South West Africa), Paper No. 4, University of Leicester, January 1975, 2–3; Barber 1973, op. cit., 230–1.
16. Bissell and Crocker 1979, op. cit., 81–2.
17. Botha said that, on the eve of Verwoerd's assassination, he asked him to 'make South Africa militarily strong'. The result was the establishment of Armscor. Interview with P.W. Botha, 18 June 1991.
18. Interview with P.W. Botha, 18 June 1991.
19. C. Coker, *South Africa's Security Dilemmas*. The Washington Papers/ 126, Center for Strategic and International Studies, Washington, D.C. (New York: Praeger 1987), 2.
20. Ibid., 79.
21. *Debates of the House of Assembly* (Hansard) 20 February 1968, (Pretoria: Government Printers) cols 856–7; ibid., 20 February 1968, ibid., cols 3295–309 and 3318–24; ibid., 24 April 1968, (Pretoria: Government Printers) cols 4055–7; ibid., 9 February 1971, ibid., cols 530–50.
22. Ibid., 23 July 1970, cols 294–6.
23. Republic of South Africa 1971, *Report of the Commission of Inquiry into Matters Relating to the Security of the State* (Abridged), (Pretoria: Government Printers), 34.
24. Republic of South Africa 1973, *White Paper on Defence and Armament Production*, (Pretoria: Government Printers), 1.
25. See C. Legum, *Vorster's Gamble for Africa: How the Search for Peace Failed*, (London: Rex Collings 1976).
26. *Debates of the House of Assembly* (Hansard) 17 April 1978, (Pretoria: Government Printers), cols 4852.
27. D. Geldenhuys, Some Foreign Policy Implications of South Africa's 'Total National Strategy' with Particular Reference to the "12 Point Plan"', Braamfontein: South African Institute of International Affairs, March 1981, 6–7.
28. *Debates of the House of Assembly* (Hansard) 20 April 1977, (Pretoria: Government Printers) col. 5644.
29. Geldenhuys 1981, op. cit., 6–7.
30. Republic of South Africa 1977, *White Paper on Defence and Armaments Production*, (Pretoria: Government Printers), 4.

31. Ibid., 7.
32. Beaufre 1965, op. cit., 30.
33. Ibid., 31.
34. Ibid., 22.
35. Ibid., 125.
36. See the relevant works of P. Frankel and K. Grundy.
37. Beaufre 1965, op. cit., 30.
38. A. Beaufre, *A Strategy for Action*, (London: Faber & Faber 1967), 19–25.
39. Lt.-General C.F. Fraser was the sponsor of these lectures. According to Professor Deon Fourie, Lt.-General Fraser's first exposure to Beaufre's work was via a book review Fraser himself penned on Beaufre's *Introduction to Strategy*. Subsequently, Fraser asked the UNISA strategist and a colleague at the University of the Witwatersrand to lecture on the topic to the SADF. Interview with Professor D. Fourie, 16 October 1990.
40. Interview Professor D. Fourie, 16 October 1990.
41. See Admiral Biermann, 'Die Politieke en Militer-Strategiese rol van die Republiek', *Paratus* September 1972, 10ff.; D. Fourie, 'Strategie – "n Oorsig",' *Paratus* December 1971, 14–15; D. Fourie, 'Strategie – "n Oorsig",' *Paratus* January 1972, 24ff.
42. Fourie, D. 'Strategie – 'n Oorsig', *Paratus*, January 1972, 61.
43. Interview with Professor D. Fourie, 16 October 1990.
44. Interview with P.W. Botha, 18 June 1991.
45. J. Roherty, *State Security in South Africa Civil-Military Relations under P.W. Botha*, (London: M. E. Sharpe 1992), 61.
46. *Debates of the House of Assembly* (Hansard) 9 February 1971, (Pretoria: Government Printers), cols 546–7.
47. Republic of South Africa 1973, *White Paper on Defence and Armaments Production*, (Pretoria: Government Printers), 1.
48. Republic of South Africa 1975, *White Paper on Defence*, (Pretoria: Government Printers), 3.
49. Republic of South Africa 1977, *White Paper on Defence and Armaments Production*, (Pretoria: Government Printers), 4–5.
50. Ibid., 5.
51. Ibid.
52. Ibid.
53. Ibid., 9.
54. Ibid., 3.
55. Ibid., 8.
56. Ibid.
57. Interview with General H. du Toit, 7 March 1990.
58. Interview with senior military officer.
59. K. Grundy, *The Militarization of South African Politics*, (Oxford: Oxford UP 1988), 17.

CHAPTER 3

1. Botha's statement was widely reported in the press in 1979; how-

ever, according to J. J. Scholtz, it was not until the mid-eighties that Botha actually used that particular phrase. *Fighter and Reformer: Extracts from the Speeches of P.W. Botha* compiled by J.J. Scholtz, (Pretoria: Promedia 1989), 1.

2. Ibid., 36.
3. The 'civilized labour' policy was introduced in 1924 into state sector employment practices. The Industrial Conciliation Act of 1924, amended in 1937, provided for the registration of trade union organizations and the establishment of industrial councils. Blacks were excluded from the definition of 'employee', and thus were unable to join the officially sanctioned labour movement. Their status was covered by the Masters and Servants Acts originating in nineteenth century legislation which made it illegal for an employee (or employer) to break a work contract. The 1925 Customs Tariff Act protected manufacturers based on their capacity to demonstrate the use of 'civilized labor'. See SAIRR, *Laws Affecting Race Relations in South Africa: Laws Affecting Race Relations*, (Pietermaritzburg: Natal Witness 1978).
4. M. Lipton, *Capitalism and Apartheid: South Africa, 1910–1986* Third edition (Cape Town: David Philip 1989), 112–13; 138–43. Lipton argues that while 'at certain stages, at least some aspects of apartheid were functional for growth in mining and agriculture', that manufacturing was consistently opposed to its introduction.
5. Friedman, op. cit., 52.
6. Ibid., 150.
7. The white Mine Workers Union organized an abortive strike in March 1979 to protest the forthcoming Wiehahn commission report, but it petered out as pressure from the mining houses was brought to bear. Friedman, op. cit., 163–4.
8. This would be done by redefining blacks as 'employees' – a category denied in previous labour legislation which had excluded 'pass bearers'. See SAIRR 1978, op. cit., 281.
9. See Republic of South Africa 1979(A), *Report of the Commission of Inquiry into Labour Legislation* Part I, (Pretoria: Government Printers). The Wiehahn commission released four other reports over the next eighteen months but, by virtue of their limited scope, these were not to have the impact of the initial report.
10. Many of the rank and file of emergent black unions were composed of workers defined as migrants (AFCWU, GWU and some Fosatu affiliates), there was an immediate resistance on their part to accepting the dual 'insider/outsider' split proposed by the government. By refusing to register officially, the unions threatened the government's labour reform programme and forced the government to revaluate its position. The 1981 Labour Relations Act incorporated the objections lodged by the unions and paved the way for the normalization of industrial relations.
11. This legislation was the logical outgrowth of the Stallard commission report of 1922, which established the principle that blacks should only be in urban areas to 'minister to the needs of the white man and should depart therefrom when he ceases to minis-

ter.' F. Wilson, *Migrant Labour in South Africa*, (Johannesburg: South African Council of Churches & SPRO-CAS 1972), 160.

12. Southall states that 'over one-third of all Africans employed in 'White' South Africa are laborers who migrate for work from their homes on a temporary, contract basis. This proportion extends to over one-half, if those who commute from homelands on a daily basis are included.' R. Southall, 'Migrants and Trade Unions in South Africa Today', *Canadian Journal of African Studies* XX:2 1986, 165.
13. Republic of South Africa 1979(B), *Report of the Commission of Inquiry into Legislation Affecting the Utilisation of Manpower*, (Pretoria: Government Printers), 221; 274. The Riekert Commission explicitly avoided rulings that were deemed the province of politics.
14. Republic of South Africa 1979(B), op. cit., 1; *Financial Mail* (Johannesburg) 18 May 1979, 567–8.
15. Republic of South Africa 1979(B), op. cit., 260.
16. Republic of South Africa 1979(C), *White Paper on the Report of the Commission of Inquiry into Legislation Affecting the Utilisation of Manpower*, Pretoria: Government Printers.
17. The best discussion of constitutional reform is I. Sarakinsky's 'Impulse to Reform: The South African State From Vorster to Botha', unpublished manuscript 1990. This section is indebted to Sarakinsky's work.
18. The position of the Indian community in South Africa was viewed as extremely problematic by the Nationalist party. After numerous attempts to secure the repatriation of the Indians to the sub-continent (modelled on the successful effort to do so with the Chinese between 1907 and 1910) failed, the Nationalist party came to accept that the Indian people were in South Africa to stay in 1961. See B. Sacks, *South Africa: An Imperial Dilemma, Non-Europeans and the British Nation 1902–1914*, (Albuquerque, NM: UP New Mexico 1967); S. Bhana and B. Pachai, eds, *A Documentary History of Indian South Africans* (Cape Town: David Philip 1984).
19. The Separate Representation of Voters Act of 1951 provoked a bitter constitutional debate and did not come into force until 1956.
20. Verwoerd's explicit denial of this perspective – he favoured the establishment of a Coloured 'homeland' – was disavowed by the Cape branch of the Nationalist party following his death in 1966. In fact, P.W. Botha himself took up the cause of the Coloureds by explaining in 1972 that they were part of the *nasie* (nation) but not of the *volk* (people). H. Giliomee and L. Schlemmer, *From Apartheid to Nation-Building*, (Cape Town: Oxford UP 1990), 98–9.
21. W. Vosloo, 'The Coloured Policy of the Nationalist Party', in *South African Dialogue*, N. Rhoodie, ed., (Pretoria: McGraw-Hill 1972), 370–371.
22. *Debates of the House of Assembly*. (Hansard) 7 February 1969 (Cape Town: Government Printer), col. 369.
23. The Coloured Persons Representative Council replaced the Union Council for Coloured Affairs established as an interim body in 1959 to advise the government on issues related to the Coloured population. It was in fact established by statute in 1964 but was only

brought into actual institutional being after the passage of the Political Non-Interference Act of 1968.

24. The SAIC established in 1968 consisted of 25 members, all appointed by the government, and had only advisory powers. SAIRR 1975, op. cit., 22.
25. *Debates and Proceedings of the Coloured Persons Representative Council* vol. 28, Seventh Session of First Council, 8–15 November 1974, 4–5.
26. Interview with Dr W. Vosloo, 5 July 1991. The discussion group consisted of luminaries from a range of professions within the Afrikaner community all of whom participated in the 'no holds barred' political debating sessions. Among the participants in this monthly discussion group were the editors of *Die Burger* and *Die Beeld.*
27. See Republic of South Africa 1976, *Recommendations of the Commission of Inquiry into Matters Relating to the Coloured Population Group,* (Pretoria: Government Printers).
28. The report pointed out that the CRC had passed only three laws in six years, none of which was deemed significant. The principal flaw, the report stated, was the overlap between existing authorities and that of the nascent Coloured political bodies and the absence of mechanisms for joint decision-making between them. Republic of South Africa 1976, op. cit., 139–40.
29. Republic of South Africa 1976, op. cit., 136–7.
30. One constitutional expert declared: 'One of the most profoundly significant developments in the comparative study of political systems over the past two decades is the cumulative empirical evidence supporting the argument that consociational democracy is the only non-authoritarian political system feasible for many plural societies of the non-Western world.' W. Vosloo, 'Consociational Democracy as a Means to Accomplish Peaceful Political Change in South Africa: an Evaluation of the Constitutional Changes proposed by the National Party in 1977', *Politikon* 6:1 June 1979, 13.
31. P.W. Botha, Public Address to the National Party Federal Congress in Bloemfontein 30–31 July 1982, 8.
32. Interview with Dr W. Vosloo, 5 July 1991. According to Vosloo, it was his hope that the same kind of pressures which ultimately induced the British government to widen representative government in the nineteenth century through a series of reform acts would act in the case of South Africa to broaden political participation to the African population.
33. SAIRR 1976, op. cit., 11.
34. Republic of South Africa, 'South Africa's New Constitutional Plan', Johannesburg: Perskor 1978; SAIRR 1977, op. cit., 7–11.
35. Chris Heunis identifies the rejection of the 1977 constitutional proposals by the leaders of the Coloured community as the critical factor in stalling the implementation of the constitution. Interview with C. Heunis, 10 September 1991.
36. Commenting on this period, P.W. Botha states rather obliquely that '[w]ithout pointing to parties responsible for this state of affairs, I want to say that despite the Government's good intentions, no

progress was made [on implementing the 1977 Constitution].' P.W. Botha 1982, op. cit., 9.

37. The Commission of Inquiry on the Constitution, or Schlebusch commission, was established on 4 July 1979.
38. P.W. Botha 1982, op. cit., 9.
39. SAIRR 1980, op. cit., 6–7.
40. C. Heymans, 'The Political and Constitutional Context of Local Government Restructuring' in *Government By the People?: The Politics of Local Government in South Africa*, C. Heymans and G. Totemeyer, eds, (Johannesburg: Juta 1988), 35.
41. Giliomee characterizes the reforms as 'the first government admission that the urban blacks are a permanent, integral part of South African society, i.e. *industrial* citizens, if not political citizens.' H. Giliomee, *The Parting of the Ways: South African Politics 1976–1982* (Cape Town: David Philip 1982), 48.
42. Botha says that the specific impetus for 'rationalization' came from a combination of three sources or incidents: the Information Scandal, the political debacle which surrounded the Angolan affair of 1975–6, and the directives of Beaufreian strategy. At the same time, he points out that he had always been motivated by a sense of order when approaching his ministerial appointments and, consequently, had reorganized both the Ministry of Coloured Affairs and the Ministry of Defence upon arrival. Interview with P.W. Botha, 18 June 1991.
43. *Debates of the House of Assembly.* (Hansard) 6 February 1980 (Pretoria: Government Printers), col. 233–4.
44. It was formerly known as the Department of the Prime Minister.
45. Initially, five cabinet committees were established – Economic Affairs, Social Affairs, Fiscal Affairs and Internal Affairs – but within eighteen months Fiscal Affairs was merged into Economic Affairs and Internal Affairs was renamed Constitutional Affairs. I have chosen to under-emphasize this point of nomenclature for the sake of clarity of presentation.
46. The Department of National Security (DONS) was temporarily established during the interim period between the demise of BOSS and the establishment of the National Intelligence Service (NIS) in June 1980. Geldenhuys 1984, op. cit., 149.
47. Swilling and Phillips 1989, op. cit., 35.
48. Nevertheless, the reform programme encountered stiff resistance amongst some bureaucrats, particularly those responsible for 'black affairs' bureaux in the reconstituted Bantu Affairs Administration Boards successfully blocked the implementation of reforms for years. Venter 1989, op. cit., 84.
49. F. Cloete, 'Characteristics of the Policy Process Aimed at Political Change in South Africa', paper prepared for presentation at the Conference of the Political Science Association of South Africa on 10 and 11 October 1989 in Port Alfred, 11.
50. Ibid., 11.
51. Geldenhuys 1984, op. cit., 90. Also see M. Swilling and M. Phillips 1989, op. cit., 34–5.

52. J. du Plessis, 'Administratiewe Vernuwing: Beleidvereistes', *Journal of Public Administration* 15:3 (1980), 112–13.
53. Interview with General A. van Deventer, 6 June 1991. The Taiwanese government's management of national security also exerted an influence on the actual implementation process, but this factor only came into play following the strengthening of relations between the two countries in 1980.
54. A. van Deventer, 'State Security Council: Not Sinister!' *Paratus,* November 1983, 11.
55. M. Malan, 'Die Aanslag Teen Suid-Afrika', address to Institute for Strategic Studies, University of Pretoria, 3 September 1980.
56. Ibid., 8; 13–14; Beaufre 1965, op. cit., 30.
57. Van Deventer, op. cit., 11.
58. Interview with Lt.-General A. van Deventer, 6 June 1991.
59. Private communication.
60. A. Seegers, 'Extending the Security Network to the Local Level: A Clarification and Some Further Comments', *Politeia,* University of South Africa 7:2 (1988), 52.
61. Republic of South Africa 1971, op. cit., 9–10.
62. Geldenhuys 1984, op. cit., 147.
63. Republic of South Africa 1971, op. cit., 90.
64. Ibid.
65. Van Deventer called the Public Service Commission a study of 'the shortcomings of the state machinery for combating threats to national security.' Van Deventer, op. cit., 10.
66. 'Many of [the Public Service Commission's report] more important provisions were eventually incorporated into the national security management system which was finally adopted and which is currently operating in the Republic of South Africa.' Van Deventer, op. cit., 10.
67. Van Deventer, op. cit., 10,
68. Interview with Lt.-General A. van Deventer, 6 June 1991. Van Deventer says that the military's dominance of the process in the van Dalsen Committee (of which he was a member) was due principally to the fact that the SADF was the only participating department with expertise in strategic matters and the only one with the requisite strategic overview.
69. Act 64/1972 in Hough and van der Merwe 1988, op. cit., 6.
70. Grundy, op. cit., 54.
71. Interview with Lt.-General A. van Deventer, 6 June 1991. According to van Deventer, the SSC met on a Monday, the Cabinet met on a Wednesday and by Thursday the Cabinet's decisions on various recommendations from the SSC would be made.
72. Interview with Lt.-General A. van Deventer, 6 June 1991. Van Deventer says that in the early days of the NSMS, the SSC had trouble putting its case before the Cabinet. With delays of up to three weeks before the Cabinet would first review a particular SSC report or proposal, the Secretary of the SSC decided to co-opt Director Generals from Foreign Affairs, the NIS and other departments onto the SSC's

Work Committee. This had the effect of both speeding up the policy review process and elevating the status of the nascent SSC.

73. The result was the financing of the Khayelitsha housing project.
74. Grundy, op. cit., 49.
75. Interview with Lt.-General A. van Deventer, 6 June 1991.
76. Ibid.
77. The actual composition of the Secretariat has been a matter of controversy amongst scholars. In a parliamentary debate, the Prime Minister stated that the staff of the Secretariat was composed primarily of officials from the National Intelligence Services (56 per cent), with the rest consisting of members of the SADF (16 per cent), the Security Policy (11 per cent), the Department of Foreign Affairs (11 per cent), the Railway Police (5 per cent), and the Prison Services (1 per cent). This contradicts assertions by Shelton and Grundy which put the staff of the Secretariat as 70 per cent SADF, 20 per cent NIS, and 10 per cent Department of Foreign Affairs. See G. Shelton, 'Theoretical Perspectives on South African Foreign Policy Making', *Politikon* 13:1 (June 1986), 5; Grundy, op. cit., 15.
78. *Hansard Questions and Answers* 8 April 1986 (Pretoria: Government Printers), col 913.
79. Interview with senior military officer, 6 August 1991. Also see Geldenhuys and Kotze 1983, op. cit., 41. The authors identify 10 Joint Management Centres (JMCs) within South Africa (including Walvis Bay), one for the whole of Namibia, and three for neighbouring countries. Apparently the JMCs for neighbouring countries were never activated.
80. *Hansard Questions and Answers* 11 March 1986 (Pretoria: Government Printers, 460–1. Reportedly, these JMC boundaries were ultimately to be altered so as to correspond with the Regional Services Councils.
81. Interview with senior military officer, 6 August 1991.
82. *Hansard Questions and Answers* 11 March 1986 (Pretoria: Government Printers), col 461.
83. Interview with senior military officer 6 August 1991. He suggests that it was in fact the SAP's lack of training in the area of counter-revolutionary warfare that kept it from playing a key part in the command of JMC structures. Despite this perception, the senior military officer indicates that in the case of his own command he made a point of establishing a co-chairmanship of the JMC with the local SAP commander. According to another source, a contributing factor was that the SAP were unwilling to take on the responsibility of running the JMCs. Personal communications.
84. Senior military sources insist that the overwhelming majority of JMC activity was devoted specifically to 'welfare' issues. This became a particularly taxing aspect of the NSMS structure for the military as a whole as the SADF found itself to be involved in a growing range of issues which fell outside of traditional military training – for example, housing and infrastructural concerns (sewage,

water, telephones and roads).

85. Interview with senior military officer, 6 August 1991.
86. J. Selfe, 'The Total Onslaught and the Total Strategy: Adaptation to the Security Intelligence Decision-making Structures under P.W. Botha's Administration', (MA dissertation, University of Cape Town 1987), 158.
87. Interview with senior military officer, 6 August 1991. Selfe says plenary meetings were once every *three* months. Selfe, op. cit., 159–160.
88. Selfe, op. cit., 159–60.
89. JMC official cited in Selfe, op. cit., 162.
90. Interview with senior military officer, 6 August 1991. The Intelligence Committee (GIK) consisted of members of military intelligence branch, the police's intelligence branch, and the NIS.
91. *Hansard Questions and Answers* 11 March 1986 (Pretoria: Government Printers), cols 460–1.
92. Selfe, op. cit., 168.
93. Interview with senior military officer, 6 August 1991; Seegers, op. cit., 60.
94. Seegers, op. cit., 60.
95. *Hansard Questions and Answers* 11 March 1986 (Pretoria: Government Printers), cols 460–1.
96. Selfe, op. cit., 168.
97. Seegers, op. cit., 61.
98. Hough and van der Merwe, op. cit., 11.
99. D. Geldenhuys and H. Kotze, 'Aspects of Political Decision-making in South Africa', *Politikon* 10:1 June 1983, 39.
100. Grundy, op. cit., 1.
101. Cloete, op. cit., 9–11.
102. M. Swilling and M. Phillips 1989, op. cit., 36.
103. Interview with Dr. F. Cloete, 5 April 1990.
104. Interview with P.W. Botha, 18 June 1991. Botha emphatically stated that the Twelve Point Plan was the blueprint for the direction his administration would take South Africa in the decade of the eighties.
105. D. Geldenhuys, 'Some Foreign Policy Implications of South Africa's "Total National Strategy", with Particular Reference to the "12-point plan"' SAIIA Special Study, Braamfontein (March 1981), 60–2.
106. Christian Nationalism calls for separate, ethnically composed schools as one of its fundamental tenets. For a summary of Christian Nationalist ideals, see the Broederbond's 'Declaration on Behalf of Volkorganisasies' issued in 1941. D. Moodie, *The Rise of Afrikanerdom: Power, Apartheid, and the Afrikaner Civil Religion* (Berkeley: University of California Press 1975), 218–19.
107. Interview with P.W. Botha, 18 June 1991.
108. Interview with C. Heunis, 10 September 1991.
109. Interview with Dr F. Cloete, 5 April 1990.
110. H. Adam and H. Giliomee, *The Rise and Crisis of Afrikaner Power* (Cape Town: David Philips 1979), 209–10.

CHAPTER 4

1. Minister of Constitutional Development and Planning, Chris Heunis, Opening Statement on South Africa Constitution Bill, 5 May 1983. *Debates of the House of Assembly* (Hansard) 2–6 May 1983 Weekly Edition (Cape Town: Government Printers), col. 6365.
2. H. Giliomee, *The Parting of the Ways: South African Politics 1976–82* (Cape Town: David Philip 1982), 160; A. Lemon, *Apartheid in Transition* (Aldershot: Gower 1987), 101.
3. One commentator said of the 1981 election results that, 'The New Right's meagre parliamentary representation, therefore, is not a true reflection of its strength.' S. Uys, 'Whither the White Oligarchy?' in *South Africa in Crisis.* J. Blumfeld, ed., (London: Croom Helm 1987), 62; Lemon, op. cit., 104–5.
4. T. Lodge, *Black Politics in South Africa since 1945* (Johannesburg: Ravan 1983), 295; 306–10. The SAP's complacency towards the PAC caused one senior police officer to say: 'We [the security police] don't pay much attention to the PAC because it is such a small faction.' Cited in 'Courts', *Work in Progress* No. 16, February 1981 (Johannesburg: Sached), 4.
5. For a thorough account of ANC diplomacy in exile see S. Thomas, 'The Diplomacy of Liberation: the International Relations of the African National Congress of South Africa, 1960–1985', unpublished doctoral dissertation, University of London 1990.
6. Barrell, op. cit., 65. On the security implications of the ANC–SACP alliance, see S. Ellis, 'Mbokodo: Security in ANC Camps, 1961–90,' *African Affairs* 93:271 1994. For another perspective on Mogorogo's importance see K. Somerville, *Southern Africa and the Soviet Union: From Communist International to Commonwealth of Independent States* (London: Macmillan 1993), 211–12.
7. Stage one is political mobilization, stage two is terrorism (or 'armed propaganda'), stage three is guerrilla warfare, and stage four is conventional warfare.
8. Barrell, op. cit., 85.
9. Ibid., 86.
10. Ibid., 87.
11. Ibid., 88.
12. Ibid., 87.
13. Ibid., 85.
14. Williamson, op. cit., 282; *Sechaba*, December 1981.
15. Official government statistics on 'terrorist' incidents: 1978 – 13 incidents; 1979 – 22; 1980 – 19; 1981 – 55; 1982 – 39; 1983 – 56; 1984 – 44. Cited in R. Jaster, *South Africa and its Neighbours: the Dynamics of Regional Conflict.* Adelphi Paper 209, London: International Institute for Strategic Studies 1986, 53.
16. SAIRR 1980, op. cit., 280.
17. Lodge 1983, op. cit., 340; Karis, op. cit., 214–15.
18. 'Indeed, many witnesses in political trials, testifying on ANC strategy, have confirmed that the general policy of the organization is

to attack strategic and symbolic installations rather than to kill or injure those who are not involved. With the exception of the killing of police informers and ex-ANC members who have actively assisted the police, most incidents which have led to court cases have born out this general policy.' Anonymous, 'Total War', in *Work in Progress* No. 8 May 1979 (Johannesburg: Sached), 1.

19. Lodge 1983, op. cit., 340–1.
20. Jaster 1986, op. cit., 53.
21. Davis, op. cit., 29.
22. Interview with senior military official, 17 October 1991.
23. Ibid.
24. Ibid.
25. Interview with senior military official, 6 August 1991.
26. However, for reasons unknown, this re-structuring process was never completed.
27. Interview with senior military official, 6 August 1991; A. Seegers, 'The Government's Perception and Handling of South Africa's Security Needs', in *South Africa: The Challenge of Reform.* D. van Vuuren, N. Wiehahn, N. Rhoodie, M. Wiechers, eds., (Pinetown, SA: Burgess 1988), 413.
28. Interview with Lt.-General C. Lloyd, 10 September 1991.
29. Interview with senior military official, 6 August 1991.
30. According to military officials, the selection of national servicemen with necessary skills such as teaching was sometimes put off until they had completed their formal training. They were then employed in the Civic Action programme in their area of expertise. Interview with senior military official, 17 October 1991.
31. Ibid.
32. K. Grundy, *The Militarization of South African Politics*, (Oxford: Oxford UP 1988), 30.
33. J. Pauw, *In the Heart of the Whore: The Story of Apartheid's Death Squads* (Johannesburg: Southern 1991), 122, pp. 145–7.
34. Anonymous, 'Total War', *Work in Progress* No.8 May 1979, (Johannesburg: Sached), 3.
35. Grundy, op. cit., 22.
36. I.W. Zartman, *Ripe for Resolution: Conflict and Intervention in Africa*, (New York: Oxford UP 1985), 130.
37. R. Davies and D. O'Meara, 'Total Strategy in Southern Africa: Regional Policy Since 1978', *Journal of Southern African Studies*, 11:2 1985, 185.
38. The United States, West Germany, France, Canada and Britain.
39. The Democratic Turnhalle Alliance (DTA) grew out of a constituent conference held in September 1975 which put together a proposal for an independent Namibian state based on the principles of confederalism in March 1977. Following the conference's dissolution, the DTA was formed under the leadership of National party secretary Dirk Mudge and Chief Kapuuo. Zartman, op. cit., 157.
40. Jaster 1985, op. cit., 45.
41. Zartman, op. cit., 167.

42. J. Barber and J. Barratt. *South Africa's Foreign Policy: The Search for Status and Security, 1945–1988* (Johannesburg: Southern 1990), 265–6. From the mid-seventies onwards, the SADF had been encouraging the establishment of ethnically-based Namibian units. By 1979 four units – the 31st (Bushman), 33rd (Caprivi), 34th (Kavango) and the 35th (Ovambo) – were in place and a year later the SWATF was founded as a separate command. In October 1980 conscription into the military was made mandatory for all Namibians between the ages of 16 and 24. This new influx of local manpower was designed to build the basis for an independent Namibian defence force, 'assist in counter- insurgency and gradually help reduce the number of white South African troops required to engage in combat against Swapo and to defend the Namibia-Angola border.' Jaster 1985, op. cit., 53–5.
43. Jaster, ibid., 52.
44. G. Evans, 'SADF and the Civic Action Program', *Work in Progress* No. 29, October 1983 (Johannesburg: Sached), 20.
45. The Angolan intervention of 1975 was unique in that it had as its objective (with the support of American and other interests) the prevention of communist rule in Luanda; subsequent interventions were more narrowly focused on objectives directly pertaining to South African interests in Namibia.
46. Jaster 1985, op. cit., 20; Zartman, op. cit., 166.
47. Jaster 1985, op. cit., 49–50.
48. J. Roherty, *State Security in South Africa: Civil–Military Relations under P.W. Botha* (London: M.E. Sharpe 1992), 47.
49. See C. Crocker, *High Noon in Southern Africa: Making Peace in a Rough Neighborhood* (Johannesburg: Jonathan Ball 1992).
50. Zartman, op. cit., 191; 198.
51. Jaster 1986, op. cit., 36; *Africa Contemporary Record: Annual Survey and Documents 1982–1983*, op. cit., A24.
52. Somerville, op. cit., 93–4. In November the Angolan government presented its preconditions for a phased withdrawal of Cuban troops northward over a two year period: the withdrawal of South African troops from southern Angola and termination of support for Unita; the implementation of Security Council Resolution 435; the limitation of South African military forces in Namibia to 1500; and the introduction of a UN Transition Force in Namibia to supervise the process.
53. Pik Botha quoted in Barber and Barratt, op. cit., 259.
54. Ibid., 259–60.
55. Jaster 1986, op. cit., 12.
56. The Lancaster House Agreement of 1979 included a promise by the Patriotic Front leaders to disavow the use of Zimbabwe as a forward base for South African liberation organizations. H. Nelson, ed., *Zimbabwe: A Country Study* (US Government: 1983), 46 and 226.
57. Jaster 1986, op. cit., 10.
58. Martin and Johnson, op. cit., 68–9. South Africa subsequently reversed

its position on the locomotives, lending them to several countries in the region to move their goods through Zimbabwe.

59. Ibid., 49.
60. Ibid.
61. Three whites from SADF's 5th Recce unit, an SADF force made up of former members of Rhodesian Special Forces, were intercepted and killed by Zimbabwean troops on 18 August 1982. After this embarrassing disclosure, the SADF apparently ceased such operations. Ibid., 50.
62. Embittered by the electoral defeat by Mugabe's Shona-dominated Zanu party, some Ndebele nationalists from Nkomo's Zapu party clashed with the Zimbabwean military in the period immediately following independence. This rebellion culminated in a failed bid to take the traditional capitol of Matabeleland in February 1981. Factoring into the conflict was Nkomo's unwillingness to accept the secondary status conferred upon him by fellow revolutionary Mugabe in the newly formed government in Harare. His displeasure over the situation resulted in his demotion within the cabinet and eventually his ousting from the government in January 1981. Nelson, op. cit., 210–12.
63. Martin and Johnson, op. cit., 56. By 1983 the Zimbabwean government had evidence of 16 cases of SADF-trained dissidents operating in Matabeleland. Davis contends that 5000 Zapu guerrillas received training by the SADF. Davis, op. cit., 42.
64. *Africa Contemporary Record: Annual Survey and Documents 1982–83*, op. cit., B882.
65. Martin and Johnson, op. cit., 62.
66. Tariffs of 40 per cent were placed on goods travelling through the Northern Transvaal.
67. T. Ranger, 'Matabeleland since the Amnesty', *African Affairs* 88:351 (April 1989), 162.
68. As one scholar notes: 'There is ample evidence of [the South African government's] readiness to strike, and a corresponding apprehension in Harare that a South African armoured column could not be stopped and might even be welcomed all the way to Bulawayo by those who have reason to oppose the Zanu Patriotic Front government.' D. Austin, *South Africa 1984*, Chatham House Paper 26, Royal Institute for International Affairs (London: Routledge & Kegan Paul 1985), 58.
69. R. Jaster, *The Defence of White Power: South African Foreign Policy under Pressure*, (London: Macmillan 1988), 119–20.
70. The origins of the Mozambican National Resistance (MNR) or Renamo as it was later called lay in the Rhodesian government's efforts combat the establishment of a Zanu sanctuary in neighboring Mozambique. Sanctions introduced in 1976 against neighbouring Rhodesia had cut traffic between the land-locked state and the vital port of Beira. While Zanu guerrillas, utilizing the sanctuary of Tete province, brought further pressure to bear on the embattled Smith regime the Rhodesians countered by engineering direct military incursions into Mozambican territory as well as establishing an armed guerrilla movement from amongst dissident elements

within Mozambican society. See K. Flower, *Serving Secretly: Rhodesia's CIO Chief on Record* (Alberton, SA: Galago 1987).

71. Martin and Johnson, op. cit., 13.
72. Ibid., 12; 19.
73. Williamson, op. cit., 282.
74. Defence Minister M. Malan, *Debates of the House of Assembly* (Hansard) 23 to 27 May 1983, No. 16, Weekly Edition, (Cape Town: Government Printer).
75. R. Davies, 'South African Strategy Towards Mozambique in the Post-Nkomati Period: A Critical Analysis of Effects and Implications', Research Report No. 73, Scandinavian Institute of African Studies, Uppsala 1985, 14.
76. Martin and Johnson, op. cit., 29.
77. Jaster 1988, op. cit., 119–20.
78. See G. Erasmus, 'The Accord of Nkomati: Context and Content' Braamfontein: South African Institute of International Affairs (October 1984), 15–21.
79. Chan, op. cit., 50.
80. Jaster 1986, op. cit., 30.
81. According to a participant in the negotiation process, the Portuguese supporters of Renamo sabotaged the delicate talks. Private communication.
82. B. Magubane, 'Botswana, Lesotho, and Swaziland: Hostages in Revolt', in *South Africa in Southern Africa: The Intensifying Vortex of Violence,* T. Callaghy, ed., (New York: Praeger 1983), 355–69.
83. Martin and Johnson, op. cit., 159.
84. According to Lodge, PAC activists utilized the country as a base for military training in the early sixties. Lodge 1983, op. cit., 316. Davis indicates that the ANC used Botswana as a conduit for its cadres. Davis, op. cit., 28–9.
85. Martin and Johnson, op. cit., 157.
86. The Botswanan Foreign Minister, A. Mogwe, said of the Nkomati Accord: 'The deal was concluded with Mozambique in order to isolate and compartmentalize one country after another in this region along the lines of the so-called homelands . . . [but] . . . we are not so dumb as to allow the ANC or any other anti-South African body to use our territory. We do not want to be placed in the position of also having to sign a non-aggression pact.' Austin, op. cit., 56.
87. Martin and Johnson, op. cit., 140.
88. Ibid., 145.
89. Ibid., 140; Karis, op. cit., 209.
90. Magubane, op. cit., 365.
91. According to some sources, the South African government's plan to transfer the homeland of KaNgwane to Swaziland was part and parcel of the security accord signed between the two states. Austin, op. cit., 54.
92. Davis, op. cit., 29; 30.
93. *Southern African Record.* No. 36, August 1984, Braamfontein: South African Institute of International Affairs, 3–6.

94. J. Barber and C. Hill, *The West and South Africa*, Chatham House Report 14, Royal Institute of International Affairs (London:Routledge & Kegan Paul 1982), 26.
95. Ibid., 3.
96. Somerville, op. cit., 242–3.
97. D. Howlett and J. Simpson, 'Nuclearisation and Denuclearisation in South Africa', *Survival* vol. 35:3, pp. 155.
98. B. Rabert, 'South Africa's Nuclear Weapons – A Defused Time Bomb?' *Aussenpolitik*, 44:3 1993, pp. 234–6.
99. Ibid., pp. 235.
100. Ibid., 236.
101. Ibid., 239
102. Ibid.
103. D. Howlett and J. Simpson, op. cit., 162.
104. M. Bennett, 'The Super Federation: Independent Unionism Comes of Age', *Indicator South Africa* 3:2 (Spring 1985), 2–3; R. Smith, 'The Black Trade Unions: From Economics to Politics', in *South Africa in Crisis*, J. Blumfeld, ed., (London: Croom Helm 1987), 94–5.
105. S. Friedman, *Building Tomorrow Today: African Workers in Trade Unions 1970–1984*, (Johannesburg: Ravan 1987), 180–241.
106. Ibid., 316.
107. E. Webster, 'The Rise of Social-movement Unionism: The Two Faces of the Black Trade Union Movement in South Africa', in *State, Resistance and Change in South Africa*, P. Frankel, N. Pines, and M. Swilling, eds, (Johannesburg: Southern 1988), 183.
108. For a discussion of the gradual lifting of one aspect of 'petty apartheid' see V. Cadman, 'Open Beaches: The Receding Tide of Apartheid', *Indicator South Africa* 3:3 (Summer 1986).
109. Pottinger, op. cit., 120; Barber and Hill 1982, op. cit., 30.
110. Cilliers 1986, op. cit., 8. Blacks who held 'section ten' rights were henceforth allowed freedom of movement between 'white' cities (formerly 'section ten' rights were granted for a specific urban area). The requirements for the obtainment of 'section ten' rights were lowered: blacks who had worked for more than one employer over the designated time period were granted residential rights (formerly blacks had to work continuously for one employer alone in order to qualify for 'section ten' rights). Finally, 'section ten' rights were restored to some blacks who lost them through such actions as homeland consolidation or relocation.
111. SAIRR 1985, op. cit., 252–3.
112. Republic of South Africa 1985(A), *Report of the Committee for Constitutional Affairs of the President's Council on an Urbanisation Strategy for the Republic of South Africa*, (Cape Town: Government Printers).
113. Lemon, op. cit., 239.
114. Cloete, op. cit., 13.
115. J. Grest, 'The Crisis of Local Government in South Africa', in *State, Resistance and Change in South Africa*, P. Frankel, N. Pines and M. Swilling, eds, (Johannesburg: Southern 1988), 105.
116. Cited in P. du Toit, 'Regional Services Councils: Control at Local

Government Level', *Government By the People?: The Politics of Local Government in South Africa,* C. Heymans, and G. Totemeyer, eds. (Johannesburg: Juta 1988), 69.

117. Interview with C. Heunis, 10 September 1991.
118. Grest, op. cit., 95.
119. Republic of South Africa 1982(C), op. cit., 42.
120. The Yeld Commission in 1977 followed by the T.J. Schlebusch Commission and the Browne Commission.
121. H. Venter, 'Assistance to Black Local Authorities', unpublished manuscript, Annexure A.
122. Republic of South Africa 1982(C), op. cit., 105. See Appendix One.
123. Ibid., 115–18.
124. Grest, op. cit., 97.
125. According to a report of the Auditor General in 1984, the development boards were R120 million in debt to the government. SAIRR 1984, op. cit., 164.
126. SAIRR 1984, op. cit., 151.
127. Interview with C. Heunis, 10 September 1991; SAIRR 1983, op. cit., 246.
128. Interview with C. Heunis, 10 September 1991.
129. SAIRR 1983, op. cit., 246.
130. SAIRR 1984, op. cit., 152.
131. SAIRR 1985, op. cit., 82.
132. Republic of South Africa 1982(C), op. cit., 114–15.
133. *Debates of the House of Assembly.* (Hansard) 6 May 1985, (Pretoria: Government Printers), col. 4902.
134. Ibid., cols 4905–7.
135. *Citizen* 7 May 1985.
136. SAIRR 1985, op. cit., 69.
137. Heunis told the Natal provincial council that the inclusion of African participation in the new provincial system had to be 'seriously considered'. *Citizen* 14 October 1985.
138. SAIRR 1985, op. cit., 70.
139. Republic of South Africa 1988, 'Regional Services Councils', issued on behalf of the Department of Development Planning and the Constitutional Development Services (Parow, South Africa: June 1988), 1; Adlem, op. cit., 76.
140. The RSCs were empowered to levy a services tax, based on the remuneration paid out to employees, and an establishment tax, based on business sales.
141. According to the final version of the RSC Bill (1985): [E]very local body represented on an RSC may nominate one member for every 10 per cent, or part of 10 per cent, of the total number of votes it is entitled to, although no local body may appoint more than five members. However, if there are two or more local bodies represented on an RSC, no local body is entitled to more than 50% of the votes. The costs of regional functions provided in industrial areas or central business districts are excluded from the calculations . . .' The chairman of the RSC, appointed by the pro-

vincial administrator, does not have voting rights. Decisions within RSCs are taken on the basis of a two-thirds majority vote. SAIRR 1985, op. cit., 74.

142. SAIRR 1984, op. cit., 161.
143. Ibid., 161.
144. Concurrent with the launching of constitutional initiatives by the South African government was the convening of a separate effort sponsored by the province of Natal and the homeland of KwaZulu. This initiative was actively discouraged by the government.
145. Republic of South Africa 1982(A), *First Report of the Constitutional Committee of the President's Council*. Cape Town: Government Printer).
146. The President's Council was elected by the different houses of parliament on the following basis: 20 white members, 10 Coloured members and 5 Asian members. The State President appointed the 25 remaining members of the institution.
147. Interview with C. Heunis, 10 September 1991; *Debates of the House of Assembly* (Hansard) 18 May 1983 (Pretoria: Government Printers), cols 7382 & 7386–7. The same day that the President's Council tabled its report – 12 May 1982 – the Prime Minister and the Minister of Constitutional Development and Planning had the first of many meetings with leaders of Labour party, the Freedom party and the Executive Committee of the Indian Council. According to Heunis, 'Only on 4 June did the Cabinet approve of provisional guidelines for submission [of the constitutional proposals] to its caucus. That caucus took place 5 June.' *Debates of the House of Assembly* (Hansard) 18 May 1983 (Pretoria: Government Printers), col. 7387. The major flaw in this process of consultation was that these leaders of the Coloured and Indian communities were not considered to be representative of those communities by some people. This would become evident as the UDF marshalled protest against the constitution.
148. Anonymous, 'Labour Party: A Constitutional Decision?' *Work in Progress* 25 (February 1983), Johannesburg: Sached.
149. Pottinger, op. cit., 105.
150. An account of the momentous split is carried in Pottinger, op. cit., 138–45.
151. P. Hugo and K. O'Malley, 'Political Parties and Pressure Groups: a Selective Overview', in *South African Government and Politics: An Introduction to its Institutions, Processes and Policies*, A. Venter, ed., (Johannesburg: Southern 1989), 130–1.
152. Giliomee, op. cit., 159.
153. Minister of Constitutional Development and Planning, C. Heunis, 16 May 1983, *Debates of the House of Assembly* (Hansard) Weekly Edition (Cape Town: Government Printers), col. 7053.
154. SAIRR 1983, op. cit., 88.
155. Alan Henrickse, leader of the Coloured Labour party, suggested that an election would be a sufficient test of the Coloured community's support for the new constitutional dispensation. SAIRR 1984, op. cit., 122. Amichand Rajbansi, leader of the Asian National Peo-

ple's Party, expressed disappointment at the cancellation of the referendum but vowed to participate in the upcoming election. SAIRR 1984, op. cit., 34.

156. Ibid., 127–8.
157. SAIRR 1984, op. cit., 130.
158. The Black State Citizenship Act of 1970 mandated that all blacks residing in South Africa were to be considered citizens of one of the homelands. The homelands were given self-governing status through the passage of the Constitution of National States Act of 1971.
159. 'The reality which we must face is that it is impossible to consolidate the geographic areas of each population group in such a way on its own so that it will satisfy the material aspirations of its people within geographic boundaries.' P.W. Botha, 21 October 1980. Cited in Pottinger, op. cit., 116.
160. Lemon, op. cit., 182–9; SAIRR 1986, op. cit., 42–56.
161. S. Coetzee, (Interview) 'A New Animal on the Sub-Continent: The Development Bank of South Africa', *Indicator South Africa* 3:2 (Spring 1985), 1–4; Lemon, op. cit., 191.
162. N. Engelbrecht and E. Kruger, 'The Role and Future of the Development Bank of Southern Africa', *Strategic Review for Southern Africa* X:2 (November 1988), 15.
163. C. Heunis, speech to National party congress in Natal, 15 August 1985. Lemon, op. cit., 192.
164. SAIRR 1984, op. cit., 142. On this point, also see P.W. Botha, 'South Africa – Some Perspectives for the Future', *Aussen Politik* 35 (Third Quarter 1984), 277–8.
165. Botha 1984, op. cit. 278–9.

CHAPTER 5

1. T. Lodge et al., *All, Here, and Now: Black Politics in South Africa in the 1980s*, South Africa Update Series, Ford Foundation/Foreign Policy Association 1991, 51.
2. R. Schrire, *Adapt or Die: The End of White Politics in South Africa*, South Africa Update Series, Ford Foundation/Foreign Policy Association 1991, 155–8.
3. J. Seekings, 'The Origins of Political Mobilisation in PWV Townships, 1980–84', *Popular Struggles in South Africa*, W. Cobbett and R. Cohen eds (London: James Currey 1988), 60.
4. Anonymous, 'Rents: Soweto', *Work in Progress* 15 (October 1980) Johannesburg: Sached, 22.
5. The absence of any kind of any industrial or commercial base upon which taxes might be levied, coupled with the 'temporary sojourner' status of black residents which obviated the use of a property tax, placed severe restrictions upon local government in the townships. As a result, the primary sources of revenue over the years had been the collection of rents and the sale of sorghum beer by a white-controlled monopoly. Ibid., 22.

6. J. Poto, 'The Viability of Black Local Authorities', in *Government by the People? The Politics of Local Government in South Africa*, C. Heymans and G. Totemeyer, eds (Johannesburg: Juta 1988), 97–8.
7. SAIRR 1982, *Survey of Race Relations in South Africa*, (Pietermaritzburg: Natal Witness 1983), 23; SAIRR 1983, op. cit., 258–9; Lodge 1991, op. cit., 42. According to the SAIRR, the overall percentage poll for the 29 councils up for election in 1982 was 21 per cent versus 30 per cent in 1978. The UDF contested these figures, claiming for example that the supposed 36 per cent poll in Kagiso was actually 3 per cent. SAIRR 1983, op. cit., 260.
8. Survey data from the period supports this conclusion. According to opinion polls conducted between 1979 and 1985, urbanized Africans experienced an increasing level of alienation during the period which coincided with the heart of the Botha reform programme. When asked to identify where 'most African people like yourself (in your township) feel about life in South Africa today', in 1977 39 per cent said they were 'angry', in 1979 44 per cent responded this way, in 1984 50 per cent and in 1985 66 per cent. Cited in R. Price, *The Apartheid State in Crisis: Political Transformation in South Africa 1975–90*, (Oxford: Oxford UP 1991), 153–4.
9. Schlemmer 1985, op. cit., 4–5.
10. On different theorists of revolution see J. Goldstone, ed., *Revolutions: Theoretical, Comparative, and Historical Studies*, (New York: Harcourt, Brace, Jovanovich 1986).
11. Schlemmer 1985, op. cit., 5.
12. *Work in Progress* 13 (July 1980) Johannesburg: Sached, 1–6. These student protests in the Western Cape were, by the early eighties, a feature of township life in the PWV area. F. Meer, ed., *Resistance in the Townships*, (Durban: Institute for Black Research, Madiba 1989), 25–6.
13. While the government initially branded the students' activities as the work of leftist agitators, by the year's end they were acknowledging the validity of many of the student's grievances. SAIRR 1980, op. cit., 502; 518. By way of contrast, the proto-civic organization the Committee of Ten appealed to students in Soweto to return to classes, a call which students by and large heeded.
14. *Work in Progress* 10 (November 1979) Johannesburg: Sached, 7. The Soweto Civic Association grew out of the Soweto Committee of Ten, an organization which was formed in July 1977 by groups (among them Black Parents Association, Black People's Convention and the South African Students Organization) which had emerged at the time of the 1976 rebellion. Thirty-three branches of the SCA were envisioned at the time of the founding of the organization. *Work in Progress* 11 (February 1980) Johannesburg: Sached, 13.
15. SAIRR 1980, op. cit., 58.
16. The Cape Housing Action Committee and the Durban Housing Action Committee slated the black local authorities. SAIRR 1982, op. cit., 30.
17. The Zwide Residents' Association and the Kwaford Residents' Association formed the nucleus of Pebco. C. Cooper and L. Ensor,

Pebco: A Black Mass Movement, (Johannesburg: SAIRR 1981), 27–8.
18. *Work in Progress* 11 (February 1980) Johannesburg: Sached, 13.
19. Cooper and Escor, op. cit., 20.
20. Ibid., 20; 25; 37.
21. Lodge 1991, op. cit., 43–5.
22. Ibid.
23. G. Moss, 'SAIC: Participation or Boycott', *Work in Progress* 10 (November 1979) Johannesburg: Sached, 1–6.
24. M. Swilling, 'The United Democratic Front and Township Revolt', *Popular Struggles in South Africa,* W. Cobbett and R. Cohen, eds (London: James Currey 1988), 96.
25. Swilling 1988, op. cit., 101.
26. SAIRR 1983, op. cit., 248; 258–9.
27. Swilling 1988, op. cit., 101.
28. The origins of many civics in the black conciousness movement underscores this point. See the earliest positions of Soweto's Committee of Ten. *Work in Progress* 10 (November 1979) Johannesburg: Sached, 7–10.
29. SAIRR 1984, op. cit., 54.
30. *Africa Contemporary Record: Annual Survey and Documents, 1983–84,* C. Legum, ed. (London: Africana 1985), B747.
31. Speaking in an interview, UDF Publicity Secretary 'Terror' Lekota admitted that, '[R]elations with Azapo are far from what one would like them to be. They have attacked the UDF on its non-racial approach.' Cited in 'Lekota on UDF', *Work in Progress* 30 (February 1983) Johannesburg: Sached, 8.
32. G. Howe, 'Deadlock in Emergent States: 1960/61 and 1984/85: Township Uprising, Armed Occupation', *Indicator SA* 3:2 (Spring 1985(A)), 2.
33. In spite of the relatively high level of publicity which accompanied the school protests in 1984, only 7 per cent of all black pupils were involved in the actions. SAIRR 1984, op. cit., 1.
34. An estimated 100 persons were injured at the polling station in Lenasia when police fired rubber bullets and tear gas and used sjamboks (whips) on the crowd. Ibid., 70–1.
35. Ibid., 65. It was estimated that anywhere from 35 per cent to 65 per cent of the township residents responded to the strike.
36. SAIRR 1985, op. cit., 65. Of the 137 deaths related to civil disturbances over the period between September 1984 and November 1984, 96 were due to security force actions, 30 were considered to be intra-civilian strife and 7 occurred during attacks on policemen and town councillors. Howe 1985(A), op. cit., 3.
37. Cited in L. Nathan, 'Troops in the Townships, 1984–87', in *War and Society: The Militarisation of South Africa.* L. Nathan and J. Cock, eds (Cape Town: David Philip 1989), 68.
38. M. Evans and M. Phillips, 'Intensifying Civil War: the Role of the South African Defence Force', *State, Resistance and Change in South Africa,* P. Frankel, N. Pines and M. Swilling, eds (Johannesburg: Southern 1988), 129; SAIRR 1984, op. cit., 752.

39. SAIRR 1984, op. cit., 65. The trade unions used the higher estimate of 800 000 participants in the strike. See S. Friedman, *Building Tomorrow Today: African Workers in Trade Unions 1970–84* (Johannesburg: Ravan 1987), 448.
40. SAIRR 1984, op. cit., 77.
41. Howe estimates that civil unrest between August and November 1984 cost an estimated R30–R50 million damage to public property alone. Howe 1985(A), op. cit., 5.
42. M. Bennett, 'Countdown to State of Emergency: A Chronology of Township Revolt, 1985', *Indicator SA* 3:2 (Spring 1985), 6.
43. One contemporary observer states: 'During the build-up to the (State of) Emergency, the security forces had become embroiled in a spiral of violence and counter-violence, emerging as an undeniably subjective element of the raging political conflict . . . By July this year (1985), the police had acknowledged responsibility for 336 out of 455 civilian deaths over 11 months of unrest, a figure more akin to a civil war "body count" than any conceivable "civilian riot" death toll. Preceding forms of tough security action had also failed to break the momentum of rebellion: more than 14,000 arrests and almost 1,500 detentions were made over the same period'. Howe 1985(A), op. cit., 2; 4.
44. Most of the boycotts were organized by the UDF and its affiliates. SAIRR 1985, op. cit., 556.
45. M. Tyala, 'The New Frontier: Rebellion in the Eastern Cape', *Indicator SA* 3:4 (Autumn 1986), 18.
46. M. Bennett, 'Countdown to State of Emergency: a Chronology of Township Revolt, 1985', *Indicator SA* 3:2 (Spring 1985), 6.
47. Attacks on policemen and town councillors' homes rose from 56 during the first phase of the rebellion to 288 during the second phase. Howe, op. cit., 2–5. A study by the Institute of Strategic Studies at the University of Pretoria showed that there had been a dramatic increase in the use of weapons such as hand grenades, AK-47s and limpet mines since the start of the township rebellion in September 1984. 'Terrorism and Sabotage in the RSA: 1976–1986', ISSUP *Bulletin*, University of Pretoria (April 1986), 5–6.
48. SAIRR 1985, op. cit., 541.
49. G. Howe, 'Cycles of Civil Unrest 1976/84: Triggers, Targets and Trends', *Indicator SA* 3:1 (Winter 1985(B)), 9.
50. Tyala, op. cit., 19.
51. M. Khwela, 'Resistance and Containment', *Resistance in the Townships*, (Durban: Institute for Black Research 1989), 208.
52. One commentator offered this explanation of the black trade unions behaviour: 'The unions had indeed spent the decade [the seventies] ignoring politics, but not because they thought it evil; their founders had launched the new movement precisely because they wanted political change. But they know that it would be tactical suicide to voice political demands when even factory battles invited police action – and that they could hardly win political rights if they were not strong enough to gain a say in the factories.'

Friedman, op. cit., 430.

53. Ibid., 440.
54. Lodge 1991, op. cit., 73.
55. It was not until the decision of the central executive committee at the Ipelegeng Centre in Soweto held in February 1986 to adopt an overtly political stance that Cosatu began to fully involve itself in politics of the day. According to the resolution adopted by the committee the current economic and political crisis required that Cosatu and the working class 'take political action' in alliance with other 'progressive organizations' which operated according to democratic principles. J. Barkin, *Striking Back: A History of Cosatu,* (Johannesburg: Ravan 1991), 91–4.
56. Ibid., 53–67.
57. T. Mazwai, 'Caught in the Crossfire: African Local Authorities twixt Government and Community', *Indicator SA* 3:2 (Spring 1985), 10.
58. Schlemmer 1985, op. cit., 2.
59. According to one critic, the lack of training and under-staffing in the police resulted in 'frequent over-reaction on the part of (very often) young, under-trained and frightened men who simply do not have the numbers, means or disposition to tackle rioting crowds through the phased use of force'. S. Baynham, 'Just the Usual Sunday Sports? The Controversy over Methods of Riot Control', interview with Major-General B. Wandrag, H. Heitman, and S. Baynham, *Indicator SA* 3:2 (Spring 1985), 15.
60. SAIRR 1985, op. cit., 496–501. A state coroner disclosed that in his opinion, many of the deaths listed officially as suicides were in fact the result of wanton police brutality. *Sunday Times* 26 July 1992.
61. See J. Pauw, *In the Heart of the Whore: The Story of Apartheid's Death Squads* (Johannesburg: Southern 1991).
62. Private communication.
63. Private communication.
64. Private communication.
65. Interview the Lt.-General P. van der Westhuizen, 24 March 1992.
66. M. Swilling and M. Phillips, 'The Powers of the Thunderbird: Decision-making Structures and Policy Strategies in the South African State', in *South Africa at the End of the Eighties: Policy Perspectives 1989* (Johannesburg: Centre for Policy Studies 1989), 48.
67. The concept of a National Welfare Management System had developed over the first few years of the Botha administration's term in office. It consisted of the three major cabinet committees devoted to 'welfare' issues: Economic, Social and Constitutional. A 'welfare' secretariat, mirroring the SSC's secretariat, coordinated the three cabinet committee policies and liaised through the NCC with the secretariat of the SSC.
68. A. Seegers, 'The Government's Perception and Handling of South Africa's Security Needs', in *South Africa: The Challenge of Reform,* D. van Vuuren, N. Wiehahn, N. Rhoodie, M. Wiechers, eds (Pinetown, RSA: Owen Burgess 1988), 420.
69. Swilling and Phillips 1989, op. cit., 46.

70. Ibid., 46.
71. Section 3(1)(a) of the Public Safety Act allowed the State President to issue by proclamation 'such regulations as appear to him to be necessary or expedient for providing for the safety of the public, or the maintenance of public order and for making adequate provisions for terminating such emergency or for dealing with any circumstances which in his opinion have arisen or are likely to arise as a result of such emergency.' SAIRR 1985, op. cit., 456.
72. According to one researcher, when the partial state of emergency was first declared 'it seemed that the government anticipated that the "situation" would soon be under control, and that no further measures would be needed against the media in the coverage of the "unrest".' R. Tomaselli, 'A Pressing Emergency: The Commercial Media under the Bureau', *Indicator SA* 4:3 (Summer 1987), 19.
73. Crocker, op. cit., 259.
74. M. Bennett, 'Curbing the Fourth Estate', *Indicator SA* 4:3 (Summer 1986), 18.
75. Interview with General P. Groenewald, 7 October 1991.
76. M. Hough, 'Revolt in the Townships', *Challenge: Southern Africa within the African Revolutionary Context,* A. Venter, ed. (Gibraltar: Ashanti 1989), 393.
77. They were: (Eastern Cape) Adelaide, Albany, Alexandria, Bathurst, Bedford, Cradock, Fort Beaufort, Graaff-Reinet, Hankey, Humansdorp, Jansenville, Kirkwood, Pearston, Port Elizabeth, Somerset East, Steytlerville and Uitenhage; (Orange Free State) Sasolburg; (Transvaal) Alberton, Balfour, Benoni, Boksburg, Brakpan, Delmas, Germiston, Heidelberg, Johannesburg, Kempton Park, Nigel, Randburg, Randfontein, Roodeport, Springs, Vanderbijlpark, Vereenigning and Westonaria. SAIRR 1985, op. cit., 456.
78. The SADF reportedly spent R22 971 out of its budget on the introduction of sports facilities. SAIRR 1985, op. cit., 424.
79. The banning order was extended to ten more groups in December 1985. SAIRR 1985, op. cit., 434–5.
80. Ibid., 441. According to the Ministry of Law and Order, 1700 persons were arrested over contravening section 46 of the Internal Security Act, hundreds of whom were under 18 years old. Ibid., 435; 440. Howe reports the figure of persons arrested in 1985 to be over 10 000. Howe, op. cit., 11. Among those serviced a banning order was Trevor Manuel, a member of the UDF's national executive.
81. One researcher declares that 'the emergency seriously crippled the work of organizations opposed to the Government. More than 4,000 activists were detained by the end of September under the emergency powers, and many activists went under ground.' B. Mthombothi, '"Introduction"', in *Resistance in the Townships,* F. Meer, ed. (Durban: Institute for Black Research 1989), 6. By the end of 1985, 11 UDF officials and activists had disappeared or were assassinated, and 136 UDF activists had been detained. SAIRR 1985, op. cit., 41.
82. With the discovery of the men's bodies, the two organizations sus-

pended their quarrel once again, blaming government vigilantes for their deaths. Subsequent evidence has demonstrated that the Cradock activists were murdered at the behest of the Eastern Cape JMC. *New Nation* 8–14 May 1992.

83. Cosas was banned at the end of August.
84. SAIRR 1985, op. cit., 576–7.
85. Ibid., 422.
86. Between June 6 and December 12 some 33 township residents did step forward and file complaints against the SADF. Of these claims, four went to trial and the defendants were found guilty, two were dealt with internally and the rest were dismissed on various grounds. SAIRR 1985, op. cit., 424–85.
87. Howe 1985(A), op. cit. 2.
88. It was lifted in (Eastern Cape) Alexandria, Hankey, Humansdorp and Steytlerville; (Transvaal) Balfour and Westonaria. The next day the emergency was imposed on (Western Cape) Bellville, Goodwood, Kuils River, Paarl, Simon's Town, Cape Town, Worcester and Wynberg.
89. It was lifted in (Eastern Cape) Adelaide, Bathurst, Bedford, Jansenville and Pearston; (Orange Free State) Sasolburg; (Transvaal) Delmas and Heidelberg. SAIRR 1985, op. cit., 456.
90. It was lifted in (Eastern Cape) Graaff-Reinet, Kirkwood, Somerset East; (Western Cape) Kuils River, Paarl and Simon's Town. Ibid., 456.
91. *Sunday Times* 28 August 1994; J. Pauw, *In the Heart of the Whore: The Story of Apartheid's Death Squads* (Johannesburg: Southern 1991), 177.
92. *Debates of the House of Assembly.* (Hansard) Weekly Edition 3–6 March 1986 (Cape Town: Government Printers), col. 1446. Botha goes on to plead for black participation in the negotiation process: 'In addition I have also announced a clear basis on which all South Africans who reject violence can come to the conference table to negotiate jointly a new constitutional dispensation for our country.'
93. See N. Haysom, *Mabangalala: The Rise of Right-Wing Vigilantes in South Africa* (Johannesburg: University of the Witwatersrand 1986).
94. T. Thulo, 'Violence in Pietermaritzburg, 1985–1988', in *Resistance in the Townships* F. Meer, ed. (Durban: Institute for Black Research 1989), 194–206.
95. Sparks, A. *Tomorrow is Another Country: The Inside Story of South Africa's Road to Change* (New York: Hill & Wang 1995), 165–8.
96. D. Quin, 'From One Emergency to Another: A Brief "Interlude", 7 March-11 June 1986', *Indicator SA* 4:1 (Winter 1986), 26.
97. P. Laurence, 'Rural Revolt: Transvaal's Homelands in Ferment', *Indicator SA* 4:2 (Spring 1986), 26.
98. SAIRR 1986, op. cit., 518. The daily rate of killing was 3.8 persons between 1 January 1986 and 6 March 1986 (partial state of emergency); 6.41 persons between 7 March 1986 and 11 June 1986 (no emergency); and 2.11 persons between 12 June 1986 and 31 December 1986 (full state of emergency).

99. H. Heitman, *War in Angola: The Final South African Phase* (Gibraltar: Ashanti 1990), 15.
100. *Africa Contemporary Record: Annual Survey and Documents 1985–1986*, C. Legum, ed. (London: Africana 1987), B699.
101. Jaster 1985, op. cit., 65.
102. *Africa Contemporary Record: Annual Survey and Documents 1986–1987.*, op. cit., B710.
103. P. Esterhuysen, 'Overcoming the Obstacles of the 1980s', *Namibia 1990: An Africa Institute Country Survey* E. Leistner and P. Esterhuysen, eds (Pretoria: Africa Institute of South Africa 1991), 57.
104. SAIRR 1985, op. cit., 433.
105. *Africa Contemporary Record: Annual Survey and Documents 1984–1985*, op. cit., B923.
106. *Africa Contemporary Record: Annual Survey and Documents, 1985–86*, B925–B929.
107. A. Vines, *Renamo: Terrorism in Mozambique*, (London: James Currey in association with Centre for Southern African Studies 1991), 26.
108. See C. Alden, 'Mozambique: An Abiding Dependency', in *Southern Africa at the Crossroads: Security and Development in the 1990s* (Johannesburg: Justified 1992).
109. According to South African intelligence, Botswana in particular acted as a conduit for the transmission of ANC cadres and weaponry following the Nkomati Accord. See *South African Digest* 4 October 1985; 'Botswana "Activated" by ANC', *Paratus* (July 1985), 19–21.
110. 'ANC Terror Hide Outs Destroyed', *Paratus* (July 1985), 18.
111. SAIRR 1985, op. cit., 431.
112. *Africa Contemporary Record: Annual Survey and Documents 1985–86*, op. cit., B658.
113. Ibid., B876.
114. S. Chan, 'Foreign Policies in Southern Africa: The History of an Epoch', in *Exporting Apartheid: Foreign Policies in Southern Africa, 1978–88* (Hong Kong: Macmillian 1990), 99–100. According to Chan, the Commonwealth's Economic Affairs Division – the largest department within the Commonwealth structure – had devoted no significant resources to the issue of sanctions by 1985.
115. Private communication.
116. N. Mandela, *Long Walk to Freedom: the Autobiography of Nelson Mandela* (New York: Little, Brown 1994), 457.
117. Barber and Barratt, op. cit., 329–30.
118. Interview with P. W. Botha 18 June 1991; Interview with P. van der Westhuizen, 24 March 1992.
119. Sparks, op. cit., 35.
120. *Sunday Times* 29 January 1995.
121. See the Commonwealth Group of Eminent Persons, *Mission to South Africa: The Commonwealth Report* (Harmondsworth: Penguin 1986).
122. Restrictions included a prohibition on the sale of technology that could be put to use by South African security forces, a halt in the export of nuclear technology, a prohibition on the purchase of Krugerrands, and an end to all new loans (save those which were

perceived to benefit all races).

123. M. Bennett 1986, 'Countdown to Sanctions: South Africa's Growing Isolation, 1984/86', *Indicator SA* 4:2 (Spring 1986), 17.
124. Private communication.
125. Private communication.
126. R. Price, *The Apartheid State in Crisis: Political Transformation in South Africa 1975–1990* (Oxford: Oxford UP 1991), 222.
127. Ibid., 222–3; 225.
128. SAIRR 1985, op. cit., 533.
129. Republic of South Africa 1985, *Report on the Investigation into Education for Blacks in the Vaal Triangle following upon the Occurrences of 3 September 1984 and Thereafter*, (Pretoria: Government Printers), 58.
130. S. van der Merwe, '. . . And What About the Black People?', Federal Information Service of the National Party, April 1985.
131. Ibid., 1–15.
132. *Debates of the House of Assembly* (Hansard), 25 January to 1 February 1985, Weekly Edition (Cape Town: Government Printers), 11–14.
133. Republic of South Africa 1985(A), *Report of the Committee for Constitutional Affairs of the President's Council on an Urbanisation Strategy for the Republic of South Africa* (Pretoria: Government Printers). The report states: 'Therefore the Committee, concurring with the preponderance of evidence before it, considers that the housing and work requirements as proposed by the Riekert Commission, cannot be implemented without modification.' Republic of South Africa 1985(A), op. cit., 172.
134. Republic of South Africa 1985(B), *White Paper on Urbanisation* (Pretoria: Government Printers).
135. Ibid., 16; 18–21.
136. SAIRR 1984, op. cit., 473–4. The Strydom Committee had been established on 27 November 1981 to examine the Group Areas Act, the Reservation of Separate Amenities Act, the Community Development Act and the Slums Act as they related to whites, Coloureds and Indians.
137. Interview with Chris Heunis, 10 September 1991.
138. SAIRR 1986, op. cit., 98.
139. 'There are some people who quite simplistically advocate a fourth chamber, but a fourth chamber would deny one thing which we all accept, and that is the multinationalism . . . of the country's population. If we believe in the self-determination of nations . . . there cannot be a fourth chamber . . .' C. Heunis, *Debates of the House of Assembly* (Hansard) 2 February 1983 (Pretoria: Government Printers), col. 213.
140. Interview with Dr D. Prinsloo, 24 April 1991.
141. SAIRR 1984, op. cit., 146.
142. Interview with C. Heunis, 10 September 1991.
143. Ibid.
144. SAIRR 1984, op. cit., 146–8. The Secretary of the Cabinet Committee on the Constitution, Dr W. Breytenbach, reported that by January

1985 sixteen meetings of the committee had been held with leaders of the African homelands, businesses and local authorities. In addition, the committee had heard testimony from a diversity of opinion, including the Urban Foundation and the Association of Commerce of South Africa and, in August 1985, met with opposition PFP leadership.

145. Ibid., 147.
146. *South African Digest* 28 August 1985.
147. Ibid., 27 September 1985.
148. Ibid., 4 October 1985.
149. See, for example, Crocker, op. cit., 274–6. While speculation persists that Botha was dissuaded from delivering the 'Rubicon speech' by conservative members of the cabinet, the fact remains that the rather parochial setting of the address – a gathering of officials from one of four provincial wings of the National party – argues against this interpretation.
150. Cited in M. Mann, 'The Giant Stirs: South African Business in the Age of Reform', in *State, Resistance and Change in South Africa,* P. Frankel, N. Pines and M. Swilling, eds (Johannesburg: Croom Helm 1988), 80.
151. *House of Assembly Debates* (Hansard) 25 January 1985 to 19 June 1985, Weekly Edition, (Cape Town: Government Printers), 15–16.
152. Ibid., 15.
153. *Sunday Times* 29 June 1986.
154. *Business Day* 23 May 1986.
155. Cited in J. Smith, *Buthelezi: The Biography,* (Melville, South Africa: Hans Strydom 1988), 236.
156. SAIRR 1985, op. cit., 530; SAIRR 1986, op. cit., 94–8.
157. N. Mandela, *Long Walk to Freedom: the Autobiography of Nelson Mandela* (New York: Little, Brown 1994), 455.
158. SAIRR 1986, op. cit., 92–3.
159. *House of Assembly Debates* (Hansard) 14 April 1986 to 18 April 1986, Weekly Edition (Cape Town: Government Printers), cols 3605–6.
160. SAIRR 1985, op. cit., 39.
161. Smith, op. cit., 246.
162. In the meantime, Buthelezi continued to pursue alternatives to the government sponsored reform process. In addition to the attempts to tie KwaZulu and Natal administratively together, Buthelezi and PFP leader van Zyl Slabbert established a National Convention of opposition leaders in September 1985. Calling for Mandela and Botha's participation in this forum, Buthelezi and van Zyl Slabbert hoped to break the political impasse facing the country. The UDF's outright and hostile derision of the National Convention sank the project almost immediately.
163. P.W. Botha, 'Address by State President P.W. Botha DMS on the Occasion of the Opening of the Tranvaal Congress of the National Party', Pretoria, 19 September 1986, 2.
164. Ibid., 3.

CHAPTER 6

1. *Sunday Times* 29 June 1986.
2. J. Smith, *Buthelezi: The Biography* (Melville, South Africa: Hans Strydom 1988), 236.
3. SAIRR, *Race Relations Survey 1987/88*, (Johannesburg: SAIRR 1988), 478.
4. See W. de Klerk's article, 'Comments on the Election: The Political Map of South Africa', *South African Election 1987: Contest, Process and Prospects*, D. van Vuuren, L. Schlemmer, H. Marais and J. Latakgoma, eds (Pinetown, South Africa: Owen Burgess 1987).
5. *Debates of the House of Assembly* (Hansard) 19 May 1987, (Pretoria: Government Printers 1988), col. 18.
6. In the case of Alexandra, activists established 'yard committees' as the basic political unit in the liberated township. Each yard committee would have two representatives on a 'block committee' and four representatives from the block committee would participate in the 'street committee'. The street committee was envisaged as electing two representatives to the Alexandra Action Committee, which would serve as an executive body for the township. K. Jochelson, 'Reform, Repression and Resistance in South Africa: a Case Study of Alexandra Township, 1979–1989', *Journal of Southern African Studies* 16:1 (March 1990), 7.
7. Ibid., 6.
8. The popular name for the battle between the 'comrades' and the security forces in February 1986.
9. Cited in C. Carter, 'Community and Conflict: The Alexandra Rebellion of 1986', *Journal of Southern African Studies* 18:1 (March 1991), 126.
10. K. Beck, 'Democratizing the United Democratic Front: The Muddy Slope', in *Apartheid Unravels*, H. Davis, ed. (Gainsville, FL: University of Florida Press 1991), 107.
11. Beck, op.cit., 102.
12. J. Muller, 'People's Education and the National Education Crisis Committee', *South African Review* 5 (Johannesburg: Ravan 1987), 18. The author explains the role of the NECC and 'people's education' as 'articulat[ing] a common vocabulary of hope and protest for educational aspiration. This leads in turn to a collective search for a new range of opposition tactics.'
13. A. Marx, *Lessons of Struggle: South African Internal Opposition, 1960–1990*, (Oxford: Oxford UP 1992), 175–8.
14. Ibid., 177.
15. Ibid., 178.
16. Ibid., 178.
17. Ibid., 155.
18. Ibid., 154–5.
19. 'Excerpts from the Political Report of the National Executive Committee at the National Consultative Conference, June 1985', *Sechaba* October 1985, 3.

20. T. Lodge, 'People's War or Negotiation? African National Congress Strategies in the 1980s', *South Africa Review* 5 (Johannesburg: Ravan 1989), 44.
21. Ellis and Sechaba, op.cit., 171–2.
22. T. Lodge et al., *All, Here and Now: Black Politics in South Africa in the 1980s*, South Africa Update Series, Ford Foundation/Foreign Policy Association 1991, 190.
23. Lodge 1989, op.cit., 48.
24. See extracts from an address by G. Starushenko of the USSR Academy of Social Sciences on South Africa, Moscow, 1986, *Southern African Record* No. 46, 76–82.
25. D. Caldwell, *No More Martyrs Now: Capitalism, Democracy and Ordinary People*, (Johannesburg: Conrad Business 1992), 180–1.
26. Sir Robert Thompson also exerted influence over the process. See, for example, P. Groenewald, 'Counter-revolutionary Action in South Africa: 1984–1990', *American Review* 10 (second quarter 1990), 17–26.
27. J.J. McCuen, *The Art of Counter-revolutionary War: The Strategy of Counter-insurgency* (London: Faber & Faber 1966), 30–45.
28. Ibid., 43–4.
29. Ibid., 195–6.
30. Interview with Lt.-General C. Lloyd, 10 September 1991.
31. Ibid.
32. *Weekly Mail* 23 June 1989 – 29 June 1989.
33. G. Evans, 'SADF and Civic Action: Black in the Defence Force', *Work in Progress* 28 August 1983, 35.
34. Interview with General C. Lloyd, 10 September 1991.
35. Ibid.
36. M. Swilling and M. Phillips, 'The Emergency State: Its Structure, Power and Limits', *South African Review* 5 (Johannesburg: Ravan 1989), 80–1.
37. SAIRR 1986, op.cit., 517–18.
38. Ibid., 816–17; *South Africa Digest* 20 June 1986; 27 June 1986.
39. SAIRR 1986, op.cit., 817.
40. Ibid., 831.
41. Ibid., 830–45.
42. Interview with Lt.-General P. van der Westhuizen, 24 March 1992.
43. SAIRR 1986, op.cit., 838–42.
44. Interview with Dr D. Prinsloo, 21 July 1992; P. Groenewald, 'Counter-revolutionary Action in South Africa: 1984–1990', *American Review* 10 (second quarter 1990), 22.
45. Groenewald, op.cit., 22. Operating above the NJMC, by 1986 the OSP consisted of key components of the government, among them: the National Priorities Committee, which established budgetary priorities for the state; the Commission for Administration, which exercised control over the state bureaucracy and coordinated the ongoing privatization efforts; the Ministry of Information, which administered the state propaganda apparatus linked to the NSMS; and the National Intelligence Service, which was principally engaged in the collection and analysis of intelligence data.

46. Groenewald, op.cit., 22; Swilling and Phillips 1989, op.cit., 50.
47. Swilling and Phillips 1989, op.cit., 50.
48. Interview with Lt.-General P. Groenewald, 7 October 1991.
49. Groenewald, op.cit., 22.
50. Stability was defined by government security officials as: 'the absence of physical manifestations of unrest, a situation where few incidents of unrest occurred.' By way of contrast, normality was defined as follows: '[N]ormality required that the causes of unrest be discovered and removed. In other words, when a youngster with a stone in his hand does not throw the stone because a policeman is standing next to him, then there is stability. If he does not throw the stone because he does not want to do so, normality exists.' Ibid., 19.
51. Ibid., 23.
52. *Die Burger* 27 May 1986.
53. SAIRR 1986, op.cit., 517.
54. SAIRR 1987/88, op.cit., 521.
55. The *kitskonstabels* (instant constables), so named because of their six-week training course and subsequent deployment, were notorious for their deviation from internationally acceptable police standards.
56. Seegers 1988, op.cit., 60.
57. SAIRR 1986, op.cit., 521–4.
58. Ibid., 524.
59. Beck, op.cit., 105–6.
60. For example, in May the home of the general secretary of the UDF, Patrick 'Terror' Lekota, was fire bombed, allegedly by a white man. SAIRR 1987–88, op.cit., 536.
61. Ibid., 22.
62. Cited in B. Pottinger, *The Imperial Presidency: P.W. Botha, the First Ten Years*, (Johannesburg: Southern 1988), 304.
63. Interview with Roelf Meyer, 20 November 1990.
64. SAIRR 1987–8, op.cit., 522.
65. Jochelson, op.cit., 22.
66. SAIRR 1987–88, op.cit., 457–8.
67. Jochelson, op.cit., 25.
68. Ibid., 28.
69. Ibid., 26–7.
70. *Weekly Mail*, 1 August 1986–7 August 1986.
71. Ibid.
72. Ibid.
73. Ibid.
74. Ibid.
75. Ibid., 3–8 October 1986.
76. R. Humphries and K. Shubane, 'A Tale of Two Squirrels: The 1988 Local Government Elections and Their Implications', in *South Africa at the End of the Eighties: Policy Perspectives 1989* (Johannesburg: Centre for Policy Studies 1989), 98–9.
77. Jochelson, op.cit., 30; Humphries and Shubane, op.cit., 99.
78. SAIRR 1988–9, op.cit., 513.

79. Humphries and Shubane, op.cit., 94–5.
80. Ibid., 95.
81. Ibid., 96. Humphries and Shubane believe that the '[f]ailure by opposition groups to mount an organized boycott on the same scale as in 1983 testifies, inter alia, to the strength of the forces the state deployed against boycotts. On the whole therefore intimidation could not have been a significant factor influencing the outcome of the election.'
82. Ibid., 97.
83. SAIRR 1988–9, op.cit., 514. The internationally respected South African Institute for Race Relations concluded that: 'The polls appear to show . . . that even in the absence of a boycott campaign, township residents remain at best indifferent to the official local authorities: in the absence of a boycott campaign, apathy, which may stem from a perception that the councils lack the power to improve conditions in the townships, may well have been a more important reason for the low poll than the desire to make a political point by boycotting elections.' H. Mashabela, op.cit., 10.
84. SAIRR 1988–9, op.cit., 514.
85. Ibid. 515.
86. Interview with Roelf Meyer, 20 November 1990.
87. SAIRR 1987/88, op.cit., 25.
88. J. Aitchison, 'The Civil War in Natal', *South African Review* 5 (Johannesburg: Ravan 1989), 457–73. Also see M. Kentridge, *An Unoffiicial War: Inside the Conflict in Pietermaritzburg* (Cape Town: David Philip 1990).
89. See for example F. Meer, ed., *Resistance in the Townships*, Institute for Black Research, (Durban: Madiba 1989), 137–8; 177–82.
90. Ibid., 18.
91. An SAAF plane was shot down in combat and 12 white SADF troops were killed in the battle for Cuito Carnavale.
92. G. Crown, 'Success of the Arms Embargo', in *South Africa: the Sanctions Report*, Documents and Statistics, J. Hanlon, ed., (London: Commonwealth Secretariat 1990), 169.
93. For the ANC–SACP analysis of events in Angola see S. Ellis and T. Sechaba, *Comrades Against Apartheid: The ANC and the South African Communist Party in Exile* (London: James Currey 1992), 183–90. For Castro's perspective, see F. Castro, 'The Angolan Debacle', in W. Steenkamp, *South Africa's Border War, 1966–1989* (Gibraltar: Ashanti 1989), 255–6.
94. B. Seery, 'Security Council Resolution 435 and the Namibian Independence Process', *South African Review* 5 (Johannesburg: Ravan 1989), 232.
95. *Africa Contemporary Record: Annual Survey and Documents, 1986–87*, C. Legum, ed. (London: Africana 1987), B632.
96. Crocker, op.cit., 392–446.
97. Ellis and Sechaba, op.cit., 191.
98. Ibid., 191.
99. S. Chan, 'Foreign Policies in Southern Africa: The History of an

Epoch', in *Exporting Apartheid: Foreign Policies in Southern Africa, 1978–1988* (Hong Kong: Macmillan 1990), 85.
100. Ibid., 85.
101. J. Barber and J. Barratt, *South Africa's Foreign Policy: The Search for Status and Security, 1945–1988* (Johannesburg: Southern 1990), 335.
102. The circumstances surrounding Machel's death still generate controversy. The Mozambican government itself admitted that three years after the event its inquiry 'into the plane crash on South African soil that killed President Samora Machel on October 19, 1986 is still continuing.' *Mozambique File* 157 (August 1989).
103. 'Botha, Chissano Meet in Mozambique', *Washington Post* 13 September 1988.
104. L. Maveneka, 'Marching with Pretoria', *Southern African Economist* (April/May 1989), 18. Joint Mozambican and South African cooperation on the replacement of more than 500 damaged pylons for the Cahora Bassa project was denounced by Renamo and, within two month's time, a further 891 pylons were destroyed by its guerrillas. A. Vines, *Renamo: Terrorism in Mozambique* (London: James Currey 1991), 28.
105. Mozambique Information Office 'News Review' 158, 13 July 1989.
106. SAIRR 1988–9, op.cit., 559.
107. R. Edgar, 'After the Coup: South Africa's Relations with Lesotho', *South African Review* 5 (Johannesburg: Ravan 1989), 242.
108. Ibid., 243–4.
109. United Nations, *The United Nations and Apartheid, 1948–1994* (New York, United Nations 1994), 87.
110. R. Price, *The Apartheid State in Crisis: Political Transformation in South Africa, 1975–1990* (Oxford: Oxford UP 1991), 274.
111. Ibid., 238.
112. SAIRR 1988–9, op.cit., 323.
113. D. Howlett and J. Simpson, 'Nuclearisation and Denuclearisation in South Africa', *Survival* 35:3, 161.
114. Extracts from M.S. Gorbachev's 2 November 1987 address on the 70th Anniversary of the October Revolution, *Southern African Record* no. 49, 1987, 15–16.
115. See extracts from an address by G. Starushenko of the USSR Academy of Sciences on South Africa, Moscow 24–26 1986, *Southern African Record* no. 46 1987, 76–82.
116. *Citizen* 19 March 1987.
117. Republic of South Africa 1987, *Report of the Committee for Constitutional Affairs of the President's Council on the Report of the Technical Committee, 1983 and Related Matters* (Cape Town: Government Printers), 21–2; 157.
118. Ibid., 158–61.
119. *House of Assembly Debates* (Hansard) 28 September 1987 to 7 October 1987, Weekly Edition (Cape Town: Government Printers), col. 6672.
120. SAIRR 1987/88, op.cit., 502–3.
121. The Council of Ministers' seal of approval was sought out accord-

ing to the original population reservation status of the area in question.

122. SAIRR 1987/88, op.cit., 256.
123. Ibid., 254–8; SAIRR 1988/89, op.cit., 28–36. The Conservative party gained control of 90 of the 529 white local authorities in the 1988 municipal elections.
124. A. Fine, 'Trends and Developments in Organised Labour', *South African Review* 4 (Johannesburg: Ravan 1987), 220.
125. J. Baskin, *Striking Back: A History of Cosatu* (Johannesburg: Ravan 1991), 176–7.
126. A. Fine and E. Webster, 'Transcending Traditions: Trade Unions and Political Unity', *South African Review* 5 (Johannesburg: Ravan 1989), 263; 271–86.
127. Fine 1987, op.cit., 220–1.
128. Fine and Webster, op.cit., 264.
129. Ibid., 262.
130. Ibid., 263.
131. SAIRR 1988/89, op.cit., 511.
132. After the municipal elections of 1988, the Conservative party won control over a few white local authorities and used their position to block cooperation with the RSC system.
133. *South Africa Digest* 17 October 1986.
134. SAIRR 1988/89, op.cit., 117. Pretoria maintained an equivocal stance on the KwaZulu/Natal Indaba, at times offering support through such actions as the passage of the Joint Executive Authority for KwaZulu and Natal Act of 1986 and on other occasions acting to stifle the process. During his short stint as Acting State President in 1989, Heunis hinted at the possibility of the establishment of other Joint Executive Authorities at the provincial level and the airing of the possibility of creating multi-racial legislatures within each of the provinces. This would apparently take place within the context of the dismemberment of the provinces as constituted into nine development regions.
135. SAIRR 1988/89, op.cit., 218; 52.
136. *South Africa Digest* 29 May 1987.
137. Ibid. 12 June 1987.
138. Ibid. 17 July 1987.
139. In September 1987, Heunis claimed to have discussed the National Council with over 250 persons and organizations since the publication of the Bill the previous May. *South Africa Digest* 18 September 1987.
140. Ibid.
141. Ibid.
142. Fida, it was disclosed years later, received substantial government support.
143. *Debates of the House of Assembly.* (Hansard) 21 April 1988 (Pretoria: Government Printers), col. 6817.
144. *South Africa Digest* 18 September 1987.
145. Ibid. 15 August 1986.
146. Smith 1988, op.cit., 246.

147. *South Africa Digest* 7 February 1986.
148. Ibid.
149. SAIRR 1987/88, op.cit., 113.
150. Swilling and Philips 1989, op.cit., 58.
151. Ibid., 58.
152. Interview with Dr D. Prinsloo, 4 June 1992.
153. *Debates of the House of Assembly* (Hansard) 9 May 1986 (Pretoria: Government Printers), cols 5277–8.
154. SAIRR 1988/89, op.cit., 505–6.
155. Ibid., 507–8.
156. Botha had reverted to this approach in 1985 and 1986 when the House of Representatives blocked his efforts to introduce the states of emergency.

CHAPTER 7

1. *Sunday Times*, 8 March 1992, 2.
2. Ibid.
3. *Die Beeld* 19 February 1992 (interview with Niel Barnard).
4. Informal contacts between the government and opposition figures had been a feature of secret diplomacy as far back as 1985, if not earlier. Crocker, op.cit., 492.
5. A. Sparks, *Tomorrow is Another Country: The Inside Story of South Africa's Road to Change* (New York: Hill & Wang 1995), 72–82; S. Friedman, *The Long Journey: South Africa's Quest for a Negotiated Settlement* (Johannesburg: Ravan 1993), 9–10.
6. *Die Beeld* 19 February 1992 (interview with Niel Barnard).
7. Ibid.
8. SAIRR, *Race Relations Survey 1987/88* (Johannesburg: South African Institute of Race Relations 1988), 707.
9. Sparks, op. cit., 82.
10. *Debates of the House of Assembly* (Hansard) 13 August 1987 (Pretoria: Government Printers), cols 3752–5.
11. See *Op Reis na de ANC: Verlae oor 'n besoek aan Windhoek, Harare en Lusaka,* compiled by C. Louw (Cape Town: JC Louw 1989); *Praat met die ANC,* complied by G. Olivier (Emmarentia: Taurus 1985); *Four Days in Lusaka: Whites from 'Home' in talks with the ANC,* R. Louw, ed. (Excom: Five Freedoms Forum 1989).
12. *Die Beeld* 18 February 1992 (interview with Niel Barnard).
13. Ibid. 19 February 1992 (interview with Niel Barnard). Mandela met with the 'contact group' 47 times. Sparks, op. cit.
14. S. Ellis and T. Sechaba, *Comrades Against Apartheid: The ANC and the South African Communist Party in Exile* (London: James Currey 1992), 175.
15. N. van Heerden, 'The New Diplomacy', photocopy 1991.
16. SAIRR 1988/89, op.cit., 642–4.
17. Ibid., 643.
18. Ibid., 502.

19. Ibid., 689.
20. *Die Beeld* 19 February 1992 (interview with Niel Barnard)
21. Ibid.
22. The personal persistence of Nelson Mandela, despite his incarceration, in pursuing a negotiated settlement with the Botha administration is a case in point.
23. See C. Alden 'From Liberation Movement to Political Party: ANC Foreign Policy in Transition', *South African Journal of International Affairs,* vol. 1:1 1993.
24. Ellis and Sechaba, op.cit., 204.
25. D. Howlett and J. Simpson, 'Nuclearisation and Denuclearisation in South Africa', *Survival* 35:3, 161.

Select Bibliography

I. SECONDARY SOURCES

Adam, H. and Giliomee, H., *The Rise and Crisis of Afrikaner Power.* Cape Town: David Philips 1979

Africa Contemporary Record: Annual Survey and Documents 1975–1976. Legum, C. (Ed.) London: Rex Collings 1976

Aitchison, J., 'The Civil War in Natal', *South African Review* No.5, Johannesburg: Ravan 1989

Alden, C., 'Mozambique: an Abiding Dependency', in *Southern Africa at the Crossroads: Prospects for Stability and Development in the 1990s.* Johannesburg: Justified 1992

——, 'ANC Foreign Policy in Transition', *The South African Journal of International Affairs,* 1:1 Spring 1993

Austin, D., *Britain and South Africa.* London: Oxford UP 1966

Barber, J., *South Africa's Foreign Policy, 1945–1970.* London: Oxford UP 1973

——, and Hill, C., *The West and South Africa* Chatham House Report 14, Royal Institute of International Affairs: Routledge & Kegan Paul 1982

——, and Barratt, J., *South Africa's Foreign Policy: The Search for Status and Security, 1945–1988.* Johannesburg: Cambridge 1990

Barrell, H., 'The Turn of the Masses: The African National Congress' Strategic Review of 1978–79', *Journal of Southern African Studies* vol. 18:1 March 1991

Baskin, C., *Striking Back: A History of Cosatu.* Johannesburg: Ravan 1991

Baynham, S., 'Political Violence and the Security Response', in *South Africa in Crisis.* Blumfeld, J. (Ed.) London: Croom Helm 1987

Beaufre, A., *An Introduction to Strategy.* London: Faber & Faber 1965

——, *A Strategy for Action.* London: Faber & Faber 1967

Beck, K., 'Democratizing the United Democratic Front: The Muddy Slope', *Apartheid Unravels.* Davis, H.R. (Ed.) Gainsville, FL: University of Florida Press 1991

Bennett, M., 'Countdown to Sanctions: South Africa's Growing Isolation, 1984/86', *Indicator SA* Vol 4:2 Spring 1986

——, 'Curbing the Fourth Estate', *Indicator SA* Vol. 4:3 Summer 1986

——, 'Countdown to State of Emergency: A Chronology of Township Revolt, 1985', *Indicator SA* Vol. 3:2 Spring 1985

Bissell, R., *South Africa and the United States: The Erosion of an Influence Relationship* New York: Praeger 1982

Botha, P.W., 'South Africa – Some Perspectives for the Future', *Aussen Politik* vol. 35, third quarter 1984

——, 'Address by State President P.W. Botha DMS on the Occasion of the Opening of the Tranvaal Congress of the National Party', Pretoria, 19 September 1986

——, 'Public Address' to the National Party Federal Congress in Bloemfontein 30–31 July 1982

——, *Fighter and Reformer: Extracts from the Speeches of P.W. Botha*, compiled by J.J. Scholtz, Pretoria: Promedia 1989

Callaghy, T., 'Apartheid and Socialism: South Africa's Relations with Angola and Mozambique', in *South Africa in Southern Africa: The Intensifying Vortex of Violence.* Callaghy, T. (Ed.) New York: Praeger 1983

Carter, C., 'Community and Conflict: The Alexandra Rebellion of 1986', *Journal of Southern African Studies* vol. 18:1, March 1991

Chan, S., 'Foreign Policies in Southern Africa: The History of an Epoch' in *Exporting Apartheid: Foreign Policies in Southern Africa, 1978–1988.* Chan, S. (Ed.) Hong Kong: Macmillan 1990

Cloete, F. 'Characteristics of the Policy Process Aimed at Political Change in South Africa'. Paper prepared for presentation at the Conference of the Political Science Association of South Africa on 10 and 11 October 1989 in Port Alfred

Commonwealth Group of Eminent Persons, *Mission to South Africa: The Commonwealth Report.* Harmondsworth, England: Penguin 1986

Cooper, C. and Ensor, L., *Pebco: A Black Mass Movement.* Johannesburg: SAIRR 1981

Crocker, C., *High Noon in Southern Africa: Making Peace in a Rough Neighborhood.* Johannesburg: Jonathan Ball 1992

Davies, R. and D. O'Meara, 'Total Strategy in Southern Africa: Regional Policy Since 1978', in *Journal of Southern African Studies,* 11:2 1985

Davis, S., *Apartheid's Rebels: Inside South Africa's Hidden War.* Craighall, SA: Donker 1987

Du Toit, P., 'Regional Services Councils: Control at Local Government Level', *Government By the People?: The Politics of Local Government in South Africa.* Heymans, C. and Totemeyer, G. (Eds) Johannesburg: Juta 1988

Dubow, S., *Racial Segregation and the Origins of Apartheid in South Africa, 1919–36.* Hong Kong: Macmillan 1989

Ellis, S. and Sechaba, T., *Comrades Against Apartheid: The ANC and the South African Communist Party in Exile.* London: James Currey 1992

Evans, G., 'SADF and Civic Action: Blacks in the Defence Force', *Work in Progress* no. 28 August 1983

——, 'SADF and the Civic Action Programme,' *Work in Progress* no. 29 October 1983

Evans, M. and Phillips, M., 'Intensifying Civil War: the Role of the South African Defence Force', *State, Resistance and Change in South Africa.* Frankel, P., Pines, N. and Swilling, M. (Eds) Johannesburg: Southern 1988

Fine, A. and Webster E., 'Transcending Traditions: Trade Unions and Political Unity', *South African Review* no. 5, Johannesburg: Ravan 1989

Fourie, D., 'Strategie – 'n Oorsig,' *Paratus* December 1971

——, 'Strategie – 'n Oorsig', *Paratus* January 1972

Frankel, P., *Pretoria's Praetorians: Civil–Military Relations in South Africa,* Cambridge: Cambridge UP 1984.

Friedman, S., *Building Tomorrow Today: African Workers in Trade Unions 1970–1984.* Johannesburg: Ravan 1987

—— (Ed.), *The Long Journey: South Africa's Quest for a Negotiated Settlement.* Johannesburg: Ravan 1993

Geldenhuys, D., 'Some Foreign Policy Implications of South Africa's "Total National Strategy" with Particular Reference to the "12 Point Plan"', Braamfontein: South African Institute of International Affairs, March 1981

——, *The Diplomacy of Isolation: South Africa's Foreign Policy Making.* Johannesburg: Macmillan 1984

—— and Kotze H., 'Aspects of Political Decision-making in South Africa', *Politikon* vol. 10:1 June 1983

Geldenhuys, D. and Venter D., 'Regional Cooperation in Southern Africa: A Constellation of States?', *International Affairs Bulletin* 3(3) December 1979

Giliomee, H., *The Parting of the Ways: South African Politics 1976–1982.* Cape Town: David Philip 1982

—— and Lawrence Schlemmer, *From Apartheid to Nation-Building.* Cape Town: Oxford UP 1989

Grest, J., 'Crisis of Local Government' in *State, Resistance and Change in South Africa.* Frankel, P., N. Pines and M. Swilling (Eds). Johannesburg: Southern 1988

Groenewald, P., 'Counter-revolutionary Action in South Africa: 1984–1990', *American Review* vol. 10, second quarter 1990

——, 'The Development of the Security Situation in South Africa Since January 1990', *American Review* vol. 10, third quarter 1990

Grundy, K., *The Militarization of South African Politics.* Oxford: Oxford UP 1988

Hanlon, J., *Mozambique: The Revolution Under Fire.* London: Zed 1984

—— (Ed.), *South Africa: The Sanctions Report,* Documents and Statistics. London: Commonwealth Secretariat 1990

Haysom, N., *Mabangalala: The Rise of Right-Wing Vigilantes in South Africa.* Johannesburg: University of the Witwatersrand 1986

Heitman, H., *War in Angola: The Final South African Phase.* Gibraltar: Ashanti 1990

Heymans, C., 'The Political and Constitutional Context of Local Government Restructuring', *Government by the People? The Politics of Local Government in South Africa.* Heymans, C. and Totemeyer, G. (Eds) Johannesburg: Juta 1988

Hough, M. and van der Merwe, M., *Selected Official South African Strategic Perceptions, 1976–1987.* Ad hoc Publication No.25, Institute for Strategic Studies, Pretoria, May 1988

Howe, G., 'Deadlock in Emergent States: 1960/61 and 1984/85: Township Uprising, Armed Occupation', *Indicator SA* 3:2 Spring 1985(A)

——, 'Cycles of Civil Unrest 1976/84: Triggers, Targets and Trends', *Indicator SA* 3:1 Winter 1985(B)

Humphries, R., 'Intermediate State Responses to the Black Local Authority Legitimacy Crisis' in *Government By the People?: The Politics of Local Government in South Africa.* Heymans, C. and Totemeyer, H. (Eds), Johannesburg: Juta 1988.

Humphries, R. and Shubane K., 'A Tale of Two Squirrels: The 1988 Local Government Elections and Their Implications', *South Africa at the End of the Eighties: Policy Perspectives 1989*. Johannesburg: Centre for Policy Studies 1989

Huntington, S., 'Reform and Stability in a Modernizing, Multi-Ethnic Society', *Politikon* vol. 8:2 December 1981.

Innes, D., 'State, Repression and Reform', *Work in Progress* no. 24, October 1982 Johannesburg: Sached

Jaster, R. *The Defence of White Power: South African Foreign Policy Under Pressure* London: Macmillan 1988

——, *South Africa in Namibia: The Botha Strategy*. Lanham, MD: UP of America 1985

——, *South Africa and its Neighbours: the Dynamics of Regional Conflict*. Adelphi Paper 209, London: International Institute for Strategic Studies 1986

Jochelson, K., 'Reform, Repression and Resistance in South Africa: a Case Study of Alexandra Township, 1979–1989', *Journal of Southern African Studies* vol. 16:1, March 1990

Karis, T., 'The Resurgent African National Congress: Competing for Hearts and Minds in South Africa', in *South Africa in Southern Africa: The Intensifying Vortex of Violence*. Callaghy, T. (Ed.) New York: Praeger 1983

Kentridge, M., *An Unofficial War: Inside the Conflict in Pietermaritzburg*. Cape Town: David Philip 1990

Khwela, M., 'Resistance and Containment', *Resistance in the Townships*. Durban: Institute for Black Research 1989

Laurence, P., 'Rural Revolt: Transvaal's Homelands in Ferment', *Indicator SA* vol. 4:2, Spring 1986

Legum, C., *Vorster's Gamble for Africa: How the Search for Peace Failed*, London: Rex Collings 1976.

——, *The Battlefronts of Southern Africa*, New York: Africana 1988

Lemon, A., *Apartheid in Transition*. Aldershot, England: Gower 1987

Leonard, R., *South Africa at War: White Power and the Crisis in Southern Africa*. Westport, CT: Lawrence Hill, 1983

Lipton, Merle, *Capitalism and Apartheid: South Africa, 1910–1986* Third Edition. Cape Town: David Philip 1989

Lodge, T., *Black Politics in South Africa since 1945*. Johannesburg: Ravan 1983

——, 'People's War or Negotiation? African National Congress Strategies in the 1980s', *South Africa Review* no. 5 Johannesburg: Ravan 1989

Lodge, T. et al., *All, Here, and Now: Black Politics in South Africa in the 1980s*. South Africa Update Series, Ford Foundation/Foreign Policy Association 1991

Magubane, B., 'Botswana, Lesotho, and Swaziland: Hostages in Revolt', in *South Africa in Southern Africa: The Intensifying Vortex of Violence*. Callaghy, T. (Ed.) New York: Praeger 1983

Malan, M., 'Die Aanslag Teen Suid-Afrika', address to Institute for Strategic Studies, University of Pretoria, 3 September 1980

Mandela, N., *Long Walk to Freedom: The Autobiography of Nelson Mandela* (New York: Little, Brown 1994)

Mann, M., 'The Giant Stirs: Business in the Age of Reform', in *State, Resistance and Change in South Africa*, Frankel P., Pines, N. and Swilling, M. (Eds) (Johannesburg: Southern 1988)

Martin, D. and P. Johnson, 'Mozambique: To Nkomati and Beyond', in *Destructive Engagement: Southern Africa at War*. Martin, D. and Johnson, P. (Eds) Harare: Zimbabwe Publishers 1986

Mashabela, H., *Fragile Figures? The 1988 PWV Township Elections*, Johannesburg: SAIRR 1989

Mazwai, T., 'Caught in the Crossfire: African Local Authorities Twixt Government and Community', *Indicator SA* vol. 3:2 Spring 1985

McCuen, J.J., *The Art of Counter-revolutionary Warfare: The Strategy of Counterinsurgency*. London: Faber & Faber 1966

Meer, F. (Ed.), *Resistance in the Townships*. Institute for Black Research, Durban: Madiba 1989

Meredith, M., 'The Black Opposition,' *South Africa in Crisis*. Blumfeld, J. (Ed.), London: Croom Helm 1987

——, *In the Name of Apartheid: South Africa in the Post War Period*. London: Hamish Hamilton 1988

Moodie, T.D., *The Rise of Afrikanerdom: Power, Apartheid, and the Afrikaner Civil Religion*. London: University of California 1975

Moss, G., 'SAIC: Participation or Boycott', in *Work in Progress* no. 10 November 1979, Johannesburg: Sached

Mthombothi, B., 'Introduction', *Resistance in the Townships*. Meer, F. (Ed.) Durban: Institute for Black Research 1989

Nathan, L., 'Troops in the Townships, 1984–1987', in *War and Society: The Militarisation of South Africa*. Nathan, L. and Cock, J. (Eds) Cape Town: David Philip 1989

Nelson, H. (Ed.), *Zimbabwe: A Country Study* US Government: 1983

Nolutshungu, S., *South Africa in Africa: A Study in Ideology and Foreign Policy*. Manchester: Manchester UP 1975

Pauw, J., *In the Heart of the Whore: The Story of Apartheid's Death Squads*. Johannesburg: Southern 1991

Poto, J., 'The Viability of Black Local Authorities', in *Government by the People? The Politics of Local Government in South Africa*. Heymans, C. and Totemeyer, G. (Eds) Johannesburg: Juta 1988

Pottinger, B., *The Imperial Presidency: The First Ten Years* Johannesburg: Southern 1988

Price, R., *The Apartheid State in Crisis: Political Transformation in South Africa 1975–1990*. Oxford: Oxford UP 1991

Quin, D., 'From One Emergency to Another: A Brief "Interlude", 7 March–11 June 1986,' *Indicator SA*. 4:1 Winter 1986

Roherty, J., *State Security in South Africa Civil–Military Relations under P.W. Botha*. London: M.E. Sharpe 1992

Schlemmer, L., 'South Africa's Urban Crisis: The Need for Fundamental Solutions', *Indicator SA* 3:1 Winter 1985

——, 'South Africa's National Party Government', in *A Future South Africa: Visions, Strategies, and Realities*. Berger, P. and Godsell, B. (Eds) Boulder, CO: Westview 1988

Schrire, R., 'South Africa: Bureaucracy and the Process of Reform', *Journal of Contemporary African Studies* 5:1/2 April/October 1986

——, *Adapt or Die: The End of White Politics in South Africa*. South Africa Update Series, Ford Foundation/Foreign Policy Association 1991

Seegers, A., 'The Government's Perception and Handling of South Africa's Security Needs', in *South Africa: The Challenge of Reform.* Van Vuuren, D., Wiehahn, N., Rhoodie, N., Wiechers, M. (Eds) Pinetown, RSA: Owen Burgess 1988

——, 'Extending the Security Network to the Local Level: A Clarification and Some Further Comments', *Politeia* University of South Africa vol. 7:2, 1988

Seekings, J., 'The Origins of Political Mobilisation in PWV Townships, 1980–84', *Popular Struggles in South Africa.* Cobbett, W. and R. Cohen (Eds) London: James Currey 1988

Selfe, J., 'The Total Onslaught and the Total Strategy: Adaptation to the Security Intelligence Decision-making Structures under P.W. Botha's Administration', unpublished MA University of Cape Town 1987

Shelton, G., 'Theoretical Perspectives on South African Foreign Policy Making', *Politikon* vol. 13:1, June 1986

Smith, J., *Buthelezi: The Biography.* Melville, South Africa: Hans Strydom 1988

Smith, R., 'The Black Trade Unions: From Economics to Politics', in *South Africa in Crisis.* Blumfeld, J. (Ed.) London: Croom Helm 1987

Somerville, K., *Southern Africa and the Soviet Union: From Communist International to Commonwealth of Independent States.* London: Macmillan 1993

South African Institute of Public Administration, 'White Paper on Rationalisation of the Public Service and Related Institutions', *Journal of Public Administration* vol. 15:2 June 1980

South African Institute of Race Relations (SAIRR) 1978, *Laws Affecting Race Relations in South Africa.* Pietermaritzburg: Natal Witness 1978

——, *Survey of Race Relations.* (An annual publication) Johannesburg: Natal Witness

Sparks, A., *Tomorrow is Another Country: The Inside Story of South Africa's Road to Change.* New York: Hill & Wang 1995

Spence, J., *Republic Under Pressure: A Study in South African Foreign Policy.* Royal Institute of International Affairs, Chatham House Essays, No. 9. London: Oxford UP 1965

——, *The Political and Military Framework,* Study Project on External Investment in South Africa and Namibia (South West Africa), Paper No. 4, University of Leicester January 1975

Steenkamp, W., *South Africa's Border War, 1966–1989.* Gibraltar: Ashanti 1989

Stultz, N., *The Apartheid Issue at the Security Council,* UN and South Africa Series, Braamfontein: South African Institute for International Affairs, September 1989

Swilling, M., 'The United Democratic Front and Township Revolt', *Popular Struggles in South Africa.* Cobbett, W. and Cohen R. (Eds) London: James Currey 1988

——, and Phillips M., 'The Emergency State: Its Structure, Power and Limits', *South African Review* No. 5, Braamfontein: Ravan 1989

——, 'The Powers of the Thunderbird: Decision-making Structures and Policy Strategies in the South African State' in *South Africa at the End of the Eighties: Policy Perspectives 1989.* Johannesburg: Centre for Policy Studies, University of the Witwatersrand 1990

Thompson, L., *The Political Mythology of Apartheid.* New Haven, CT: Yale UP 1985

Thompson, R., *Defeating Communist Insurgency: The Lessons of Malaya and Vietnam.* New York: Praeger 1966

Thulo, T., 'Violence in Pietermaritzburg, 1985–1988', *Resistance in the Townships.* Meer, F. (Ed.) Durban: Institute for Black Research 1989

Tyala, M., 'The New Frontier: Rebellion in the Eastern Cape', *Indicator SA* vol. 3:4 Autumn 1986

United Nations, *The United Nations and Apartheid, 1948–1994,* New York: United Nations 1994

Van der Merwe, S., '. . . And What About the Black People' Federal Information Service of the National Party, April 1985

Van Deventer, A., 'State Security Council: Not Sinister!' *Paratus* November 1983

Van der Ross, R., *The Rise and Decline of Apartheid: A Study of Political Movements among the Coloured People of South Africa, 1880–1985,* Cape Town: Tafelberg 1986

Van Niekerk, P., 'The Trade Union Movement in the Politics of South Africa', in *South Africa: No Turning Back.* Johnson, S. (Ed.), Bloomington, IN: Indiana UP 1989

Vines, A., *Renamo: Terrorism in Mozambique.* London: James Currey in association with the Centre for Southern African Studies 1991

Vosloo, W., 'Consociational Democracy as a Means to Accomplish Peaceful Political Change in South Africa: an Evaluation of the Constitutional Change Proposed by the National Party in 1977', *Politikon* 6:1 June 1979

——, 'The Coloured Policy of the National Party', *South African Dialogue.* Rhoodie, N. (Ed.), Pretoria: McGraw-Hill 1972

Webster, E., 'The Rise of Social-Movement Unionism: The Two Faces of the Black Trade Union Movement in South Africa', in *State, Resistance and Change in South Africa.* Frankel, P., Pines, N. and Swilling, M. (Eds), Johannesburg: Southern 1988

Wilson, M. and Thompson, L. (Eds), *The Oxford History of South Africa.* vol. I & II, Oxford: Clarendon 1969–71

Young, T., 'The MNR/Renamo: External and Internal Dynamics,' *African Affairs* 1990

II. SOUTH AFRICAN GOVERNMENT DOCUMENTS

Debates and Proceedings of the Coloured Persons Representative Council (An annual publication) Pretoria: Government Printers

Union House of Assembly Debates (Hansard) (An annual publication) Pretoria: Government Printers

Debates of the House of Assembly (Hansard) (An annual publication) Pretoria: Government Printers

House of Assembly Questions & Answers (Hansard) (An annual publication) Pretoria: Government Printers

Republic of South Africa 1971, *Report of the Commission of Inquiry into*

Matters Relating to the Security of the State (Abridged), Pretoria: Government Printers 1971

Republic of South Africa 1973, *White Paper on Defence and Armaments Production*, Pretoria: Government Printers 1973

Republic of South Africa 1975 *White Paper on Defence*, Pretoria: Government Printers 1975

Republic of South Africa 1976, *Recommendations of the Commission of Inquiry into Matters Relating to the Coloured Population Group*, Pretoria: Government Printers 1976

Republic of South Africa 1977, *White Paper on Defence and Armaments Production*, Pretoria: Government Printers 1977

Republic of South Africa 1978, 'South Africa's New Constitutional Plan', Johannesburg: Perskor 1978

Republic of South Africa 1979(A), *Report of the Commission of Inquiry into Labour Legislation* Part I, Pretoria: Government Printers 1979

Republic of South Africa 1979(B), *Report of the Commission of Inquiry into Legislation Affecting the Utilisation of Manpower*, Pretoria: Government Printers 1979

Republic of South Africa 1979(C), *White Paper on the Report of the Commission of Inquiry into Legislation Affecting the Utilisation of Manpower*, Pretoria: Government Printers 1980

Republic of South Africa 1979(D), *White Paper on the Commission of Inquiry into Labour Legislation*, Pretoria: Government Printers 1979

Republic of South Africa 1980, *Commission for Administration: Annual Report*, Pretoria: Government Printers 1979–1980

Republic of South Africa 1981, *Report of the President's Council on the Group Areas Act 1966 (Act 36 of 1966) with Special Reference to Zonnebloem (District Six) and Pageview*, Cape Town: Government Printers 1981

Republic of South Africa 1982(A), *First Report of the Constitutional Committee of the President's Council*, Cape Town: Government Printer, 1982

Republic of South Africa 1982(B), *Report of the Commission of Inquiry into the Mass Media*, Pretoria: Government Printers 1982

Republic of South Africa 1982(C), *Joint Report of the Committee for Economic Affairs and the Constitutional Committee of the President's Council on Local and Regional Management Systems in the Republic of South Africa*, Cape Town: Government Printers 1982

Republic of South Africa 1985(A), *Report of the Committee for Constitutional Affairs of the President's Council on an Urbanisation Strategy for the Republic of South Africa*, Cape Town: Government Printers 1985

Republic of South Africa 1985(B), *White Paper on Urbanisation*, Cape Town: Government Printers, 1985

Republic of South Africa 1985(C), *Report on the Investigation into Education for Blacks in the Vaal Triangle following upon the Occurrences of 3 September 1984 and Thereafter*, Cape Town: Government Printers 1985

Republic of South Africa 1987, *Report of the Committee for Consitutional Affairs of the President's Council on the Report of the Technical Committee, 1983 and Related Matters*, Cape Town: Government Printers 1987

Republic of South Africa 1988, 'Regional Services Councils', issued on behalf of the Department of Development Planning and the Constitutional Development Services, Parow, South Africa: June 1988

III. NEWSPAPERS AND MAGAZINES

Business Day (SA)
Citizen (SA)
Die Beeld (SA)
Die Burger (SA)
Financial Mail (SA)
Financial Times (SA)
New Nation (SA)
Paratus (SA)
Sechaba (SA)
South African Digest (SA)
Star (SA)
Sunday Times (SA)
Weekly Mail (SA)

IV. ARCHIVES

The Papers of P.W. Botha, Institute of Contemporary History, University of the Orange Free State, Bloemfontein, Orange Free State

V. INTERVIEWS

Former State President P.W. Bötha, 18 June 1991
Professor F. Cloete, 5 April 1990
General H. du Toit, 7 March 1990
Professor D. Fourie, 16 October 1990
General P. Groenewald, 7 October 1991
M. Hough, 11 March 1990
C. Heunis, 10 September 1991
General C. Lloyd, 10 September 1991
R. Meyer, 20 November 1990
Dr D. Prinsloo, 24 April 1991 and 21 July 1992
Professor Rautenbach, 9 June 1992
Senior military official, 6 August 1991
Senior military official, 17 October 1991
General A. van Deventer, 6 June 1991
General P. van der Westhuizen, 24 March 1992
Dr W. Vosloo, 5 July 1991

Index